John

John

by

Robert W. Yarbrough

MOODY PRESS
CHICAGO

All Scripture quotations, unless noted otherwise, are from the *Holy Bible: New International Version*. Copyright © 1973, 1978, 1984, International Bible Society. Used by permission of Zondervan Bible Publishers.

Library of Congress Cataloging in Publication Data

Yarbrough, Robert W.
    John / by Robert W. Yarbrough.
        p.   cm.   —   (Everyman's Bible commentary)
    Includes bibliographical references.
    ISBN 0-8024-2096-6
    1. Bible. N.T. John—Commentaries. I. Title. II. Series.
BS2615.3.Y37   1991
226.5'07—dc20   91-26352
                                                                        CIP

1 2 3 4 5 6 7 Printing/EP/Year 96 95 94 93 92 91

Printed in the United States of America

To the memory of
Mitchell Steven Fritz

CONTENTS

PREFACE

Recent polls suggest that knowledge of the Bible is waning in North American society. While religious fervor seems to be in a stable or even growing pattern, personal familiarity with the single most important book, religious or otherwise, in the history of humanity is declining.

A modern best-seller reflects this ignorance or perhaps just cavalier indifference. Jesus is said to have taught, "Know thyself," or, "Know thyself and that truth will set you free." It is claimed that Jesus taught the theory of reincarnation. In another passage, Jesus is listed along with Anwar Sadat, Martin Luther King, Buddha, Mother Teresa, Gandhi, Thomas Jefferson, Thoreau, and Voltaire. What could these figures possibly have in common? "All these people personally believed in a higher cosmic design which enabled them to take up a positive belief in human potential."[1]

Anyone with even a basic understanding of the New Testament should recognize that none of these claims about Jesus has much if any grounding in its pages. Yet such claims are apparently widely believed and accepted as plausible.

This commentary is addressed to the average reader who is tired of second-hand knowledge about the Bible and wants to know for himself what it says.

It is not a substitute for the gospel of John, which needs to be open alongside this commentary whenever it is read. The commentary's aim is not to replace but to clarify John's gospel, shedding light

1. Shirley MacLaine, *Out on a Limb* (Toronto/New York/London/Sydney: Bantam, 1983). The above quotes may be found, in the order in which they appear here, on pp. 301, 121, 235, and 365.

on each verse and chapter so that the reader will be better equipped to develop his own informed grasp of its message.

Complex theories, arcane facts, and technical explanations of fine details have their place among scholars who deal with John and the rest of the New Testament. But this commentary is not for scholars (though it is hoped that scholars will recognize some of their contributions to our knowledge of John's gospel in its pages). Academically trained readers will quickly realize that much more could have been achieved in the area of interaction with current theories. But as George R. Beasley-Murray concedes, "It is a disturbing fact that the effect of more than a little contemporary scholarly discussion on the Fourth Gospel is to confuse both laity and clergy; it leads some to disregard the Gospel's significance for life and for ministry."[2] Robert Kysar examines modern scholarly work on John and concludes that scholars have not yet found even the basic "categories" and "presuppositions" that would enable them to understand what the gospel is trying to convey.[3]

In much the same vein, Jacob Jervell writes, "An examination of the literature dealing with this gospel leads us to observe that scholarship, to a certain extent, has had to grope in the dark, and that the mystery connected with the Fourth Gospel is far from being solved."[4] A leading scholar's characterization of one of his own seminal studies is "to suggest some of the gains that may be had if one will be reckless enough to try to ride uphill and downhill on three horses at once, and, much of the time, by night."[5]

All of this points to the futility, if not outright folly, of too ambitious an attempt to incorporate "scholarship" into a basic-level commentary on John—at least a commentary written from an orthodox theological perspective. Although I have made some attempt, therefore, to reflect contemporary scholarship's debates and findings, this task has not

2. George Beasley-Murray, *John*, Word Biblical Commentary 36 (Waco: Word, 1987), p. liii.

3. Robert Kysar, *The Fourth Evangelist and His Gospel* (Minneapolis: Ausgburg, 1975), p. 279.

4. Jacob Jervell, *Jesus in the Gospel of John* (Minneapolis: Augsburg, 1984), p. 86.

5. J. Louis Martyn, "Source Criticism and Religionsgeschichte [History of Religions] in the Fourth Gospel," in John Ashton, ed., *The Interpretation of John* (Philadelphia/ London: Fortress/SPCK, 1986), pp. 99-121.

been the chief priority. For the debates are highly confusing, even to specialists, and as yet tend to lead only to more debates, as the scholars above freely concede.

This commentary is rather for those seekers of truth who realize that in today's world of popular ideas more and more people are embracing unlikely and distorted views of what the Bible and Jesus are all about. It is for those clear thinkers who see the dangers of common but misguided notions and wish to avoid them, not by ignoring them but by overcoming them with a better knowledge of the gospel than they presently possess.

Many fine commentaries and reference works have been consulted in the production of this book. Most of these are included in the annotated bibliography. Other works have been specified in footnotes. Please be aware that full bibliographical data is given when a book first appears in a footnote; in subsequent footnotes throughout the commentary a shortened reference note is given.

The person who studies the gospel of John along with this commentary will, it is hoped, be in a position to lessen contemporary confusion about Jesus Christ and His message instead of contributing to the existing surplus.

Thanks are due to my friend and former Moody editor Terry Miethe for inviting me to contribute to the Everyman's Bible Commentary series. My student assistant Dawn Campion (now Dawn Burnett) read earlier versions of the manuscript, as did Matthew L. Strauser of Santiam Christian Schools in Corvallis, Oregon. Both made helpful suggestions. My wife and two sons suffered, as a writer's family always does, as these pages took shape. They bore it with grace.

ABBREVIATIONS

KJV – King James Version

NEB – *New English Bible*

NPNF – Nicene and Post-Nicene Fathers

NT – New Testament

OT – Old Testament

SCM – Student Christian Movement

SPCK – Society for the Propagation of Christian Knowledge

INTRODUCTION TO JOHN'S GOSPEL

The Four Gospels

We are about to embark on an exciting investigation of the gospel of John. But what exactly is a "gospel"? For Christians a "gospel" is any of four historical accounts preserved in the New Testament, which recount the life and teachings of Jesus Christ. A gospel is an authoritative presentation of the "good news" (the literal meaning of the Greek word for *gospel*) that through Jesus Christ, God has fulfilled His ancient promises to bring salvation to His people.

In the ancient world there were, to be sure, more than just four gospels. A number of works claiming to be "gospels" appeared in the second, third, and subsequent centuries among various groups trying to legitimize their versions of religion, some of which resembled Christianity at points. In bookstores today one can often find volumes containing such works as the *Gospel of Thomas,* or other so-called "secret" gospels of Jesus. From their earliest appearance, these writings were looked on with suspicion by true Christians. Modern scholars widely agree that they are spurious, containing little, if any, dependable historical information about Jesus or about the church He founded. As R. Wilson states, "Even a slight acquaintance is enough to make it clear that they cannot (apart from the earliest) be considered as reliable historical sources for the life of Jesus or the apostles."[1]

There are, then, only four true gospels. There are, and since the times of the apostles have been, only four accounts of Jesus' life with

---

1. R. Wilson, "New Testament Apocrypha," in Eldon Epp and George MacRae, eds. *The New Testament and Its Modern Interpreters* (Philadelphia/Atlanta: Fortress/Scholars, 1989), p. 446.

convincing claims to have been written in the first century by authors with personal acquaintance of the things they relate.[2] Although there were other early written records containing information about Jesus' life (Luke 1:1), only the accounts eventually preserved in the New Testament have survived. The gospel of John is one of these priceless accounts.

DISTINCTIVES OF JOHN'S GOSPEL

Each of the four gospels makes its own distinctive contribution to our understanding of Jesus Christ. But the gospel of John holds a unique place. For one thing, whereas Matthew, Mark, and Luke have a good deal of information in common, more than 90 per cent of John is without direct parallel in the other three gospels.

For another, the author is a personal eyewitness of much of what he describes. He is John the son of Zebedee, one of the first followers Jesus selected, and is most likely the figure called "the beloved disciple" in John 13:23; 19:26; 21:7, 20.[3] While many modern scholars dispute John's authorship, it is the unanimous verdict of ancient witnesses and continues to be the choice that explains the most data in the most plausible way.[4] Both evangelical modern commentators such as Leon Morris and more liberal interpreters such as J. A. T. Robinson continue to defend the view that the apostle John is the direct source of much, if not all, of what the gospel named for him contains.[5] In the absence of more weighty evidence to the contrary, there is good reason to continue to understand this gospel as the literary and theological testimony of one of Jesus' closest followers.[6]

2. This point was made powerfully years ago in a German work by Adolf Schlatter, *The History of the Christ* (Stuttgart: Calwer, 1923), p. 8, and retains its cogency today.

3. Vernard Eller, *The Beloved Disciple* (Grand Rapids: Eerdmans, 1987) is representative of some who argue that someone besides John is the author. Eller suggests Lazarus. For a survey of other proposals see Robert Kysar, *The Fourth Evangelist and His Gospel* (Minneapolis: Augsburg, 1975), pp. 86-101.

4. After recounting the possibilities, Gary Burge, "John," in Walter A. Elwell, ed., *Evangelical Commentary on the Bible* (Grand Rapids: Baker, 1989), p. 841, concludes, "the best solution is the traditional one."

5. Leon Morris, *The Gospel According to John* (Grand Rapids: Eerdmans, 1977); J. A. T. Robinson, *The Priority of John* (Oak Park, Ill.: Meyer-Stone, 1987).

6. The classic argument for Johannine authorship is still B. F. Westcott, *The Gospel According to St. John* (Reprint; Grand Rapids: Eerdmans, 1978), pp. v-xxxii.

John served as a "pillar" in the Jerusalem church for many years following Christ's ascension (Gal. 2:9). Later, ancient sources say, he was a leader in the church at Ephesus. Just when he put his gospel in the form we have it is unknown. Many scholars argue that he labored over it at different times over a period of years or even decades, perhaps assisted by scribes or other co-workers.

In any case, John's gospel reflects the distinctive insights of someone well qualified to report things "which we have heard, which we have seen with our eyes, which we have looked at and our hands have touched" (1 John 1:1). John speaks not from hearsay or popular speculation but from first-hand experience (note especially 1:14; 19:35; 20:8; 21:24).

A third reason that John's gospel holds a unique place is that it preserves a wealth of accounts of Jesus' discussions with various listeners and opponents. John gives us page after page of wisdom from Jesus' lips (in John's words, to be sure) that is preserved with the same clarity and fullness in no other source. Moreover, much of this material comes from exchanges that took place in the Jerusalem area over the span of two or three years leading up to the final weeks of Jesus' ministry. The other three gospels, by contrast, preserve extensive knowledge of only the final days of Jesus' work in Jerusalem. Were it not for John, we might think Jesus' ministry lasted only a year and was confined first to Galilee, after which it ended in Judea. John's gospel makes clear that Jesus moved freely between Galilee and Jerusalem a number of times and that His public ministry was two or three years in duration.

JESUS AND GEOGRAPHY

IN JOHN'S GOSPEL

1:28 — Jesus baptized at Bethany on the east side of the Jordan (precise location uncertain today)

1:43 — Jesus leaves for Galilee

2:1 — Attends wedding at Cana of Galilee

2:12 — Goes to Capernaum with mother and brothers

2:13 — Goes up to Jerusalem

3:22 — Jesus and disciples go out into the Judean countryside

4:3 — Leaves Judea and heads back to Galilee

4:4 — Heads through Samaria

4:43 — After two days departs for Galilee

4:45 — Arrives in Galilee

4:46 — Returns to Cana in Galilee

5:1 — Visits Jerusalem once more

6:1 — Crosses to the far shore of the Sea of Galilee

6:17 — Crosses back to Capernaum

7:1 — Itinerant ministry in Galilee (purposeful avoidance of Judea and the Jews there)

7:10 — Returns to Jerusalem for feast of Tabernacles (September–October)

10:22 — In Jerusalem for the feast of Dedication (December 25)

10:40 — Back to where John the Baptist had once baptized

11:7 — Decides to go back to Judea to minister to Lazarus

11:17 — Arrives at Bethany, less than two miles from Jerusalem

11:54 — Withdraws to Ephraim (fifteen miles north of Jerusalem?)

12:1 — Six days before the Passover, Jesus arrives in Bethany once more

12:12 — Triumphal entry into Jerusalem, site of betrayal, trial, and crucifixion (until chap. 21 Jesus' ministry is in the vicinity of Jerusalem)

21:1 — Jesus appears by the Sea of Tiberius

IN THE OTHER GOSPELS

Matthew, Mark, and Luke track Jesus' movements mainly in the following sequence. Many modern scholars see this as the outline originally used by Mark ("the Marcan outline"), then adapted by Matthew and Luke when they later wrote gospels of their own using Mark as a source.

> John the Baptist's ministry
> Jesus' ministry in Galilee
> Jesus and disciples journey to Jerusalem
> Last week in Jerusalem

JOHN'S APPEAL TO THE READER

It is stimulating to know that John's account is important and that we can depend on what he tells us. Yet there are strings attached to his message, and the reader of John might as well know at the outset what these are.

John tells us that he has a distinct purpose in all he recounts. He aims to convince the reader that Jesus is the Christ, the Son of God, so that he or she might believe and have life in His name (20:31).

Questions immediately arise. Just what does "Christ" mean? And "Son of God"? Why is it important to "believe," and why would John wish his readers to have "life"—if someone is alive enough to be reading John, he can hardly be "dead," can he?

The gospel of John raises, and addresses, these and many other questions. But the point is that John is not concerned merely with conveying information, important as that is. What he writes, he insists, is totally trustworthy (21:24), but it should also be life-changing. Jesus Christ has radically transformed John's own life along with the lives of countless others. This is what Jesus came for. Jesus appointed John, along with others, to spread the life-changing truth that Jesus conveyed to them. The reader of John's gospel will be challenged again and again to come to terms with Jesus Christ in his personal life and setting as those who first encountered Jesus did in theirs.

SUGGESTION FOR READING JOHN'S GOSPEL

We read this gospel aright, then, when we do two things.

First, we seek to understand the "then and there." We are interested in the facts, the history, the meaning of words like "witness" and "Jew," the identity of groups like "Pharisees." We are eager to observe with new understanding the impact of Jesus' life-imparting utterances on those who first heard them.

Second, we are attentive also to our position in the "here and now." We cooperate, as best we can, with John's stated purpose in writing. He wants to challenge us. He wants us to invite Jesus Christ to claim our lives as, John testifies, He has every right to do. We have not begun to understand the gospel until we wrestle seriously and honestly with the meaning of its message, not only for others in the first century but for us as we enter the twenty-first.

The gospel of John tells of Jesus calling men and women to believe. This may sound elementary. Yet if it were, John would probably not have written twenty-one chapters to drive home his point. As we turn to John's opening words, we are aware that we are about to encounter not merely a story but a Person who wishes to claim and change our lives.

Through John's gospel, then, Jesus Christ is about to invite us to let Him transform our understanding, our priorities, and the way we live as He has been doing steadily, faithfully, remarkably ever since John first encountered Him. John's gospel tells how Jesus revolutionized life for many in His time and setting. John's wish, we may be certain, is that his gospel would do likewise for many more today.

1

IN THE BEGINNING (1:1-51)

In the first chapter of his gospel, John opens a panoramic vista stretching from eternity past (v. 1) to the mysterious glories of Jesus' earthly ministry (v. 51). He describes in summary form who Jesus is, what marks Him as unique, what His earthly life accomplished, and how His ministry got underway. All this sets the stage for the chapters following. John's stated intention (20:31) is to commend Jesus to us as deserving our rapt attention, personal loyalty, and complete obedience. In Him and Him alone we find forgiveness for sins and our highest destiny in life as servants, not of our personal goals and interests, but of Christ's.

JESUS' DEITY (1:1-5):
WHO HE IS

RELIGIONS, PHILOSOPHIES—AND THE SON OF GOD (1:1-3)

The ancient world, like ours today, swarmed with religious movements and leaders.[1] Official Roman religion honored the emperor and the Roman state. Local pagan deities were worshiped for the benefit they were thought to bring to the communities that venerated them. For example, in Acts 14:13 we read of a priest and temple honoring the Greek god Zeus. Various philosophies abounded, promising deliverance from ignorance and evil by indoctrination into noble and transforming ideas.[2]

---

1. See Jack Finegan, *Myth and Mystery: An Introduction to the Pagan Religions of the Biblical World* (Grand Rapids: Baker, 1989).
2. See Frederick Copleston, *A History of Philosophy*, vol. 1, pts. 1 and 2 (Garden City, N.Y.: Doubleday, 1962).

John's gospel points to neither a religion nor a philosophy. It points instead to Jesus Christ.[3] To do so it first establishes His status: He is, in the words of the ancient creed, very God of very God. In other words, Jesus is divine, no less than the unseen heavenly Father Himself (v. 18). "The Word," who took on full human existence ("flesh") in the life of Jesus Christ (vv. 14, 17), "was God" (v. 1).

Jesus' divinity is seen first in this: "In the beginning," farther back than the human mind can conceive, "the Word was with God" (v. 2). For the ancient Jewish reader the Word signified God's powerful creative presence (Ps. 33:6). God's work is done with infalliable effectiveness by the Word He sends forth (Isa. 55:11). Some non-Jewish readers might find a different meaning. In Greek philosophy the Logos (word) was the coherent unity giving order to the universe. Although John may have either or both meanings in mind,[4] Jesus is greater still. He not only achieves God's purposes and gives meaning to the universe, His eternality is as unquestioned and complete as God's itself (see Ps. 90:2). This marks Him as profoundly one with the one true and living God.

Jesus' divinity is seen second in this: "Through him all things were made" (v. 3). The Old Testament states that "God created the heavens and the earth" (Gen. 1:1). John says that it is through Jesus that God did this (see also Col. 1:16-17; Heb. 1:2). Life itself has its origin in the Word. When God spoke the world into being (Heb. 11:3), Jesus Christ was actively present.

THE LIGHT OF THE WORLD (1:4-5)

Finally, Jesus' divinity is revealed by what He brings to the world. He brings light (v. 4). In Scripture light often denotes God's essence, His nature and sinless purity (1 John 1:5). Darkness (v. 5), on the other hand, refers to sin, the spiritual and moral corruption that grips mankind. God beams forth His purifying radiance, which destroys and rescues from sin, by the light that shines in the darkness. That darkness has often shunned the light or sought to repress it. But

3. Martin Albertz, a New Testament scholar imprisoned by the Nazis, pungently asserts this in his German work *The Message of the New Testament*, vol. 2, pt. 1 (Zollikon-Zurich: Evangelischer Verlag, 1954), pp. 15-21.

4. For a full discussion of John's use of *logos*, see Raymond Brown, *The Gospel According to John*, vol. 1 (Garden City, N.Y.: Doubleday, 1966), pp. 519-24.

with the tough patience of a God who loves the world He has made (3:16), the Word is a beacon of God's cleansing light.

In a darkened world full of gods and religions and philosophies, in a complex world much like ours, teeming with competing religious theories, cults, and claims, God acts to show mankind who He is and what He offers. The Word is the person in whom God cuts through all ignorance and deception to make His presence savingly known. This person is Jesus Christ.

JOHN THE BAPTIST'S WITNESS (1:6-8, 15): ESTABLISHING JESUS' UNIQUENESS

Jesus did not burst on the scene unheralded. A man called John prepared the way (see vv. 19-28 below; this is not the John who writes this gospel but John the Baptist). His job was to be a witness.[5] In the Old Testament (Deut. 19:15), as for Jesus (Matt. 18:16) and the early church (2 Cor. 13:1), it was through witnesses that facts were established. What someone said might be safely ignored if it was not confirmed by the legally sworn testimony, or witness, of others.

John was sent from God (v. 6; see Luke 1:5-25, 57-80) to furnish grounds for persons to believe in Jesus. He was sent to vouch for Jesus as the unique savior of mankind. He pointed to the light. God sent John so that "through him," through John the Baptist, "all men might believe" (v. 7).

John had much in common with Jesus. Their mothers were relatives (Luke 1:36).[6] Unusual circumstances surrounded both of their conceptions and births. From their infancies God was present with both in uncanny ways (Luke 1:15-16; 2:40-52). As they each began preaching, their messages were identical (Matt. 3:2; 4:17).

But the resemblance had its limits. John "was not the light" (v. 8). This does not mean he was unimportant. He testifies, lays down vitally important and morally binding claims, about Jesus (v. 15). Elsewhere Jesus points out what a great responsibility John fulfilled (Matt. 11:11). Still, John's highest calling was to put Jesus first. This is reasonable, for He was before John (v. 15). In antiquity old things that

5. A full-length study of the importance of "witness" in John is John M. Boice, *Witness and Revelation in the Gospel of John* (Grand Rapids: Eerdmans, 1970).

6. See J. A. T. Robinson, *Priority of John*, pp. 119-22.

had proved themselves, not new and novel ones that tickled popular fancy, commanded respect. John apparently had some sense of Jesus' timeless origins (see 8:58). For this reason he gladly called his world to get ready for who was coming and then selflessly got out of the way when He appeared on the scene. John's preparatory work marked Jesus as the unique savior of mankind whose ministry would eventually vindicate, yet overshadow, that of John (3:30).

JESUS' ACHIEVEMENT (1:9-13, 16-18): REVEALING GOD

LORD OVER ALL (1:9-13)

Jesus' coming has a universal effect; no one is untouched (v. 9). This does not mean all are saved (3:36). It means that all true knowledge of God comes about as hearts are enlightened by "the light of the knowledge of the glory of God in the face of Christ" (2 Cor. 4:6).

Many did not recognize Jesus for who He was (v. 10). There is irony and tragedy in the fact that the creator of mankind met rejection from "the world" He brought into being. The first "his own" of v. 11 refers to all aspects and objects of creation. The second "his own" seems to refer to the Jewish nation, to which Jesus belonged. Its people were God's chosen vehicle of His saving grace; "salvation is from the Jews" (4:22; see Rom. 9:4-5). But many of them, too, turned aside when He extended Himself to them as their king.

Yet many "received him." To do so they "believed in his name." John writes of "believing," always in verbal form, some ninety-eight times in his gospel.[7] He never uses the noun "faith." This may be a clue to what believing in Jesus involves. It is not a thing, a lifeless object, a static attitude of passive agreement and acceptance. It is a dynamic posture, an activity, a living devotion.

Believing "in his name" involves total commitment to what Jesus' name signifies and demands.[8] The name *Jesus* means literally "Yahweh is salvation." It points to the God of the Old Testament

---

7. See the discussion in Brown, *Gospel According to John*, vol. 1, pp. 512-14. An older but useful commentary emphasizing "believing" is Merrill C. Tenney, *John: The Gospel of Belief* (Grand Rapids: Eerdmans, 1948).

8. Note the valuable discussion in W. Bingham Hunter, *The God Who Hears* (Downers Grove: InterVarsity, 1986), pp. 191-99.

(and the New Testament too), a God of mercy and grace who offers pardon and new life yet rejects those who steadfastly reject Him (Ex. 34:6-7). To believe in the name of Jesus means to enter an all-encompassing, life-transforming relationship with the God whom Jesus has come to disclose. It means to live life no longer for oneself but instead for Jesus Christ (2 Cor. 5:15) and ultimately for the God He came to reveal.

Those who received Him were granted a new standing. From then on, God regarded them as His children. This is not a "right" that persons have in themselves or can earn. It is not a matter of natural parentage, ethnic heritage, or personal initiative. Yet the opportunity to receive it arises through believing in Jesus. Those who thus believe are born of God. Jesus will explain this "new birth" more fully in chapter 3.

THE WONDROUS INCARNATION (1:14, 16-18)

The Word made His home in the midst of mankind for a season (v. 14). The gospel writer was a personal witness of this unique event in which the unseen God "became flesh." "Grace and truth," characteristics of God Himself, filled Jesus' earthly life.[9] This same grace He offered freely to others (v. 16). "One blessing after another" is literally "grace in place of grace." This may refer to the "grace" of the gospel, the saving message of Jesus, which completes and expands the gracious covenant love God had already extended to all those who sought Him in Old Testament times.

If so, then v. 16 is restated more fully in v. 17. Moses was the channel of God's holy law and the covenant promises of the Old Testament, which according to Jesus' are more life-giving than natural food itself (Matt. 4:4; see Ps. 119:97-104). Great as the assurances of the Scriptures Moses penned are, they receive their completed meaning and saving power in the grace and truth that "came through Jesus Christ."

Jesus is the name Joseph and Mary were told to give their child, since His destiny was to "save his people from their sins" (Matt. 1:21; Luke 1:31). "Christ" is the Greek translation of the Hebrew "Messiah." It marks Jesus as the high king over all kings ever appointed by

9. On the meaning of "truth" in John see Ignace de la Potterie, "The Truth in St. John," in John Ashton, ed., *Interpretation of John*, pp. 53-66.

God to deliver His people. Other kings, such as David, were "anointed ones" or "messiahs"; Jesus is the unique Messiah, whose eternal reign fulfills God's ancient promise of deliverance by a king of David's royal line (2 Sam. 7).

John's gospel has already affirmed repeatedly the exalted status and accomplishment of Jesus Christ. Verse 18 goes even further. Although God the Father in His essence and full glory transcends man's physical and spiritual comprehension, that same God has made Himself known. Since man cannot reach Him, He has come to man. He has done so through the one who has always been "at the Father's side," in closest imaginable personal union with Him. "God the One and Only," like "the Word" an unusual designation for Jesus Christ, discloses the unseen God to mankind, who desperately needs His forgiving acceptance and transforming presence. No higher tribute could be paid to what Jesus Christ, because of who He is, is able to achieve.

JESUS' PUBLIC MINISTRY TAKES SHAPE (1:19-51): CREDENTIALS AND DISCIPLES

The rest of chapter 1 does two things. First, it clarifies Jesus' credentials. It gives reasons, based on John the Baptist's claims, why the reader should take Jesus seriously. Second, it relates how the first band of Jesus' followers was formed.

JOHN THE BAPTIST IDENTIFIES THE LAMB OF GOD (1:19-34)

From the time of the Old Testament prophet Malachi (about 440 B.C.) until John the Baptist there had been no widely accredited prophet among the Jews. For this reason John created quite a stir when he appeared on the scene. There was widespread longing among the Jews for God, the covenant God of the descendants of Abraham, to act. They wished to see Him deliver His people from Roman occupation by establishing His kingdom anew in Jerusalem (see Luke 2:25, 38; Acts 1:6). To do this, of course, would mean the defeat of the hated Romans. The Jews wondered: Was John the Baptist perhaps the first prophetic sign of what God was about to do?

The Jews of Jerusalem (v. 19) were religious authorities concerned that John might be a dangerous fanatic or imposter. John made no pretense of being the Christ, God's anointed deliverer. But the questioners persisted. Was he Elijah (v. 21)? Malachi had foretold that Elijah would return to prepare the way just before "that great and dreadful day of the Lord" (Mal. 4:5). Or was he the Prophet (v. 21)? Moses had foretold that God would one day send a prophet like Moses, only greater (Deut. 18:15).

John replied that he was neither. Quoting Isaiah 40:3, he identified his role as one of preparation for a great work the Lord was about to do (v. 23).

But there were other questioners. The priests and Levites (v. 19) represented those Jews who placed great stress on the Jerusalem Temple and its elaborate rituals as being the center of true worship of God. The Pharisees (v. 24) had a different emphasis. They stressed scrupulous adherence to an elaborate set of oral traditions. These traditions, they maintained, made proper obedience to the Old Testament possible. John's preaching called on all Jews, including the Pharisees, to repent. This was a direct challenge to their authority and social prestige, for among the Jews they were widely thought to be the most upright and pious religious group of their day.

"Why then do you baptize?" they demanded, scoffing at John as they would later scoff at Jesus (Matt. 21:23). John's reply played down his own personal significance, yet tantalized his detractors with the claim that the answer to their question was right under their noses (v. 26).

On the next day (v. 29) this answer appeared in person. "This is the one I meant," John exclaimed (v. 30). This is "the Lamb of God, who takes away the sin of the world" (v. 29). John's language identified Jesus as the innocent sacrificial victim whose suffering would atone for the sins of many (Isa. 53:4-7).[10]

John and Jesus were cousins. When John said, "I myself did not know him" (v. 31), he did not mean Jesus was an utter stranger to him. He rather indicated that until that moment he had not realized that the person whose way he had been preparing was none other than the eldest son of his aunt Mary, Jesus' mother.

But how did John single out Jesus among the crowds? God had promised to give John a sign when the right person appeared (v. 33).

---

10. For a somewhat different understanding see Beasley-Murray, *John*, pp. 24-25.

This would be the one whose work would eventually make John's water baptism alone obsolete, for he would "baptize with the Holy Spirit" (v. 33). By prophetic insight John identified Jesus.

With decisive, magisterial finality John the Baptist swore a solemn deposition, like a key witness testifying under oath on the witness stand. Using the perfect tense, which stressed the completeness and ongoing effect of the actions described, John declared he had seen and therefore testified who Jesus was. This is the first of a number of weighty proofs John's gospel will furnish for establishing Jesus' credentials, thus opening up the way for the reader to believe in Him. Jesus is both the Lamb of God (v. 29) and the Son of God (v. 34). He takes away sin, something only God can do (Mark 2:7). He can do this because as God the One and Only (v. 18)—another way of saying the Son of God—it lies within His authority and prerogative to do so.

JESUS CALLS THE DISCIPLES (1:35-51)

The day after John the Baptist proclaimed Jesus' true identity, he repeated his claim in the presence of two of his disciples (vv. 35-36). Their curiosity aroused, they tagged along behind Jesus until He noticed them and asked what they wanted (vv. 37-38). One was Andrew, Simon Peter's brother (v. 40). Each time Andrew is mentioned in John's gospel, he is bringing someone to Jesus (6:8-9; 12:22).

They did not really answer Jesus' question (v. 38); perhaps they were intimidated by the man so highly praised by their previous mentor, John the Baptist. But Jesus encouraged them in a friendly manner. "Tenth hour" was about four in the afternoon. Andrew and the other listener were highly impressed. Andrew immediately informed his brother, Simon Peter, a man destined to play a central role among Jesus' closest followers and in the early church. Jesus gave him a nickname that foreshadowed that central role (v. 42). The Greek word *Peter*, like the Aramaic *Cephas*, means "rock."

Jesus intended to set out for Galilee (v. 43), where much of His ministry described by the other three gospels took place. But He first called Philip to join His band. Later Jesus reminded His disciples that He chose them; they did not choose Him (15:16). So it was in Philip's case.

Like Andrew, Philip must share the news about Jesus with someone else. Just as the Pharisees saw John as a potential claimant to the deliverer foretold in the Old Testament, so Philip wondered whether Jesus might not be a key figure in the strange and wonderful things God was bringing about in the wake of John's electrifying preaching (v. 45).

No one today knows why Nathanael expressed rancor toward Nazareth (v. 46). Perhaps there was simply small town rivalry beween the village in which Jesus grew up and Nathanael's home town, nearby Cana (21:2).[11]

As Nathanael approached Jesus, Jesus amazed him by making pronouncements, first about his personal character (v. 47) and then about where he was standing when Philip found him (v. 48). Later (2:25; 4:17-19) it becomes clear that Jesus was at times capable of prophetic insight into the thoughts and intentions of those He addressed. He appears to have exercised that capacity here. Nathanael was dumbstruck (v. 49). He heaped lofty titles of praise, if not worship, on Him, though time would reveal that he did not really understand the ways in which Jesus would fulfill those roles. For example, Nathanael hailed him as "King of Israel," another way of saying Messiah. But like Pilate much later (18:36-37), Nathanael had little grasp of the nature of Jesus' lordship and intentions at this early point in His ministry.

Jesus did not try to enlarge Nathanael's limited understanding at this juncture. He simply made an authoritative pronouncement, "I tell you the truth" (v. 51). To sympathetic Jewish hearers this unusual expression would give Jesus' statement the weight of words from God Himself. To the unsympathetic they would make Jesus sound like a blasphemer. For the expression (Greek: "amen, amen"; KJV: "verily, verily") signifies that Jesus was setting His words on a par with those of Scripture, as in the synagogue the reading of God's Word would end with the congregation solemnly adding their "Amen!" which meant, "May it be! God's Word is ever true!"[12]

Jesus spoke not to Nathanael alone but to the entire little band surrounding Him. They "shall see heaven open." They would recognize God's presence in "the Son of Man." This title points to Jesus' messi-

---

11. See F. F. Bruce, *The Gospel of John* (Grand Rapids: Eerdmans, 1983), p. 60.
12. Beasley-Murray, *John*, p. 21, states that Jesus used the expression "to introduce important statements, implying that behind them stands the authority of 'the God whose name is Amen' " (NEB, Isa. 65:16).

anic (Dan. 7:13-14) and divine status (3:13; 5:27). It also suggests His humble identification with fallen man through suffering (12:23; 13:31).[13]

Nathanael and the others had no idea of what lay ahead for Jesus and for them. This was just the beginning. But the way was prepared for specifics to begin to take shape. Two important incidents from Jesus' early public ministry gave concrete form to the claims and testimony already recorded. We encounter these incidents in the gospel's next chapter.

---

13. The literature surrounding the meaning of "Son of Man" is voluminous. A solid though dated starting point for further study is Morris, *The Gospel According to John*, pp. 172-73. Much more thorough is Schnackenburg, *The Gospel According to John*, vol. 1, pp. 529-42. For a different treatment with implications for what Son of Man means in John's gospel, see Wayne A. Meeks, "The Man from Heaven in Johannine Sectarianism," in John Ashton, ed., *Interpretation of John*, pp. 141-73.

2

GLORY AND SIGNS (2:1-25)

In the first chapter of John, a number of indicators point to Jesus Christ's unique origin, insight, and destiny. How will these indicators work themselves out in real life experience? Do they really merit the reader's serious attention and his personal commitment to Jesus Christ (20:31)? Chapter two begins to answer these questions. The reader has already heard of Jesus' glory (1:14); now he will see an expression of it. The reader has also encountered John the Baptist's lofty claims about Jesus. Now he will consider a report—Jesus' prediction of His own resurrection—which may make the Baptist's claims seem if anything too modest.

WATER TO WINE (2:1-11)

NOT YET TIME (2:1-10)

"On the third day" (v. 1) has no mysterious meaning. It merely links this incident with the two preceding days when Jesus first began to gather disciples. Cana was a small village some nine miles to the north of Nazareth, where Jesus had spent the bulk of His life up to that point.

The question arises why Jesus' mother[1] spoke to Him when the wine supply ran out (v. 3). Although Jesus may have been invited to the gathering all along, there could have been no advance planning for

---

1. On the role of Jesus' mother and other women in John's gospel, see the feminist perspective offered by Turid Karlsen Seim, "Roles of Women in the Gospel of John," in Lars Hartman and Birger Olsson, eds., *Aspects on the Johannine Literature* (Uppsala: Almquist & Wiksell International, 1987), pp. 56-73.

His disciples, for they had come together only the day before. In that case, it was partially Jesus' fault that there was not enough wine.

Jesus gently rebuffed Mary (v. 4). It was not yet His time, He replied. In the overall sweep of John, Jesus' time (literally "hour") is that period focused on His crucifixion and resurrection.[2] It is the point when He would fulfill the ultimate purpose for which God sent Him. Mary, who like John the Baptist must have sensed that God's hand was on Jesus in an unusual way, presumed on His ability and willingness to perform a dramatic act. Jesus' response shows that His goal was to fulfill His ultimate mission of redeeming mankind, not to be at the beck and call of anyone who might wish to capitalize on the power of God at work in Him.

Yet Jesus, who would later observe that He always did what pleased His Father (8:29), found liberty to comply with the request. Huge stone crocks were at hand, common in a kosher household, where many items must be continually purified (see Mark 7:3-4). Some may have already held water. Jesus insisted that they all be "filled . . . to the brim" (v. 7). Then the servants were to remove some of the contents and take it to the person in charge of the wedding feast (v. 8).

The "master of the banquet" (v. 9) knew nothing of what had been going on behind the scenes. He had likely been absorbed in his own embarrassment at presiding over a festive gathering where there was nothing left to drink. Upon sampling the sudden new supply, he excitedly summoned the groom, who probably had final responsibility for food and beverages at the feast. Near the end of such celebrations palates become less and less discriminating. One would expect the last rounds of wine to be of lower quality (v. 10). But this situation was quite different. The wine was excellent, even better than what was served before. The day was saved, and the merrymaking could continue.

THE FIRST SIGN (2:11)

John's gospel is not primarily interested, however, in Jesus' ability to transform ordinary water into fermented drink (there is no evi-

2. For discussion of all of John's twenty-six uses of the word, see Brown, *Gospel According to John*, 1:517-18.

dence that the wine was nonalcoholic[3]). John is interested in the significance of what Jesus' action implied. He refers to it as "the first of his miraculous signs" (v. 11). A "sign" is a deed or occurrence that points beyond itself to a reality more significant than the occurrence alone.[4] At least as far as Galilee is concerned, this is the first public manifestation of God's awe-inspiring personal presence, His glory, through Jesus.

Some point to the symbolic significance of Jesus' act: He transforms the ordinary water of Jewish ritual into the new wine that points men to Himself.[5] It is not necessary, however, to see a put-down of Jewish customs in what Jesus does. John underscores not the uselessness of ritual washings, but the awesome divine glory that Jesus' deed reflected, which filled the disciples' hearts with new respect and trust in Him.

No doubt it was an incomplete faith. They had barely begun their time of intensive instruction and ministry that would cover the next several dozen months. But the preaching and claims of their former leader John the Baptist had already been vindicated in grand fashion. "The glory of the One and Only, who came from the Father, full of grace and truth" (v. 1:14), was truly in their midst. Jesus' prediction of 1:51 had already begun to be fulfilled.

TEMPLE CLEANSING (2:12-25)

WORSHIP CENTER OR BAZAAR? (2:12-14)

From Cana, site of the wedding feast, it was but a dozen miles down to the coastal village of Capernaum. In addition to "his disciples," Jesus' "mother and brothers" also went along. It is likely they were all simply returning home. In any case Capernaum was known as Jesus' residence during much of His ministry (Matt. 9:1; see also 8:5).

But He did not stay long. There were three main annual feasts in Jerusalem (Deut. 16:16), and the Passover (v. 13) was one of them. It

---

3. See F. S. Fitzsimmonds, "Wine and Strong Drink," in J. D. Douglas, ed., *The New Bible Dictionary* (Grand Rapids: Eerdmans, 1979), pp. 1331-32.

4. Colin Brown, *Miracles and the Critical Mind* (Grand Rapids: Eerdmans, 1984), pp. 322-24. More comprehensively, see Rudolph Schnackenburg, *The Gospel According to John*, vol. 1 (New York: Seabury, 1980), pp. 515-28.

5. Bruce, *John*, p. 71.

was celebrated in the Jewish month of Nisan, our March-April. It commemorated the night that God spared the Israelites as He took the life of every firstborn, animal or human, in ancient Egypt (Ex. 12).[6]

Jesus "went up" to Jerusalem since Capernaum on the Sea of Galilee was 696 feet below sea level, whereas Jerusalem stands at about 2,600 feet above sea level. Upon arriving at the Temple He found at least two classes of entrepreneurs hard at work.

One group sold various animals. These would be purchased by pilgrims who had come to make Temple sacrifices. Many would have traveled hundreds of miles. They had no way of transporting suitable animals with them. So cattle and sheep were readily available on the spot—for a price. Doves were offered by those too poor to purchase the larger animals that Jewish law normally called for (Lev. 12:8). Jesus' own parents had offered doves or pigeons (Luke 2:24) when the infant Jesus was circumcised.

Another group exchanged money. The Temple authorities would not accept Roman coinage, for it bore images of the Roman rulers, whom the Jews had no desire to honor. Since the Romans did not permit the Jews to mint their own coins, officials in Jerusalem determined that money used to purchase sacrifices or to pay the annual Temple tax must be changed into Tyrian coins, the currency of the nearby coastal city of Tyre.

From childhood Jesus had possessed a strong sense of the sanctity of the Temple. At age twelve He had called it "my Father's house" (Luke 2:49). The Old Testament hallowed the Temple as "a house of prayer for all nations" (Isa. 56:7). God had ordained it to be a sacred center of worship. In Jesus' day the Temple was the scene of much honorable devotion to God by those who trusted in His promises to redeem His chosen people (see Luke 2:27, 36-37). After His ascension, Jesus' disciples continued to meet and worship God in the Temple (Acts 2:46; 3:1). Jesus harbored no ill will toward the Temple itself nor toward the true worship of God that went on there.

But not all that went on was true worship. For years Jesus would have witnessed a flea market atmosphere in some quarters as He wor-

---

6. Old Testament events, themes, and citations play a significant role throughout John's gospel. See Carson, *Gospel According to John*, p. 98.

shiped in Jerusalem in keeping with the religious calendar. For years He had allowed the sacrilege to pass unchallenged. But the time for public proclamation of God's saving grace and judgment had come. John the Baptist had broken the silence of God's prophets that had lasted for some five hundred years, since the time of Malachi in the Old Testament. Now it was Jesus' turn to further what the Baptist had begun. The time for silence was past. In proud Jerusalem an object lesson was needed to give point to Jesus' pressing claims and to dramatize that God was not some passive, tolerant observer of the holy city but powerfully present and actively aware. Many had come to ignore this fact, as God had already expressed it in His Word; now they would be confronted with it in the person of His son.

ZEAL FOR TRUE WORSHIP (2:15-17)

In the quiet strength of the Spirit Jesus deliberately "made a whip out of cords" (2:15). With it He started a stampede. Plunging livestock, fluttering birds, and scrambling pilgrims fled before this sudden burst of conviction and zeal. If it was business they wanted instead of worship, Jesus would give it to them! Counters and the money they contained were sent skidding across the cobblestones (v. 15). Addressing the dove sellers, whom Jesus might have remembered as the very hucksters who had gouged His own impoverished parents in years past, Jesus reasserted that the Temple was His Father's house (v. 16). Such a claim to unique sonship was significant, for in the broad sense God was the Father of the whole Jewish nation, not just Jesus. Jesus' statement was understood as placing Himself in a relationship with God that no one else shared. This was implicit blasphemy (5:18), a claim to be equal with almighty God.

The whole dramatic spectacle took on special meaning for Jesus' disciples (v. 17) in the light of the Old Testament. John probably described a remembering that took place later, possibly even after Jesus had risen from the grave (v. 22) and the full import of His words and actions took on greater clarity.

The immediate force of what Jesus had done was not lost on the Jews (v. 20). As in 1:19, these were the religious and to some extent civic leaders in Jerusalem. Jesus had disrupted religious proceedings at a busy time when Jerusalem was packed with pilgrims for the most solemn celebration of the entire year.[7]

Jesus also risked incurring the displeasure of Roman troops stationed in the fortress overlooking the Temple. They were always on the alert to quell disturbances that might arise (see Acts 21:31-32), as many did in the volatile years of Roman occupation. Later Jesus Himself would have to face their merciless brutality (Matt. 27:27-31). Jewish authorities realized that public disorder was unacceptable to the Romans and that if the Jews did not maintain proper order, the Romans might deprive them of what little right to self-rule they still maintained (11:48).

BY WHAT AUTHORITY (2:18-21)

So the Jews, who knew that both John the Baptist and Jesus were making prophetic claims that challenged their religious power and threatened public order, demanded that Jesus produce a "miraculous sign" to demonstrate His "authority" (v. 18).

Here it is helpful to recall what the preaching of both John the Baptist and Jesus implied about God's verdict on the Jews, the religious hierarchy with their own systems of religion and politics who never did acknowledge the prophetic authority of either the Baptist or Jesus (Matt. 21:23-27). Although many Jews responded readily to the divine call to repentance and later to the preaching of the gospel, the power echelon in Jerusalem, seemingly corrupted by their own self-importance and vested interests, were largely incapable of careful consideration of God's appointed messengers. They were generally uninterested in learning from Jesus; they sought rather to limit His influence and oppose His message by whatever means necessary. For Jesus, standing in solidarity with John the Baptist, was from the beginning an unmistakable challenge to the understanding of God's rule among His people that the Jerusalem hierarchy championed.

7. Matthew, Mark, and Luke speak of a Temple cleansing during Jesus' final week in Jerusalem, just before His crucifixion. Many interpreters suggest that John took an incident that happened late in Jesus' ministry and transposed it to the beginning for literary or theological effect. An alternative view is that Jesus cleansed the Temple twice. See Morris, *Gospel According to John*, pp. 188-91. Still highly instructive are John Calvin's observations; see *The Gospel According to St. John*, vol. 1, trans. T. H. L. Parker (Grand Rapids: Eerdmans, 1961), pp. 51-52.

The question in v. 18, then, does not necessarily reflect a serious desire to hear Jesus out or respond penitently to the misuse of God's house that He has just unmasked. It is a cautious yet stern charge that Jesus has acted in an unlawful if not blasphemous fashion. Unless He can prove Himself innocent in a way that they will accept, He is guilty of usurping their power, which they equated with God's reign, over the holy city and the worship taking place there.

Jesus honored their request but not on their terms. He referred to an event still many months in the future (v. 19). The "sign" He offered them was the sign His followers would one day preach to the whole world, His bodily resurrection (v. 21).

The Jews, however, took His words literally (v. 20). They knew that Herod the Great, who reigned 40–4 B.C., began a Temple expansion program around 20 B.C. (which dates this incident at around A.D. 28). Not until A.D. 64 was the mammoth project completed. How could any one person possibly rebuild the Temple in three centuries, let alone in three days?

UNANSWERED QUESTIONS AND SIGNS (2:22-25)

John's gospel does not tell how the confrontation continued or ended. Instead it breaks into the account to inform the reader that even the disciples did not understand what Jesus meant until after He arose and appeared to them. Then Jesus' "words" (v. 19) took on meaning, backed up by the sacred Scripture. (For an example of how the Old Testament enabled believers to interpret Jesus' death and resurrection, see Ps. 16:10, then Acts 13:34-37.)

John presents this incident, then, as a second "sign" (the first was water into wine) of the power and divine origin that John the Baptist claimed for Jesus in chapter 1.

Apparently this was only the beginning, not the end, of the stir Jesus created during that Passover. Although He refused to bow and scrape before the arrogant authorities who demanded that He meet their standards, He evidently performed a number of "miraculous signs" (v. 23) before common folk more open to His humbling message. These "believed in his name" because of the signs they saw. John does not say whether this was an enduring faith or merely a temporary commitment resulting from excitement at the signs.

In either case, though some trusted Jesus (v. 23), He knew better than to trust them (v. 24). The time would come when even the staunchest disciples would fall away. Jesus looked to His Father alone, as the prophets of old taught: "Cursed is the one who trusts in man, who depends on flesh for his strength and whose heart turns away from the Lord" (Jer. 17:5). The other gospels tell of Jesus' temptations and of the long nights of prayer by which He maintained fidelity to and unity with the heavenly Father (see John 17:22-23). Jesus was fully human, but He showed that the highest wisdom of man is to know that in God alone is deliverance.

For Jesus "knew all men." Like God in 1 Samuel 16:7, He saw beyond appearances to the heart. He saw the lurking evil, the need for purifying new beginnings, in every person (v. 25), from the everyday people round about Him at Cana and Jerusalem to the prestigious authorities among the Jews, including Nicodemus in the next chapter.

Chapter two of John's gospel, then, illustrates how Jesus' glory and signs went forth publicly and convincingly among the masses. It introduces the opposition of the national leaders. It shows that John the Baptist was justified in all he claimed for Jesus.

Chapter three will illustrate how Jesus conveyed His identity and message privately to the top level of those whose faith in their spirituality was the strongest and whose opposition to Jesus was the most decided and severe. It will also record John the Baptist's final solemn verdict on the eternal importance and entire truthfulness of the message Jesus brought.

3

NEW BIRTH (3:1-36)

Jesus aroused suspicion even before He made His public debut. The Jerusalem authorities interrogated John the Baptist closely regarding the mysterious figure whom He claimed was about to appear (1:19; 24-25). Shortly thereafter, as Jesus inaugurated His public ministry in the heartland of traditional Jewish worship—the area of Jerusalem, with its Temple—His bold actions and rebukes were not kindly received (2:18). In short order Jesus went from unknown to notorious. Although some made initial positive response to His striking deeds (2:23), John makes clear that in important respects Jesus stood alone over against those around Him (2:25). The darkness did not comprehend the light (1:5).

Chapter 3 recounts the probing private queries of an eminent religious authority of the time, Nicodemus (3:1-21). Jesus took the opportunity to impress a leader of His staunchest opponents, the Pharisees, with the nature of God's dealings through John the Baptist and Jesus Himself. He explained what is necessary for a person to see and enter the kingdom of God, which had broken upon that generation with particular force.

Chapter 3 also sums up and completes John the Baptist's strategic testimony about Jesus (3:22-36). We will hear no more from the Baptist himself in this gospel. But the witness he records will aptly describe the relationship of his ministry to that of Jesus. John will comment pungently on the lofty status, and thus authority, of Jesus. Those who turn away from, ignore, or in any way minimize His central importance, the Baptist insists, are making a foolhardy and tragic error.

INVITATION TO THE LIGHT (3:1-21)

JESUS AND THE PHARISEES (3:1)

Chapter 2 ends with the words "[Jesus] knew what was in a man" (2:25). Chapter 3 gives a specific illustration of what Jesus knew.

The man in question was Nicodemus (3:1). He was a Pharisee.[1] The Pharisees were a highly trained and dedicated group of men who sought to honor God by an elaborate system of observances and rules that affected behavior in all of life. They held that the Old Testament was God's word but that the right way to approach the God of the Old Testament had been handed down over the centuries in the form of traditions. These were called "traditions of the elders" (Mark 7:5).

At numerous points the Pharisees' views agreed with what Jesus Himself taught. Like Jesus, they believed in the bodily resurrection, the authority of the whole of the Old Testament, tithing, and the existence of angels. Also like Jesus, they taught that God was concerned with the behavior of His people at all times and in all settings. So it is not surprising that at one point Jesus tells His listeners to obey the Pharisees and observe all that they teach (Matt. 23:3).

Jesus accused the Pharisees, however, of grave errors. He warned against aspects of their teaching (Matt. 16:6). Their veneration of human traditions tended to overshadow divine commands (Mark 7:8). They too often failed to practice what they taught (Matt. 23:3).

While the conflict between Jesus and the Pharisees is prominent in all the gospels, including John, it should not be forgotten that some of their views were quite sound and that many of them eventually became Christians. Paul Himself was a Pharisee (Phil. 3:5), and Pharisees played an active, though sometimes troublesome, role in the early church (Acts 15:5). It should also not be supposed that all Jews in the time of Jesus were Pharisees. One ancient writer estimates that there were only about 6,000 of them at any one time during the first cen-

---

1. Instructive observations on the relationship of the Pharisees' views to Jesus' comments about them in John's gospel are found in Adolf Schlatter, *John the Evangelist* (Stuttgart: Calwer, 1975), pp. 83-103.

tury.[2] They were in fact a tiny minority, though they wielded great influence. Finally, it should not be forgotten that they were looked up to as paragons of doctrinal soundness and commitment by many of their countrymen. In criticizing the Pharisees Jesus was calling into question the best and most honored religious experts, not some fringe group of unsavory extremists. In this way Jesus raised questions about the integrity of all His listeners, not just the Pharisees alone.

SECRET MEETING (3:2-5)

Nicodemus met Jesus at night (v. 2). Possibly this was to avoid publicity, since he sat on the Sanhedrin, the Jewish high court in Jerusalem, and may have wanted to collect information without attracting unwanted attention. Or he may have found it necessary to come at night simply because that was when serious talk was possible, without the confusion and interruptions that Jesus' daytime appearances generated.

No one knows for sure how sincere Nicodemus's opening statement was (v. 2). Was he being honest, or was he buttering up Jesus as other Pharisees did later (Matt. 22:15-17)? Either way, Jesus' reply got to the real issue. With the solemn authority Jesus often claimed for His utterances (see remarks on 1:51 above), He declared that without a new birth (or perhaps a birth "from above"–the Greek can be translated two ways), God's kingdom in its real significance would remain invisible to the observer.

Thus, even if Nicodemus did seriously acknowledge Jesus' insight as a teacher and power as a miracle worker, that in itself was not enough. Something new and fresh, something only God alone could bring about, must take place in his own personal life.

Nicodemus immediately raised a question, perhaps trying to make Jesus' statement look absurd (v. 4). Jesus remained unshaken (v. 5). Spiritual birth, or rebirth, is required.

2. This is the estimate of Josephus. See his comments on the Pharisees (a party to which he belonged for a time) in *Jewish Wars* 2.162-66; *Antiquities* 18.12-15. See also J. Bowker, *Jesus and the Pharisees* (Cambridge: University, 1973).

NEW BIRTH (3:5-6)

A number of interpretations have been suggested for Jesus' words "born of water and the Spirit" (v. 5; literally "born of water and of Spirit"). For example, some see "water" as John's baptism and "Spirit" as the new life to which John's preaching refers and which Jesus Himself offers.

Others suggest that "water" is physical birth and "Spirit" the regeneration worked by God in the human heart. Against this, there seems to be no evidence that ancient writers associated water with physical birth in the way some do today.

Others suggest that "water" is Christian baptism and "Spirit" is God's work in the heart, which baptism signifies. This may be reading later church teaching back into a night-time exchange between Rabbi Jesus and His Pharisee questioner.

A fourth proposal is to see "water" and "Spirit" as two ways of indicating one reality, the reality of God's rejuvenating spiritual presence. One might translate this as "water, indeed the regenerating water of the Spirit of God Himself." The Old Testament sometimes links water and God's Spirit quite closely (Ezek. 36:25-27), and Nicodemus might have understood Jesus' reference in that way.[3]

The first or fourth suggestions seem most likely. In verse 6 Jesus explains further. "Flesh," or mankind in its natural sinful state, reproduces itself. Like produces like. Nicodemus with his natural experience and understanding will always be what he is at the moment, unable to see or enter God's kingdom. Yet there is hope. God's Spirit can work a great change. The Spirit can transform flesh and infuse it with a new quality of awareness and life.

BORN OF THE SPIRIT (3:7-13)

Apparently Jesus sensed that Nicodemus was not following His line of thought or was simply rejecting it. In verse 7 He seems to challenge Nicodemus's failure, or refusal, to understand. The first "you" in verse 7 is singular, addressing Nicodemus. The second is plural, in-

---

3. See D. A. Carson, *Exegetical Fallacies* (Grand Rapids: Baker, 1984), pp. 41-42. Carson cites the study of Linda L. Belleville, "'Born of Water and Spirit': John 3:5," *Trinity Journal* 1(1980): 125-40.

dicating that Jesus is applying what He says either to Jews like Nicodemus as a whole, or to mankind generally. Either way, all "must be born again." There is no alternative. It is an absolute necessity. Such authoritative pronouncement was unusual among religious teachers of the Pharisees (see Mark 1:22), who saw authority as a chain of memorized traditions and practices, not the definitive insight of any one particular person alone.

Jesus likened the Spirit's work to the wind (v. 8). Nobody questions that the wind produces definite effects, even though no one can control it or explain all the details of what causes its velocity, direction, and shifts. So it is with the Spirit. His workings are mysterious and beyond human manipulation, but this should not be any harder to accept than the fact of wind. Still, Nicodemus expressed incredulity (v. 9). What Jesus was saying, and the very tone He used, were quite out of step with much of what Nicodemus would have accepted and been accustomed to.

In verse 10 Jesus imitates Nicodemus's response with some incredulity of His own. Or perhaps He gently chides this recognized authority who has so much to learn about theological basics. For the third time Jesus invoked His special authority ("I tell you the truth"; see vv. 3, 5). The "we" of verse 11 may refer to either of three groups (or some combination of these groups): Jesus and His disciples, Jesus and His heavenly Father, or Jesus along with John the Baptist and the Old Testament prophets. In any case Jesus addressed the major problem: "you people," the Jewish hierarchy that Nicodemus represented, did not accept the testimony through which God was calling their generation, and especially themselves as self-proclaimed leaders, to repentance. They had turned away from the very means God had chosen to use for their enlightenment and redemption.

Jesus had employed earthly metaphors such as birth and the wind, yet Nicodemus refused to believe (v. 12). The "you" is plural, i.e., those Nicodemus represents. How will they possibly understand still loftier truths? Yet whether they chose to accept what Jesus (and John the Baptist before Him) said or not, He proceeded to present some of the heavenly realities that confront all mankind in God's Son. He was in a position to know what He was talking about, for His own origins, while earthly, were not merely earthly. He "came from heaven" (v. 13), a statement shedding light indirectly on the virgin birth described in Matthew and Luke. Therefore, due to His origin and His status as Son of Man (see comments on 1:51), He was qualified to speak authoritatively on realities that were presently unknown to Nicodemus.

MOSES, THE SERPENT, AND LIFE (3:14-15)

Moses was the most important Old Testament figure for the Pharisees. Through Moses God gave the Law, which was in turn the primary basis for Pharisaic belief. Jesus showed that even Moses recognized the basic dynamics of the salvation Jesus came to reveal (v. 14; see Num. 21:8-9). This is a salvation that is not gained, even in part, by human merit through the successful mental mastery of traditions and scrupulous observance of religious ritual. It is rather a salvation brought about by God's free creative act. His mysterious Spirit and grace move and enliven as God wills, and they are not bound by human systems, like the traditions of the Pharisees, designed to tame and make them subject to human control and manipulation.

As God used the upraised serpent,[4] so He will use the uplifted Son of Man (v. 14). "Must" signifies the divine will and necessity of what Jesus foretold. "Lifted up" in John's gospel (see also 8:28; 12:32, 34) has the double meaning of "being exalted" and of being crucified, that is, "lifted up" on a criminal's cross. This is an example of the use of irony common throughout John's gospel.[5]

The result of the Son of Man's exaltation is even more powerful and enduring than Moses' lifting up the bronze serpent in the wilderness. That was a cure for the bite of poisonous snakes. Those who look to Jesus, who place their trust squarely in Him, will receive not a temporary cure for physical affliction but a whole new quality of existence, "eternal life" (v. 15).

GOD SO LOVED (3:16)

Some commentators see verses 16-21 as the gospel writer's comments, not the words of Jesus Himself. Yet most modern translations extend Jesus' words to Nicodemus to the end of verse 21. There seems

---

4. For a valuable survey of ancient understandings of this OT incident, see Westcott, *Gospel According to John*, pp. 63-64.

5. See Paul Duke, *Irony in the Fourth Gospel* (Atlanta: John Knox, 1985).

to be no compelling reason why Jesus could not have uttered these words on this occasion.[6] Quite likely Nicodemus did not understand all, or even most, of what Jesus was saying. Yet the fact that Nicodemus later would defend Jesus before his peers (7:50-51) suggests that Jesus gave him plenty to chew on during this initial encounter.

Perhaps the most quoted verse in all the Bible, verse 16, explains why the Son must undergo crucifixion (v. 14) and how He will bring about redemption (v. 15). The cruel cross is the result of God's love, which He demonstrates in sending "his one and only son." He makes this sacrifice of His son, of Himself, so that man might have an alternative to condemnation and destruction before God on the day of judgment. Instead of death, there can be life, if Nicodemus and mankind generally will believe.

A further word is necessary on what John means by "believe."[7] This gospel is often called "the Gospel of faith." Yet it is significant that the noun form of the word *believe*, "belief" or "faith," never occurs. However, John uses a verb or verbal form of "believe" nearly one hundred times. What is the significance of this?

At the very least we should observe that "faith" is an action, something carried on in an ongoing fashion as opposed to a static and lifeless memory of something done sometime in the past. Faith is alive and dynamic, not a list of theories or propositions to which we give assent. Believing does involve propositions: John's statement of purpose (20:31) makes clear that saving trust in Christ has a definite content. One must believe, and thus to some extent understand and give assent to the proposition that "Jesus is the Christ, the Son of God." But this is the starting point, not the conclusion, of believing in Christ. Having eternal life, believing in Christ, is both a factual and an intensely personal matter.[8] It exists when one's deepest allegiance and affections are set on Christ and on promoting what promotes Christ, rather than on oneself and how one can further one's own aims in life.

---

6. Brown, *Gospel According to John* 1:149, agrees that "the Gospel presents Jesus as speaking and not the evangelist" in vv. 16-21.

7. For a fuller discussion see Schnackenburg, *Gospel According to John*, 1:558-75.

8. R. C. Sproul speaks in similar terms of how Christians should read the Bible in *Knowing Scripture* (Downers Grove: InterVarsity, 1977), pp. 65-68.

NOT TO JUDGE (3:17-21)

The time will come when Christ will judge all mankind (5:22, 27). But, Jesus told Nicodemus, this was not His task at the moment (3:17). It was rather His desire to seek and to save. Eternal ruin can be averted through trusting in His name (see comments on 1:12). But Nicodemus must act. There is no neutral ground. "Whoever does not believe stands condemned already" (v. 18).

The word "condemned" in verse 18 is related closely to the word "verdict" in 19. This word group often carries courtroom associations. It is as if Jesus were saying "To believe is to avoid having a death sentence pronounced; not to believe is to invite an awful judicial decree" (v. 18). And what is the basis of that decree? It is this (v. 19): God in His brilliant and saving purity has entered the world, and mankind despised that light, unwilling to have its dark deeds shown up for what they are (v. 20). Yet some seek what is good and true in God's eyes. They are attracted to the light and pursue it (v. 21). This shows plainly that God has been at work; they have been born again and are active participants in God's kingdom.

Thus, in His exchange with Nicodemus Jesus ended where He began—with the need for every person, including the religious expert Nicodemus, to allow God to renew him so that he may see and enter the sphere of God's redemptive activity on the earth, His kingdom. A leader of Jerusalem's leaders had been informed in depth, probably deeper than he could then grasp, of the intent and outcome of Jesus' mission.

In the end, Nicodemus would be unable to stop the tide of antagonism against Jesus that resulted in the Jewish ruling council's pressing successfully for His execution. Yet Jesus' words were not in vain. Nicodemus was one of the two men who removed Jesus' lifeless body from the cross and laid it in the tomb (19:39-42). The man with the courageous humility to ask seriously, "How can this be?" (3:9) found the answer to life's most crucial question because he dared to approach the light that most others, fearing that the truth about themselves would be unmasked, chose to flee (v. 20).

JOHN THE BAPTIST'S FINAL PLEA (3:22-36)

John the Baptist is a key figure in this gospel[9] from the start, for he is the prophetic voice, God's proof to His people that what the Old Testament prophets foretold has come to pass in Jesus Christ. The Baptist would now make his final statement.

JESUS' DISCIPLES BAPTIZE (3:22-30)

The setting was a difficult one for the fiery man of God. Formerly it was he alone who enjoyed center stage, calling all to repent and baptizing the multitudes who wished to prepare themselves for what God was about to do through the coming king, the Messiah. Now Jesus' disciples, too, began to baptize in the same area (3:22-23; the precise location of "Aenon near Salim" is unknown today[10]).

The Baptist's disciples expressed to Him their frustration over Jesus' rising prominence (v. 26). They had encountered someone who disputed with them about "ceremonial washings," ritual purification of the body and certain home furnishings (see Mark 7:3-4). It is not clear just how this related to Jesus. Perhaps Jesus had already begun to point out the need for inner rather than simply outer cleansing (Matt. 23:25-26), and perhaps this teaching struck John's disciples as new and strange. In any case this gave them a chance to seek their master's guidance on how they ought to react to Jesus, who was essentially upstaging the Baptist.

John was unruffled (though later he would show understandable confusion when he was thrown in prison and when Jesus seemed not to be the sort of messianic deliverer that John expected; see Matt. 11:2-3). Whatever attention he once had came his way in God's will and timing (v. 27). John had always claimed to point to the light rather than to be the light itself (v. 28). He was delighted with Jesus' rise, like the close friend of a bridegroom shares the happiness that his new-

9. He is important, of course, throughout the gospels; see Graham N. Stanton, *The Gospels and Jesus* (Oxford: University, 1989), pp. 165-76.
10. Harry Thomas Frank, ed., *Atlas of the Bible Lands* (Maplewood, N.J.: Hammond, 1984), B-26, suggests a location near the border of Perea and Decapolis approximately halfway between the Dead Sea and the Sea of Galilee.

lywed companion enjoys (v. 29).[11] Referring to the same divine necessity already seen twice in this chapter (3:7, 14), John deferred gladly to the popular recognition Jesus was receiving. John was but a prophet; Jesus, as John was the first to note, was "the Lamb of God, who takes away the sin of the world" (1:29).

BELIEVE JOHN—BUT BELIEVE IN JESUS (3:31-36)

Some commentators punctuate verses 31-36 as John the Baptist's words. Others end the quotation at verse 30 and view verses 31-36 as comments of the gospel writer himself. The message is very much the same in either case. Jesus Christ is preeminent, having His origin in the realms that transcend the bounds that confine and restrict all other persons, the Baptist included (v. 31). While many may be curious, few can bear the full impact of what Jesus had to say, though He had perfectly good grounds for saying it (v. 32). Jesus had already pointed out what those grounds were, namely His heavenly origin (v. 13).

Those who do accept Jesus for what and who He claims to be verify what both the Baptist and Jesus claim, that Jesus is the fulfillment of God's ancient promises to redeem His people—"God is truthful" (v. 33). And knowledge of His truthfulness is possible because He sends one who speaks "the words of God" (v. 34). This refers to Jesus, whose experience of the Spirit was more intense and effective than any other person's in part because He committed no act to grieve the Spirit, thus quenching His influence and force.

John the Baptist concluded: Jesus is the special object of the Father's attention and affection. Not only the Baptist's fortunes but in fact the destinies of all men and movements at all times have been placed in the Son's hands by the Father (v. 35). Jesus Christ is exalted above all (see Eph. 1:20-23).

Therefore John was not disturbed by his falling personal prestige. What was at stake was not his own pride but mankind's salvation. The Baptist's disciples could stop fretting about their master's importance compared to Jesus'. They ought rather focus on Jesus' summons to believe. Those who did would enter into the new dimension of awareness, purpose, and blessedness that Jesus personally announced to

11. The bridegroom's joy is colorfully discussed in Beasley-Murray, *John*, pp. 52-53.

Nicodemus (3:15): eternal life. To overlook that summons is to risk the grimmest of ends, God's wrath (v. 36).[12]

Up till now John's gospel has described incidents in Jesus' ministry in Galilee and in Judea. Jesus has acted in public ways, and He has also spoken quietly in private. He has laid claim to be God's active agent in mediating a salvation that extends to all persons ("God so loved the world"). This salvation results in a new quality of existence ("eternal life").

But what about those who are neither Galileans nor Judeans? It seems clear that the threat of wrath extends to all mankind; how far does God extend the invitation to eternal life? In two surprising accounts, chapter 4 of John's gospel takes up these questions.

12. It has become common even in some segments of the church to look askance at the Bible's assertions regarding God's wrath. Yet OT and NT writers alike are unanimous that God is faithful both to bless and to curse, depending on man's response. God has a zealous, benevolent, and rightful desire for the devotion of each person's heart. He yearns to deliver man from the ravages of evil and death. To reject His love is to forfeit His protection from destruction. No figure in the Bible stresses God's wrath more often or graphically than Jesus Himself. It seems inconsistent to claim allegiance to Christ but at the same time to rebel at the thought of what He clearly taught, not only about God's compassion but also about His displeasure. One may ask whether a God without the zeal to punish evil would have had the zeal to go to the cross for thankless sinners. For a brief but piercing challenge to current skepticism regarding God's wrath, see Heinz W. Cassirer, *Grace and Law: St. Paul, Kant, and the Hebrew Prophets* (Grand Rapids: Eerdmans, 1988), pp. 99-107.

4

SAVIOR OF THE WORLD (4:1-54)

Up till now John's gospel has recorded Jesus' activity within primarily Jewish areas: the Jordan, Cana, Capernaum, Jerusalem. Now the scene shifts.[1] The salvation Jesus proclaimed and brought is "from the Jews" (4:24). But it is not for the Jews alone. As the opening verses of John's gospel make clear (1:1-18), the Word who became flesh is God's salvation for all who will receive it, not just for descendants of Abraham or some one particular nation. Chapter 4 illustrates this in a memorable manner.

SALVATION FOR SAMARITANS[2] (4:1-42)

JEWS AND SAMARITANS (4:1-3)

For the modern reader, the word "Samaritan" may have a pleasant ring, as in the phrase "a good Samaritan." But this was not the case for Jews in Jesus' time in the areas where Jesus carried out His work.[3] Second Kings 17:24-40 recounts the origins of the Samaritans and why Jews detested them and their ways. In Jesus' day bitter feelings reigned between Jews and Samaritans. Suspicion was mutual, and racial prejudice was as intense as any known in modern times.

1. See "The Course of the Ministry in St. John," in Archibald M. Hunter, *According to John* (Philadelphia: Westminster, 1968), pp. 56-65.
2. On the Samaritans, John Bowman, *The Samaritan Problem* (Pittsburgh: Pickwick, 1975) is dated but useful.
3. This is brought out forcefully by Anthony Thiselton, "Understanding God's Word Today," in *Obeying Christ in a Changing World* (Glasgow: Collins, 1977), pp. 106-10. See also Gordon Fee and Douglas Stuart, *How to Read the Bible for All Its Worth* (Grand Rapids: Zondervan, 1982), p. 133.

The Samaritans' territory was sandwiched between Judea in the south and Galilee in the north, so it was hard for Jews to remain totally unaware of their presence. But Jews did all they could to avoid direct contact with them. Jesus was different. He listened to and taught them with the same sensitivity and straightforwardness that He had already shown with Nicodemus and others.

Jesus entered Samaria as the result of being forced to leave Judea, the area around Jerusalem. Apparently the Pharisees, who had long dogged John the Baptist's steps and remained skeptical of his message (1:24-25), were about to turn their full attention on Jesus (4:1-2). Had Jesus remained in Jerusalem where the Pharisees were concentrated, they might have used their influence to put a premature end to His ministry. But it was not yet time for that. Jesus wisely withdrew, setting out once more for Galilee (v. 3).

He could have avoided Samaria, as many Jews did when they traveled between Judea and Galilee. This was achieved by crossing the Jordan River near Jericho, then traveling through Perea and the Decapolis. That meant a longer distance to walk, but many Jews thought the trouble was worth it in order to avoid passing through the villages of the despised Samaritans.

WAITING BY THE WELL (4:4-12)

Jesus led His disciples on the shorter route, through Samaria (v. 4). Sychar (v. 5) is modern Shechem, some thirty miles north of Jerusalem. At about noon Jesus called a halt at a famous well (vv. 5-6). There Jesus remained while His disciples entered the village to buy food for their midday meal (v. 8).

The Samaritan woman who came to draw water in the heat of the day was taken aback when Jesus spoke to her. This was most unusual (v. 9). Yet even more unusual was the Jewish stranger's reply. One of the most bitter points of difference between Jew and Samaritan involved religious belief. But Jesus took up precisely that topic in opening the conversation (v. 10). "Living water" may be understood as meaning "water that gives life."[4] By "life" Jesus was referring to the

---

4. Brown's discussion (*Gospel According to John* 1:178-80) is useful here, though it is unnecessary to see a reference to baptism in Jesus' words.

same spiritual vitality and blessedness of which He spoke to Nicodemus using the phrase "eternal life." Ps. 36:8-9 gives a related image of God's abundance coming like a cool, refreshing drink.

The woman's reply was frank and provocative, expressing skepticism at Jesus' bold claim (v. 10). He had no way of drawing water. How could He hope to give her, or anyone else, something to drink (v. 11)? She then referred to "our father Jacob" (v. 12). That was perhaps a veiled insult, since from the Jewish viewpoint Jacob, or Israel (see Gen. 32:28), was the father of their nation, not of the Samaritans. In either case, she implied, surely Jesus was not claiming to rival one of the great Old Testament patriarchs.

WATER THAT GIVES LIFE (4:13-20)

Jesus ignored the provocation and zeroed in on the issue: the woman's desperate need for the potent water that would deeply satisfy her inner thirst (vv. 13-14). "Welling up" points to the water's dynamic power; the same verb describes the joyous leap of the healed beggar in Acts 3:8.

The woman's reply (v. 15) was once more probably one of skepticism. Fine, she said, I'll take whatever it is you're talking about if it means I won't have to lug water to the village day after day. She does not appear to have taken Jesus seriously.

That did not deter him. He merely took a different tack. He told her to fetch her husband (v. 16), to which she replied with curt finality, "I have no husband" (v. 17). She had risen to the bait. Jesus began to reel in the line. Revealing the uncanny insight into others' lives that Jesus has already shown elsewhere in this gospel (see 1:48; 2:25), He lets her know that her checkered past is an open book to Him (v. 18). Even by Samaritan standards the woman's ways had been less than nobly moral.

Jesus' startling remark caught her off guard. She recognized that Jesus must possess prophetic insight to know about her unflattering past so well (v. 19). But she recovered quickly. Even if He was a prophet, He was still a Jew. And Jews were wrong, from the Samaritan point of view, about where God was to be worshiped. If she could maintain that point, it would be easy for her to discount Jesus' eerie ability to plumb the depths of her personal life. Bitter argument is far preferable to further painful personal disclosure.

IN SPIRIT AND TRUTH (4:21-24)

Disagreement over where to worship God, on Mount Gerizim in Samaria or on Mount Zion in Jerusalem, had a long history. Indeed, Deut. 27:12 speaks of a time when worship was to take place on Mount Gerizim, although according to the Jewish Scriptures God later commanded the Temple to be built in Jerusalem. But the Samaritans, perhaps in part due to their own version and interpretation of the five Old Testament books of Moses that they recognized, had long observed a different tradition.

The difference in outlook was eventually resolved brutally in the Jews' favor. In 128 B.C., at a time when the Jews ruled over their own independent state, they destroyed the Samaritan temple on Mount Gerizim. It remained in ruins as the woman spoke. But the memory of it was alive. It was a perennial bone of contention between the two peoples, a symbol of their divergent views and mutual hostility. Jesus had tried to break into the woman's personal sphere of relationship, or lack of relationship, to God. She now sought to move the exchange back onto less threatening turf where she felt she could maintain some control over a conversation that was getting out of hand.

She did not get far, because Jesus refused to be drawn into a debate over mere geography, much less over the superiority of Jewish tradition to Samaritan belief (v. 21). It was true, Jesus insisted, that Samaritans were mistaken in their disagreement with what the Old Testament of the Jews said. For God had chosen to communicate His saving light to the world primarily through Abraham's direct descendants. In that sense, "salvation [was] of the Jews" (v. 22). Some years later the apostle Paul would make similar statements (Rom. 3:1-2; 9:4-5).

But true worship is not first of all a matter of geographical location. It is rather a matter of the inner person, the heart, the spirit. God seeks those who can see beyond externalities to the need of their own souls and to His sufficiency to meet that need (v. 23). "God is spirit" (v. 24), and to have dealings with Him means much more than squabbling over which mountain He would rather be worshiped on.

He must also be worshiped "in truth" (vv. 23-24).[5] There are, in fact, right and wrong, true and false ways to approach Him. Even the question of mountains had its place, and Jesus had already stated the ultimate answer (v. 21). But being right about facts is not all there is to acceptable worship to God. He must be worshiped with inner openness extending to the very core of one's self ("in spirit"), a point at which the Samaritan woman had not yet arrived. And He must also be approached with an understanding of His nature and character that reflects what He has revealed about Himself to prophets past and present, from Moses to David to the Son of David, who now stood before her. He must be worshiped "in truth." John's gospel makes clear later that this "truth" is present supremely in Jesus Christ Himself (14:6).

THE MESSIAH WILL DECIDE (4:25-26)

The woman appears to have realized she was out of her depth. She moved to terminate the exchange. Whatever Jesus is saying, she blurted out, it will be seen to be right or wrong in view of what the coming Messiah,[6] the deliverer and ruler sent from God, will bring to light (v. 25). He will straighten all this out.

But Jesus did not let her off the hook. "I who speak to you am he," He replied (v. 26).

How can Jesus so openly claim to be the Messiah here, whereas in other gospels He seems to avoid association with this title? It is likely that He feared the political connotations of the word in areas where Jews might understand it as an earthly political king (see 6:15) or where Romans might see it as a rival claim to authority in their provinces. Either view might bring a premature end to Jesus' freedom to move about and preach. But in Samaria there was no such danger. He was as free to own up to His identity before the woman as He was elsewhere in the privacy of His own band of followers (Matt. 16:16-17).

In any case, Jesus had already shown too much prophetic insight to be dismissed by the woman with the sarcastic laugh that she may

---

5. Morris comments, "The combination of 'spirit and truth' points to the need for complete sincerity and complete reality in our approach to God" (*Gospel According to John*, p. 271).

6. On messianic expectations among Samaritans see Schnackenburg, *Gospel According to John*, 1:441; J. Macdonald, *The Theology of the Samaritans* (London, 1964), pp. 362-71 (cited in Bruce, *Gospel of John*, p. 120 n. 15).

have uttered a few minutes earlier. She no doubt sucked in her breath with astonishment at Jesus' audacious claim.

THE DISCIPLES RETURN (4:27-38)

At this instant the disciples came shuffling back from the village. They were surprised to find Jesus talking to a woman, especially a Samaritan woman. Jewish tradition frowned on such contact, and the disciples might well have felt uncomfortable about their leader violating this taboo, for it reflected badly on them as His followers. But they observed respectful silence (v. 27).

For her part, in such haste that she left her jar (v. 28), the woman scurried back to the village and rallied her neighbors (v. 29). The response was immediate and would prove to be positive (v. 30; see v. 39). Although Jews traveling to or from Jerusalem were sometimes no more welcome to Samaritans than Samaritans were to Jews (see Luke 9:52-53), Jesus' impression on the woman had not alienated her. He had rather opened her heart to mysterious, and alluring, possibilities that she could not help relating to others.

Jesus used the next few minutes to instruct and exhort the disciples. They urged him to eat (v. 31). His attention was riveted on higher priorities (v. 32). The disciples were oblivious to what He meant (v. 33). As elsewhere, His words were overliteralized and thus misunderstood (see 2:20; 3:4; 4:15). Jesus patiently explained.

His greatest appetite was to do God's will (v. 34). God's will is to make Himself known to sinners through His Son (3:17-18). Jesus no doubt sensed that the woman would return, if for no other reason than to get the water she forgot. How could He worry about eating when the soul of a person who did not know God was on the line?

Jesus extended His own sense of urgency in that situation to His disciples. Perhaps as Jesus spoke, He was watching the Samaritans approach. If His disciples would but open their eyes, they would see the harvest lying before them (v. 35). Now was the time for "the reaper" (the follower of Jesus) to be working for heavenly reward, to be spreading the message that Jesus gave him.

Even the Old Testament teaches that pointing souls to the Lord is a virtuous pursuit (Ps. 51:13; Prov. 11:30). Now was the time to realize that eternal life, the kingdom of God, was at hand. Now was the time for the sower (Jesus, and others such as John the Baptist, who had labored to prepare His way) to celebrate with those who reaped (v. 36) as those who walked in darkness turned instead to the light. Others had prepared the way. All the disciples must do was to gather in the grain (v. 38). Could they think of nothing but their stomachs at such a time?

MANY SAMARITANS BELIEVE (4:39-42)

At that moment the Samaritans arrived. The woman's enthusiastic report had had effect: many were ready to take Jesus at His word when they first encountered Him (v. 39). In fact, they invited the whole entourage into their village, where Jesus taught for two more days (v. 40). Many more came to share the woman's own high regard for Jesus and the truths "his words" conveyed (v. 41).

In the end, the Samaritans proclaimed Jesus as Savior (v. 42). "Savior" denotes one who rescues from impending disaster. The Samaritans must have grasped that Jesus' message heralded both pardon and judgment (see 3:36). But they did not proclaim Him as merely their own Savior: He was the deliverer of "the world." They saw that Jesus, though a Jew, conveyed the message of the one true God to the one race of mankind. Though Samaritans had come to be rejected by the Jews, they were acceptable to Jesus and to the God of the kingdom Jesus preached. And if Samaritans were acceptable, whom the Jews detested perhaps even more than they detested Gentiles, then no one in the world could claim that his ways were unknown to God or that God did not desire the devotion of his heart.

Truly Jesus had come so that "whoever believes in him," whether Nicodemus or the woman or a whole isolated Samaritan village, "shall not perish but have eternal life" (John 3:16). One author carries the point a step further: "In passing . . . through one Samaritan town and talking with one sinful woman, Jesus both reaps a harvest and anticipates a greater harvest to come, the church's mission to the Gentiles."[7]

7. J. Ramsey Michaels, *John* (San Francisco: Harper & Row, 1984), p. 59.

A SECOND SIGN (4:43-54)

RETURN TO GALILEE (4:43-48)

Some believe that verses 43-54 are another version of Matthew 8:5-13/Luke 7:1-10. Others note numerous differences in detail between the account in John and the accounts in Matthew and Luke. Morris concludes, "Despite the verbal parallels the two stories are distinct."[8] It seems best to treat it as an account standing on its own merit and serving its own function within the drama John's gospel relates.

John cites miraculous deeds ("signs") done by Jesus as a means of convincing readers to trust Him and thereby receive the life He offers (20:31). After Jesus returned to Galilee (v. 43) He performed an act that supported the high acclaim that the Samaritans had just accorded Him (v. 42).

John's comment in v. 44 ("a prophet has no honor in his own country") may allude to the hardheartedness Jesus appears to rebuke in verse 48. True, He was welcomed by fellow Galileans, for none can deny that He made an impressive showing in Jerusalem (v. 45; see 2:23).

But merely acknowledging what Jesus does is not the same as committing oneself to Him and the kingdom He proclaims. Later John would point out that even Jesus' own brothers remained cynically hostile to Him, though they acknowledged the works He did (7:4-5). When a royal official from Cana requested that Jesus heal his child (vv. 46-47), Jesus felt the need to denounce the sensationalist craving for a spectacular event that He saw in the observers milling around Him. It is not wrong to be moved to faith by the sight of God's powerful hand, but how much more commendable is the heart willing to take God at His word without demanding God to submit again and again to a test of His strength (see 20:29).

REASON TO BELIEVE (4:49-54)

The official persisted in hopeful desperation (v. 49). Jesus did not hold the recalcitrance of the many against the plaintive seeking of the

8. Morris, *Gospel According to John*, p. 288.

one. He granted the request, and the official took Jesus "at his word" (v. 50).

John's gospel does not leave the reader wondering about the outcome. The power of a sign lies largely in the fact that it happened. A sign that never occurred can hardly inspire confidence in the spiritual reality to which it is supposed to point. Did what Jesus say really take place? John points out that it did. On the way home, excited servants reported the son's recovery (v. 51). Comparison of times and events confirmed that it was Jesus' word that brought about the healing (vv. 52-53).

John records this as the second sign (v. 54). Changing water to wine was the first. He is not counting the casual allusion to Jesus' works in Jerusalem (2:23), which he did not recount in detail.

But John underscores that this is yet a second weighty indicator that Jesus should be regarded with utmost seriousness. Hardhearted fools make no commitment and crave yet another titillating spectacle. John's gospel calls the reader to the response of the Samaritans, whose faith overcame the pride and cultural prejudice that cut them off in principle from Jesus and His message. It calls the reader to the straightforward commitment to Jesus that the royal official showed, despite smirks of skepticism all around. Jesus is the Savior of the world. Chapter 4 describes the devotion that that Savior calls for and gives reasons why He eminently deserves it.

5

AUTHORITY TO JUDGE (5:1-47)

Authority is a key issue in John's gospel. In 1:12 we read that those who receive Christ are given authority, or authorized, to be God's children. Jesus states that He is authorized both to lay down His life and to receive it back again (10:18). In intimate prayer Jesus affirms that God has given the Son "authority over all people," so that the Son might grant eternal life to all those God has given Him (17:2). When Pilate threatens Jesus with Roman authority (19:10), Jesus corrects him firmly: not even mighty Rome can exert power over Jesus unless God authorizes it (19:11).

In order for John's purpose in writing to be fulfilled (20:31), the reader must come to grips with Jesus Christ's authority over all persons and times and therefore over all areas and issues in the reader's personal life. For to "believe that Jesus is the Christ, the Son of God," and to "have life in His name" (20:31), means for Christ to be recognized for who He is and to be honored as He deserves. It means that the reader submit his will and direct his heart's loyalty to the one whom God has placed in the position of ultimate judge, or authority, over the reader's every act and attitude.

Chapter 5[1] addresses the matter of authority, as it came to be an issue for some religious leaders confronted by Jesus' earthly ministry,

---

1. A number of scholars have suggested that chaps. 5 and 6 make better sense if their position in John's gospel is reversed: see, e.g., Schnackenburg, *Gospel According to John* 2:5-9. Brown's comment (*Gospel According to John*, 1:236) bears repeating: "The projected rearrangement is attractive in some ways but not compelling. There is no manuscript evidence for it, and we must not forget that there are other indications that favor the present order." The traditional canonical order of the chapters is assumed below.

in three dimensions: authority to define the Sabbath, authority to grant life, and authority to interpret God's Word.

AUTHORITY TO DEFINE THE SABBATH (5:1-18)

TEST CASE: THE PARALYTIC AT BETHESDA (5:1-8)

Since before Jesus appeared on the scene, religious authorities from Jerusalem had been wary of the kingdom that John the Baptist announced (1:19-28). After the Baptist identified Jesus as the central figure in that kingdom's imminent arrival (1:29), Jesus immediately found it necessary to serve notice that the traditional seat of Jewish religious prestige and authority, the Jerusalem Temple, needed a thorough housecleaning (2:14-16). In the same vein Jesus instructed Nicodemus, a ruling Jewish teacher, of his need to undergo radical personal transformation, or spiritual rebirth.

There is a recognizable pattern developing here: John the Baptist and Jesus concur in their claim that God's authority, His living presence, and revealed will must be allowed to define religious rules. Man's religious observances, although they are not necessarily bad, must not be allowed to squelch the revealed prerogatives, the directly stated authority, of God.

This pattern continues and intensifies when Jesus travels to Jerusalem for a religious feast (5:1) and heals a paralytic. This was Jesus' second Jerusalem visit recorded by John's gospel. It is not known for sure which Jewish feast was underway.[2] John writes as though the pool he describes was still intact (v. 2); some scholars suggest that this means he was writing before the destruction of Jerusalem by Roman armies in A.D. 70. Archaeologists have discovered remains of the pool and columns of which John speaks near what is now the Church of St. Anne in the northeastern part of old Jerusalem.[3]

As Jesus approached, a great many disabled persons languished near the pool. There seems to have been a belief, preserved in some ancient copies of John, that an angel would occasionally stir the waters and restore to full health the first person who plunged in (v. 4, rightly

2. Brown, *Gospel According to John*, 1:206.
3. For the location see Barry Beitzel, *The Moody Atlas of Bible Lands* (Chicago: Moody, 1985), p. 163.

placed in the margin in modern texts and translations[4]). One man who had suffered without relief for nearly four decades (v. 5) attracted Jesus' attention (v. 6). His reply to Jesus' question (v. 7) reveals His poignant dilemma: the very illness which was the reason for his permanent residence at water's edge was also the handicap that prevented his cure.

John's gospel records, concisely and without dramatic flair, how Jesus calmly closed one chapter in the man's life and opened another (v. 8). Truly, the power of God's kingdom, which makes all things new, is present in the person of Jesus.

REACTION: JESUS' AUTHORITY REJECTED (5:9-18)

The other gospels suggest that Jesus healed various illnesses from early in His public ministry (see e.g., Mark 1:34). What marks this particular incident as significant is what follows it. Jesus chose to perform this work on Saturday, the Jewish Sabbath (v. 9).

Over the centuries prior to Jesus, since the cessation of Old Testament prophecy with Malachi (about 440 B.C.), elaborate systems of religious regulations affecting every aspect of life had arisen. These stipulated, among other things, what could and could not be done on the seventh day of each week. "The law" in verse 10 does not refer to the Old Testament. In fact, a more literal translation of the Greek is simply, "It is not permitted." Thus Jesus did not violate Moses' command (Ex. 20:8): "Remember the Sabbath day by keeping it holy." He rather ran up against current prevailing opinion of how Moses' command was to be understood. The man had violated one of some thirty-nine categories of labor forbidden on the Sabbath according to the Jewish "tradition of the elders" in force at that time.[5]

When the religious leaders spied the man joyously putting distance between himself and the poolside that had been his prison, they harassed him for carrying his bedroll on the Sabbath (v. 10). The man rightly referred them to Jesus, though he did not know Him by name (vv. 11, 13). The authorities were baffled and no doubt miffed (v. 12).

4. See Bruce M. Metzger, *A Textual Commentary on the Greek New Testament* (London/New York: United Bible Societies, 1975), p. 209.

5. Bruce, *Gospel of John*, pp. 124-25.

The mystery was cleared up when the man later met Jesus in the Temple. Jesus reminded him how God had smiled on his hopeless condition, then underscored that he dare not squander the precious gift God had granted: "Stop sinning or something worse may happen to you" (v. 14). Although physical infirmity is not necessarily the direct cause of someone's sin (see 9:2-3), it may be (see 1 Cor. 11:30). Apparently the man needed reminding not to forget the God who had delivered him. Jesus told him what he needed to hear.

Perhaps Jesus' admonition did not sit well with the man,[6] or perhaps he simply wished to clear himself of possible guilt by helping the religious authorities identify the real culprit, as they saw it, in the whole incident. In either case, He gave them Jesus' name (v. 15). They no doubt recognized Jesus by now as the one who earlier upset daily business in the Temple area (2:14-16). He must be stopped. John records that persecution of Jesus first arose at this point, over the Sabbath issue (v. 16).[7]

John also implies that they confronted Jesus. Jesus replied in a way that smoothed no ruffled feathers (v. 17). He simply made it still clearer that He was asserting a higher authority than that possessed by the religious leaders themselves.

He was, in fact, asserting the highest possible authority. He called God His own Father, which the Jews took as a blasphemous utterance (v. 18).[8] Blasphemy is when a human claims the attributes of God. Jesus implied that what He did grew directly out of what God Himself was doing (v. 17). In a setting where the one true God was so highly venerated that His name Yahweh was not even pronounced, Je-

---

6. Robert Kysar, *John*, Augsburg Commentary on the New Testament (Minneapolis: Augsburg, 1986), speaks of the man's "ungrateful act."

7. A number of scholars insist that John's gospel reflects primarily a historical situation late in the first century when Jews allegedly first began to persecute Christians, not the actual situation that existed during Jesus' life and ministry. This view tends to weaken the historical reliability of John, which straightforwardly asserts that such hostility existed even before Jesus' death. The important discussion in Robinson, *Priority of John*, pp. 72-81, points to the ample justification that exists for supposing that the sort of pitched conflict between Jews and Jesus recounted in John did not require a period of forty years or more to develop.

8. Schlatter, *John the Evangelist* (German), p. 147: "God is the father of the [Jewish] people; He is also father for all mankind. He is not, however, any individuals's own father. Anyone who calls Him that profanes His majesty."

sus' claim to reflect in His own work the actions of Almighty God sounds arrogant and obnoxious. Jesus was making Himself equal with God. He was claiming authority to define how the Sabbath, an ordinance of God revealed to Moses, should be observed.

The Jewish leaders rejected this authority, for they had already reserved it for their traditions and ultimately, therefore, for themselves. The seeds were sown that would result in Jesus' arrest and crucifixion (v. 18). For now, Jesus remained free to elaborate on the meaning of His work and words.

The next section provides Jesus' interpretation of His daring act.

AUTHORITY TO GRANT LIFE (5:19-30)

LIKE FATHER, LIKE SON (5:19-23)

Jesus answered His detractors, not by backing off or softening His claims to reflect God's very presence and will, but by making these claims more explicit. He repeated that His actions merely imitated those of God (v. 19). The Son is the special object of the Father's love, and the Son is privy to the Father's dealings in a way no one else can be. They might as well brace themselves for more of what they had just seen: Jesus' healing of the paralytic would in fact pale in significance next to still greater acts He would perform later by the Father's enabling power (v. 20).

Jesus' unique closeness to God, He continued, is demonstrated in two more ways.

First, "as the Father raises the dead and gives them life, even so the Son gives life" (v. 21). The Jews would be familiar with Old Testament accounts in which God asserted or demonstrateed His ability to raise the dead (Deut. 32:39; 1 Sam. 2:6; 2 Kings 4:33-37; 5:7). Jesus claimed the same power for Himself. In chapter 3 He told Nicodemus that eternal life is through the Son. In chapter 11 He will raise Lazarus from physical death. Whatever life-giving powers God possesses, the Son possesses those same powers. He gives life "to whom He is pleased to give it" (v. 21).

Second, the Son has authority to judge (vv. 22-23). The Old Testament makes clear that it is God and God alone who stands in judgment of His people and of all mankind (Deut. 32:36; Pss. 7:8; 9:8; Joel

3:12). Jesus states that God has delegated authority to judge to the Son, so that mankind will not overlook the Son or take Him lightly. For to dishonor the Son, the appointed judge, is to dishonor the Father who appointed Him (v. 23).

FROM DEATH TO LIFE (5:24-30)

Apparently the notion that the Son is judge needs additional explanation. Twice in two verses (vv. 24-25), Jesus gives His words the special force usually reserved for the divinely inspired written Word of God alone (see remarks on 1:51). He explains that condemnation can be averted by accepting the plain meaning of His assertions. To heed His words is to accept the Father who sent Him and to pass "from death to life" in God's eyes (v. 24). Calvin rightly states that Jesus' statement "describes the way and method by which He is to be honored, lest any should think it consists merely in some external rite and trifling ceremonies. For the teaching of the gospel is like Christ's scepter with which He governs believers, whom the Father has submitted unto Him."[9]

But the proclamation of Jesus as judge is not merely a negative threat of impending doom. It is, more important, the necessary prelude to experiencing the life Jesus has come to bring. John's gospel will later give a graphic example of how "the dead" are made alive by Jesus' life-giving words: Lazarus, dead for days, comes forth from the tomb (chap. 11). This same power can make the spiritually dead, those whose hearts remain as yet untouched by God's transforming presence, spring into a new dimension of awareness and responsiveness to God. "Those who hear will live" (v. 25). Man is dependent on God for life, because God alone "has life in himself" (v. 26; see Gen. 2:7; Job 10:12; Ps. 36:9). Yet the Son possesses life "in himself" in just the same way. As Son of Man (see remarks on 1:51) who will one day judge all mankind, He is also the dispenser of blessedness and life (v. 27).

Jesus realized that His words, which promised spiritual renewal and life, were revolutionary. "Do not be amazed," He cautioned (v. 28). There is the danger that His hearers would tune Him out. So He

9. Calvin, *Gospel According to St. John*, 1:128.

related what He was saying to a teaching that many of them already accepted: the doctrine of the resurrection of the dead. They were correct, Jesus implied, to hold that view. But they needed to clarify their understanding of what ultimate acceptance or condemnation before God will involve. In the light of Jesus' words, it will involve whether a person has "done good" (been receptive to Jesus Christ) or "done evil" (v. 29). As Jesus states elsewhere: "The work of God is this: to believe in the one He has sent" (6:29).

Jesus concluded these remarks on His unique life-giving importance by repeating that He acts not on His own but at God's personal direction. His words are therefore reliable—"my judgment is just"—because He is not speaking with merely human wisdom and insight but with the backing and agreement of God Himself (v. 30).

But why should Jesus' listeners have accepted what He said? Though Jesus claimed God's authority, was there any evidence beyond His own say-so that what He said was actually true?

Jesus was calling them to believe, but He was not indifferent to their need to know. For knowledge and faith, here as often in Scripture, are delicately yet firmly intertwined.[10] Jesus spoke to their doubts by citing a series of witnesses that establish the credibility of His authoritative claims.

AUTHORITY TO INTERPRET GOD'S WORD (5:31-47)

WEIGHTY AND WEIGHTIER TESTIMONY (5:31-40)

Jesus conceded that one person's testimony by itself is not legally binding (v. 31). He may have in mind here rabbinic laws of evidence based on Deut. 19:15, which required that facts be confirmed by two or more witnesses. But Jesus' testimony was not solitary. "There is another who testifies in my favor" (v. 32). He spoke of God the Father.

Even apart from the Father, His listeners had already been confronted with evidence that they should receive the Son. This evidence was John the Baptist, with whom they were familiar (v. 33). "Not that I accept human testimony" (v. 34) was not meant to belittle John's

---

10. Brown, *Gospel According to John*, 1:513, notes: "To a certain extent 'knowing' and 'believing' are interchangeable in John."

importance; it was rather an insistence that John's claims were not merely human in nature or authority but were grounded in God's own initiative in sending John to preach (see 1:6). John's claims were more than just human testimony, and Jesus' listeners had been illumined by John. Jesus reminded them of this once more, now in the light of the miraculous healing of the paralytic, so that they "may be saved" (vv. 34-35). Jesus' concern was for His listeners' welfare, even though they sought to harm Him (v. 16). In this He practiced what He taught (see Matt. 5:44).

But whatever they made of John, they must also come to grips with still weightier evidence. In verses 36-40, Jesus refers to three more witnesses who validate His claims. The most important is the Father Himself (v. 37). His detractors had occasion to recognize this, as Nicodemus did (3:2), by the works Jesus was doing, such as healing the paralytic. Jesus' works were, in fact, the second witness to the truthfulness of His claims (v. 36). They were one of the ways the unseen God had chosen to make His presence and will known to man.

The third witness is the Scriptures (v. 39). His listeners knew the Scriptures well and made them the focal point of much disciplined study. Yet they refused to see them as Jesus did, as witnesses to the Son of God in their midst and as indicators that they should repent and believe in the new thing God was doing in their day. They insisted on seeing them rather as the basis for the traditions their religion held dear. They were faced with a crisis of authority. Who would determine the meaning of the Scripture they rightly venerated—the teachers of the religious system they had developed, teachers who were strangers to God's voice, form, and word (vv. 37-38)? Or Jesus Christ, who embodies the unseen God (1:18) and shatters religious systems that, He charged, reduce God to human dimensions?[11]

At this point, Jesus stated, they chose to obey each other rather than God. This is not a matter of understanding; it is a matter of will. They "refuse to come" to Jesus "to have life" (v. 40). The problem was not that Jesus' teaching was too complicated for them; it was rather too demanding and humiliating given their present commitments and prestige within the religious system they upheld.

11. Kysar, *John*, Augsburg Commentary, p. 86, states: "John is here denying that those who reject Jesus have truly embraced the Old Testament tradition."

Jesus concluded the exchange by putting His finger on the issue that divided Him from His detractors—human recognition and acceptance.

PRAISE FROM MEN (5:41-47)

Jesus came with authority. This authority was backed up by a number of weighty witnesses. Yet the religious leaders who were offended by Jesus' healing of the paralytic on the Sabbath rejected both this authority and Jesus' interpretation of witnesses such as John the Baptist, Jesus' works, and Scripture. Why were the two parties, Jesus and His listeners, at such an impasse?

First, Jesus said, their hearts were not set on God (v. 42). As Paul states elsewhere, they were zealous, but their zeal was misguided (Rom. 10:2).

Second, they were more apt to believe someone who "comes in His own name" than one claiming to be sent from God and having credentials to back up the claim (v. 43). Jewish historians note that some sixty or more messianic pretenders appeared and gained a following in ancient times.[12] Jesus probably referred to this readiness to follow false prophets, both tragic and ironic given the skepticism about the true prophets John the Baptist and Jesus, who confronted them and whom they rejected. In biblical terms, salvation is, in a sense, gaining God's approval or favor. This means that to have one's heart set on gaining human approval makes complete trust in Christ impossible (v. 44).

Third, they have set their hope on a false interpretation of the Old Testament, or "Moses" (v. 45). Jesus charged them with not believing the Old Testament lawgiver whom they honored as the figurehead of their whole religion (v. 46; see 9:28). In fact, Moses' writings were highly regarded by Jesus' listeners. But the divine intent of those writings had been buried by the religious traditions used to interpret them. Instead of recognizing Christ in the light of Moses' writings, they rejected Him on the basis of their traditions.

Without a change of heart toward their skewed understanding of Scripture, they would remain blind to the divine presence in the person

12. Morris, *Gospel According to John*, p. 333 n. 122.

of Jesus before them (v. 47). They would miss the redemption Jesus' benevolent authority brought. They would instead condemn themselves by their erroneous reading of the Scriptures, which should bring them life. For they, unlike Jesus, had no life in themselves. Unless they received Him, they would fail to find the deliverance their traditions claimed, falsely in Jesus' view, to provide. As Jesus stated elsewhere, they would die in their sins (8:24).

Chapter 5 underscores Jesus' authority over the Sabbath, over judgment and life, and over Scripture. It begins with a miraculous sign and concludes with weighty words of rebuke, instruction, and challenge.

Chapter 6 will follow a similar pattern. Both the promise and the offense of who Jesus Christ is, and the life He calls His hearers to, will take on yet greater sharpness and urgency as God's divine light continues to beam forth through Jesus' acts and claims. John's gospel will continue to show how this light illumines those who receive it and blinds those who despise it.

6

A HARD TEACHING (6:1-71)

So far Jesus has spoken directly and at length to Nicodemus (chap. 3), to the Samaritans (chap. 4), and to somewhat hostile Jewish leaders in Jerusalem (chap. 5). Chapter 6 marks an abrupt change of location. Without John's express mention, Jesus has apparently traveled back north into Galilee between the end of chapter 5 and the beginning of chapter 6. As the sixth chapter opens, John relates that Jesus crossed from the western side (perhaps Capernaum) to the eastern or northeastern side of the Sea of Galilee (6:1).

As John explains, this historic fresh-water lake is also called the Sea of Tiberias, after the Roman emperor to whom a town on the southwestern shore, Tiberias, was dedicated by a local ruler[1] in about A.D. 20.

Chapter 6 contains four important incidents. First, Jesus feeds the five thousand. Next, He walks on the surface of the stormy lake. Third, He conducts a lengthy discussion with listeners who demand still more demonstrations of His power. Finally, He deals with His closest disciples, many of whom turn away from Him because they will not accept the demands He seems to be making.

Jesus' difficult teaching centered on what it takes to be His follower. This is the central point of the chapter, and it will be the central point of the discussion below. But the setting for His teaching is set forth in the three sections leading up to it. We will treat them in turn,

---

1. Herod Antipas, a son of Herod the Great (40-4 B.C.). Herod Antipas ruled (4 B.C.-A.D. 39) the regions of Galilee and Perea where Jesus conducted most of His ministry. He played an active role in Jesus' trial (Luke 23:6-12). The standard treatment is by Harold Hoehner, *Herod Antipas* (New York/London: Cambridge U., 1972).

pointing out how they set the stage for one of the Jesus' most significant self-disclosures in John's entire gospel.

"SURELY THIS IS THE PROPHET" (6:1-15)

A HOPELESS SITUATION (6:1-9)

As Jesus and His disciples left Capernaum in one or more small boats, a large crowd trailed behind in pursuit. Some may have used boats of their own, but many traveled around the north end of the lake on foot (Mark 6:33). They would have been able to keep Jesus' boat in sight from the shoreline. News of Jesus' power to heal the sick had spread far and wide (v. 2). Upon landing on the east shore, Jesus ascended a hillside with His disciples (v. 3), perhaps to instruct them. In short order the multitude that had followed Him from Capernaum drew near (v. 5).

Mention of the Passover (v. 4), the Feast of Unleavened Bread,[2] may be dramatic foreshadowing of how bread will figure prominently in the accounts which make up this chapter. As the bread of the feast is reminiscent of God's deliverance of His people in ancient times, Jesus will provide actual bread for the multitudes (v. 11). He will also claim to be the spiritual bread that imparts not just physical life but spiritual vitality and communion with God (v. 35: "I am the bread of life").

Jesus' feeding of the multitude is one of the few portions of John paralleled in other gospels (see Matt. 14:13-21; Mark 6:32-44; Luke 9:10-17). John recalls that Jesus queried Philip about where to obtain food, knowing what He was intending to do (vv. 5-6). As Philip was a native of Bethsaida (1:44), and they were in that general vicinity, He would have been the logical person to ask. Philip's reply was pessimistic, perhaps even sarcastic (v. 7).

Peter's brother, Andrew, called attention to a small boy (v. 8). Perhaps this lad had overheard Jesus' question to Philip and decided to volunteer what food He had. But it could not possibly meet the huge need (v. 9).

---

2. See Ex. 12 for the OT background of this celebration.

JESUS TAKES COMMAND (6:10-15)

Yet Jesus had a plan. He directed the people to be seated in orderly fashion (v. 10). Mark 6:39 notes that the grass on which they sat was green, supporting the idea that it was Passover time, in the spring before the hillside would have been scorched brown by summer heat. He twice offered the customary blessing, once before each course that was served (v. 11). Everyone ate as much as he wished.

So that nothing would be wasted,[3] and perhaps also so that all could see how mightily God had worked in their midst, Jesus directed that any leftovers be gathered up. The fragments filled twelve large reed baskets (vv. 12-13).

The multitude realized the extraordinary nature of what they had been part of. They hailed Jesus as "the Prophet." This was most likely a reference to the figure of whom Moses spoke (Deut. 18:15), a prophet like Moses who would appear in the last days. They will make another link between Jesus and Moses in verses 30-31.

Jesus was forced to act quickly to deflate the dangerous pressure that was mounting. If word spread that Jesus was somehow "king," both the local and the imperial (Roman) authorities would move quickly to put down the uprising. Jesus knew this was not the time or the place for His mission to draw to a close. Leaving His disciples behind, He withdrew farther into the hills alone (v. 15).

The miraculous feeding raised dramatic expectations in the hearts of the local populace: "We want Jesus to be our king!" they said in effect.[4] But Jesus' work involved pleasing the Father, not seeking the fa-

3. Calvin, *Gospel According to St. John*, 1:148, elaborates that "although it is to emphasize the miracle that Christ commands them to fill the baskets, He is at the same time exhorting His disciples to frugality when He says, 'Gather it up that nothing be lost.' For God's greater bounty ought not to incite us to luxury. Let those who abound, therefore, remember that one day they will give account of their excessive possessions if they do not carefully and faithfully apply their superfluity to a good purpose which God approves."

4. It is, however, not necessary to conclude that these expectations "may well have contributed to the Evangelist's decision to place the sacramental teaching [which many find later in chap. 6] in this setting and not in the Upper Room" (Beasley-Murray, *John*, p. 89). Quite apart from whether chap. 6 is primarily a reference to the Lord's Supper or not (see below), what John records in 6:15, and what the synoptics record about the Lord's Supper, are two fundamentally different matters.

vor of public opinion. His decision to forgo public acclaim here fore-shadow His refusal to tailor His deeds and teaching to public demand later in the chapter.

The next day Jesus would deal with the frustrated persons whose offer of kingship He spurned. But first a memorable sign took place, seemingly for the eyes of His closest disciples alone.

"It Is I; Don't Be Afraid" (6:16-24)

STORM AND DELIVERANCE (6:16-21)

At Jesus' direction (Mark 6:45), His disciples started back to Capernaum without Him (vv. 16-17). Presumably they assumed that He would make His way back on foot.

Once they were well underway on a crossing of some five miles in length, they were beset by a sudden storm (v. 18). Such disturbances still assail the lake in modern times due to its low elevation (600 feet below sea level) and the high hills surrounding it (1,200-1,500 feet above sea level).

With seasoned fishermen among them, who had grown up and made their living in boats, a violent squall was no cause for undue alarm. They braved the wind and rowed steadily along. But the wind was full in their faces. Progress was slow. By nearly daybreak (Mark 6:48), they were still being buffeted about under adverse conditions.

At the dreary hour when their fatigue and frustration were greatest, fear struck. For Jesus suddenly approached, somehow striding along the water's surface (v. 19).

Some thought they were seeing a ghost (Mark 6:49). Perhaps others had already heard the rumor that Jesus' power was demonic in nature (see John 7:20; Mark 3:22). We should not assume that the disciples understood Jesus as fully then as they would later on.

Also, the disciples would have known Ps. 107:23-30, which speaks of Yahweh's mastery over wind and stormy waves. Jesus' display of similar power must have filled them with a sense of awe and perhaps even dread. Their weariness, the sudden and astonishing spectacle of Jesus on the waves, and the fear of all they did not understand caused great anxiety.

Jesus allayed their fears (v. 20). After He took His place in the boat, the trip was immediately over (v. 21). Some think that once Jesus was with them and the wind subsided (Mark 6:51), the remaining time it took to row to shore was so brief that they reached shore in a short time. A few suggest that in the same way that Jesus demonstrated power over natural forces like gravity and water's natural density, He allowed the disciples to experience His mastery over space and time.[5]

IN SEARCH OF JESUS (6:22-24)

Jesus' disciples had just witnessed a sight that should have strengthened commitment to their leader. This confirmation might have been necessary for two reasons. First, they may have sensed disappointment that Jesus would not fulfill popular expectations (v. 15) —expectations they may have shared.[6] They needed dramatic encouragement. Second, Jesus was about to make statements that would cause massive defection from the ranks of His followers (v. 66). They needed a fresh vision that would help them trust in Jesus' words and His mission, whatever the verdict of popular opinion and the shortcomings of their own understanding.

Meanwhile, the larger crowd on the northeast side of the lake was baffled (v. 22). They knew that the disciples had departed, but where was Jesus? A flotilla of boats from relatively far-off Tiberias arrived, possibly in response to news of the miraculous feeding of the previous day (v. 23). The crowd apparently concluded that if anyone would know Jesus' whereabouts, it would be His closest followers at Jesus' headquarters in Capernaum. They piled into the available boats and

5. Westcott notes a similarity between the feeding of the multitude and Jesus' walk on the stormy lake: "Both correct limited views springing out of our material conceptions. Effects are produced at variance with our ideas of quantity and quality. That which is small becomes great. That which is heavy moves on the surface of the water. Contrary elements yield at a divine presence. Both 'signs,' in other words, prepare the way for new thoughts of Christ, of His sustaining, preserving, guiding power, and exclude deductions drawn from corporeal relations only. He can support men, though visible means fall short."

6. Is it possible that as they left Jesus behind, they shared something of the disgruntled impatience of many others that He would not do what everyone in Galilee thought He should? If so, His sudden appearance on the water would have been all the more threatening.

quickly make the crossing that had proved so troublesome to the disciples just hours before (v. 24).[7]

"UNLESS YOU EAT THE FLESH OF THE SON OF MAN" (6:25-59)

THE WORK OF GOD (6:25-29)

The crowd was surprised to discover Jesus waiting for them (v. 25). Apparently He was near or in the synagogue (v. 59). He seized the opportunity to instruct them.

The subject He took up was not complimentary.[8] He pointed out that what they sought was not eternal life but free food (vv. 26-27). They responded in a way that may reflect the influence of the Pharisees at the popular level: what good works can we do to earn the blessing of which You speak? (v. 28). They assumed that God's favor is to some extent dependent on human merit.

Jesus disagreed. He called them to an acceptance of Himself and His message that He termed "believing." Believing in Jesus is the thread that unites the rest of the chapter (see vv. 36, 47, 64, 69). All that Jesus was about to say related to what it means to believe—to devote one's whole being and future to the One who stands before them.

With some irony Jesus called believing "the work of God" (v. 29). In that believing is the antithesis of earning merit by good deeds, it is not a "work" at all. It is something God brings about by His gracious will (see 1:13; 6:65), not by man's meritorious achievement. In that it is truly God's work, it is not man's reward for his own works, as the crowd seemed to suppose.

THE CHALLENGE OF MOSES (6:30-40)

Not all of Jesus' audience was present at the miraculous feeding the day before, and it may be these who demanded another sign (v.

---

7. In Mark 6:53f, a crowd meets Jesus at Gennesaret, a couple of miles southwest of Capernaum. Apparently Mark speaks of an incident that immediately follows Jesus' teaching in the synagogue in John 6. Mark omits the verbal exchange in Capernaum that John carefully records. John does not mention that Jesus and His disciples made a short trip by boat to Gennesaret after the exchange described in John 6.

8. Kysar's suggestion (*John*, Augsburg Commentary, p. 100) that the crowd is "sincere but incorrectly oriented" seems to underestimate the hardness of heart, if not deliberate then nevertheless culpable, of Jesus' listeners.

30). If Jesus is really the Prophet foretold by Moses (v. 14), they reasoned, then He should be able to feed the children of Israel as Moses did according to the Old Testament and their traditions based on it (v. 31).

Jesus challenged their understanding of the Old Testament. It was not Moses but God who should get the credit for the "bread from heaven" (v. 32), the manna (see Ex. 16:4-5; Num. 11:7-9), to which they were comparing the bread Jesus furnished the previous day. They were missing the spiritual significance of both Moses' act and Jesus' presence. The "bread" God wished to provide was not merely to fill the bellies of Galileans but to give new life to all who respond to Jesus and His message (v. 33).

The crowd's response was probably to be understood in this sense: if what You bring is greater than what Moses gave our forefathers, then provide bread "from now on" (v. 34). They were demanding that Jesus continually furnish them food to eat, as God provided manna through Moses for nearly forty years.

Jesus countered their demand by underscoring their need to commit themselves to Him. Jesus Himself was "the bread of life" (v. 35). Those who are nourished by Him will have their deepest appetites satisfied continually. This remains true even though they could not understand it due to their unwillingness, their unbelief (v. 36).

In verses 37-40, Jesus stressed that to believe in Him requires God's work and will. This may seem a confusing or discouraging tactic. Why did He not simply exhort His listeners to overcome their misconceptions and believe?

He did not ignore the need and possibility for His listeners to exercise faith (v. 40). But He may have been responding to their assumption that they had it in themselves to do what God required (v. 28). Perhaps they needed to be confronted with their need for absolute dependence on God. Perhaps Jesus knew that their naive self-confidence needed to be shattered before they would be capable of directing their deepest loyalty away from themselves and toward Jesus. That may be why Jesus stressed God's initiative in salvation so strongly before this particular audience.

GRUMBLING LEADERS (6:41-51)

Suddenly it is clear that "the Jews" were present and that they did not like what Jesus was saying (v. 41). Of course, everyone at the scene was Jewish. John was probably referring to the Jewish teachers and leaders who shared the religious outlook of the rabbinic leaders in Jerusalem whom Jesus had already repeatedly encountered. These officials, or their Galilean allies, pointed out Jesus' humble family background (v. 42). How then could He make such exalted claims about Himself?

Jesus jolted them with the assertion that their logic could not displace His truth. He reasserted mankind's dependence on the Father for true spiritual deliverance (v. 44). To verify His claims (see 5:39), He cited the prophet Isaiah (54:13). Jesus interpreted these words as being fulfilled in His own day, in fact His own life. Those who accept Him are bearing out the accuracy and power of Old Testament prophecy (v. 45).

Jesus then carefully restated what He had already said. He knew what He was talking about, for He was sent from God (v. 46). The issue was not bread but believing (v. 47). Jesus, not barley loaves and fish, is God's provision for man's deliverance (v. 48).

Appealing to an obvious point of Old Testament history, He noted that those who ate the manna still died (v. 49). This refers to physical death but also alludes to the spiritual rebelliousness of many in Israel who partook of God's blessing but would not give Him their hearts (see 1 Cor. 10:1-5). They willfully perished outside of God's eternal acceptance and future reward. Jesus was offering bread that would deliver from such spiritual condemnation, or death, forever (v. 50).

In a climactic assertion doubtless understood by few at the time (see 2:22), Jesus foretold His death for mankind's sins (v. 51).[9] He would give His "flesh" for the world. This means that He would lay down His physical life in order to open the way for sinful mankind to meet God's approval rather than rejection (see 3:36). Jesus here laid the foundation for the apostolic preaching of the cross. But His gracious words meet a harsh response.

9. See also 10:11, 15; 11:50-52; 15:13; 17:19.

STALEMATE (6:52-59)

Sharp disagreement arose at Jesus' striking claim (v. 52). Here as elsewhere, simplistic interpretation of Jesus' words led to serious misunderstanding of His message (see 2:20-21; 3:4; 4:15).

Rather than back off and explain Himself yet again, Jesus seems to have concluded that He should make His remarks even more pointed. Perhaps He saw stubborn pride, not humble ignorance, before Him. Perhaps He sensed that His listeners were not wrestling but trifling with the priceless word of life He had been sent to share.

It was, then, time for them either to break down and accept what lay before them or else to dash themselves against the rocks of their own willful haughtiness. There comes the moment when man must get down on his knees and plead with God for understanding, not vice versa.

Since they had deliberately chosen to misconstrue His words, Jesus played along with their game. They must "eat the flesh of the Son of Man". They must "drink His blood" (v. 53). It is not necessary to see an explicit reference to the Lord's Supper here (or elsewhere in this chapter).[10] Jesus was simply calling on them to extend themselves to Him as He was extending Himself to them. They must admit His person and teachings into the inmost recesses of their souls. They needed to make His will and aims the center of their own present and future.

If they did so, they would know eternal life in the present and experience the resurrection of the righteous, not the damned, in the hereafter (v. 54). The word "real" in v. 55 is literally "true"; it denotes the unique power and authenticity of what Jesus offers. Nothing can take its place. Once Jesus is truly accepted, the difference He makes is continual and permanent (v. 56). As the Father nourishes the Son, so will the Son grant vitality to those who feed on Him (v. 57).

---

10. Morris's conclusion (*Gospel According to John*, p. 354) seems reasonable: the best interpretation is one that sees "primarily a teaching about spiritual realities . . . but does not deny that there may be a secondary reference to the sacrament." For a survey of other views and detailed examination of 6:35-59 see Brown, *Gospel According to John*, 1:272-94.

"Lord, to Whom Shall We Go?" (6:60-71)

MUTINY IN THE RANKS (6:60-66)

Jesus' disciples seem to have had as poor an understanding of Jesus' remarks as the Jewish leaders and the crowds at large. They, too, bridled at Jesus' statements (v. 60). Jesus was aware of their objections (v. 61).

He confronted them as He did the larger crowd. The words "What if you see the Son of Man ascend to where He was before!" (v. 62) admit of two interpretations. He may have been saying, "When you witness the still greater miracles yet to come, then you will realize that it was wise to believe these difficult words now." Or He may have been saying, "If you are incapable of seeing the real meaning of my words now, you will have even more trouble drawing the right conclusions once the Son of Man is resurrected and ascends."

In either case He pointed them to the spirit of His words, the meaning that they held if they will allow the Holy Spirit to impress His teaching on them (v. 63). Then they would not remain mere words: they would impart life. Bruce comments, "To try to take His words in a material sense, without attempting to penetrate beneath their surface meaning, is to miss their point. Eating the flesh of the Son of Man and drinking His blood must be understood as an attitude and activity of the spiritual realm."[11]

But many even among His followers "do not believe" (v. 64). This was no surprise to Jesus, who knew their hearts and was aware that one of them would betray him. It takes God's act, not merely man's mental or religious striving, to create the eye-opening, life-transforming trust to which Jesus calls. Many of them had not yet been enabled by the Father (v. 65).

Was it discouragement? Confusion? Misunderstanding? Anger? John does not say. He only recounts that many "turned back" (v. 66). They had not foreseen these developments. Jesus had turned down a move to make Him king. Now He was teaching about Himself in terms that were at least ambiguous, and on the surface downright disgusting. They had had enough. They "no longer followed him."

11. *Gospel of John*, p. 163.

"WE BELIEVE AND KNOW" (6:67-71)

"The twelve" (v. 67) had witnessed the miraculous feeding on the previous day (v. 13). They had heard Jesus' difficult teaching regarding what it takes to receive the life He offered. Now Jesus gave them a chance to vote with their feet just like the others. Did they wish to leave, too (v. 67)?

Perhaps more by default than by informed conviction, Peter expressed the group's sentiments. They had followed Jesus for months now. Some of them had been John the Baptist's followers prior to that. They had left everything (Luke 18:28). There was no turning back (v. 68). They recognized Jesus' unique role as God's appointed messenger or agent[12] (v. 69), even if they remained oblivious to much of what He stood for and taught (see 13:7).

The chapter ends on a foreboding note. One of Jesus' hand-picked followers would prove to be a traitor (vv. 70-71). Jesus did not seem to take pleasure in this, but He accepted it as the Father's will.

Jesus had fed the multitude, shown His mastery over the elements, and set forth richly yet starkly the terms of following Him. His committed followers had been pared down to only those with unshakable resolve. With them He was about to set out on an extensive ministry in Galilee, away from the plots of the religious officials from Judea in the south (7:1). He would then journey to Jerusalem once more. That journey and its consequences will be the subject of the next chapter.

12. See Peder Borgen, "God's Agent in the Fourth Gospel," in Ashton, ed., *The Interpretation of John*, pp. 67-78.

7

"COME TO ME AND DRINK" (7:1-53)

Chapter 6 describes a portion of Jesus' Galilean ministry. Due to opposition from hostile leaders in Judea to the south, Jesus found it prudent to extend His Galilean ministry for many months (7:1). Yet He eventually ventured south once more, selflessly and courageously proclaiming the message entrusted to Him by His Father. Despite the lack of understanding, and even hostility, of His own family, of many of the common people, and of the religious leadership, He obediently and effectively continued to invite His hearers to put their full trust in His message and ultimately in Jesus Himself.

Chapter 7 records Jesus' third appearance in Jerusalem (two earlier visits are mentioned at 2:13 and 5:1) and the mixed response He received. It continues to encourage the reader to "believe that Jesus is the Christ, the Son of God" (20:31) by calling attention in various vivid ways to how Jesus offered Himself to His hearers as God's promised royal deliverer, the Messiah prophesied from days of old.

SECRET JOURNEY SOUTH (7:1-13)

PROPHET WITHOUT HONOR (7:1-5)

The time span between the end of chapter 6 and the activity of chapter 7 is some six months. John does not record every incident in Jesus' ministry (see 21:25). After Jesus had spent several months to the north in Galilee (v. 1), the Feast of Tabernacles (sometimes called Feast of Booths) approached (v. 2). This feast took place in early autumn (September-October) and was one of the three great religious observances of the Jewish year. It celebrated the successful ingathering of the entire growing season's harvest. Jesus was to use this festival to further His work in the midst of the people.

His brothers appear to have taunted Him (vv. 3-4). John explains that they did so because they remained skeptical of their brother's controversial message and claims (v. 5). Jesus' brothers were James, Joseph, Simon, and Judas (Matt. 13:55). He had sisters as well (Matt. 13:56). The resurrected Jesus later appeared to James (1 Cor. 15:7), who became a leader of the Jerusalem church (Acts 15:13) along with John and Peter (Gal. 2:9). He wrote the New Testament book of James. Judas (or Jude) appears to be the author of the New Testament epistle that bears his name.

Eventually, therefore, the hardness of at least two of Jesus' brothers melted away. But for now Jesus was personally experiencing the family division that He said His teaching was likely to bring (see Luke 12:51-53; 14:26).

THE TIME HAS NOT YET COME (7:6-13)

John's gospel repeatedly stresses that Jesus had a sense of divine timing (see comments on 2:4). Unlike His brothers, who lived apart from the intimacy with God that Jesus knew, Jesus must be sensitive to the Father's promptings and timetable for Him (v. 6). His brothers were in no danger of a "world" in Judea that was hostile to them as it was to Jesus. This was because the brothers were walking in step with that world, whereas Jesus was telling it what it did not wish to hear (v. 7).[1] Jesus must remain behind for the present time, and He did so (vv. 8-9).

As preparation for Jesus' surprise appearance in Jerusalem (v. 14), John's gospel describes three different spheres of activity taking place behind the scenes.

First was Jesus' covert journey (v. 10). To avoid detection and possible arrest, He went "in secret" rather than traveling in a larger group as seems to have been customary (see Luke 2:44).

Second, the Jews were lying in wait for Him to appear (v. 11). Their designs were obviously not benevolent. They had been seeking

1. See Westcott, *Gospel According to St. John*, p. 117: "They were in sympathy with the world, while Christ was in antagonism with the world."

to remove Jesus from the public eye for some months, and they were prepared to apprehend Him immediately if they got the chance (v. 32). As Jesus headed south, they secretly prepared to terminate His troublesome influence.

Third, the crowds were abuzz with rumors about the startling movement building under Jesus' leadership. Some took up for Him. Others favored the theory that He was evil and dangerous (v. 12).

In this highly charged atmosphere of secrecy, suspicion, controversy, and fear (v. 13) where every precaution was being taken to ensure that Jesus was prevented from disrupting the proceedings, the Man both loved and despised suddenly exploded on the scene.

CONTROVERSIAL CLAIMS (7:14-53)

MAKE A RIGHT JUDGMENT (7:14-24)

The feast of Tabernacles lasted for a week (Lev. 23:34). When it was halfway along, Jesus appeared (v. 14). "The Jews" who were so amazed at Jesus' learning (v. 15) were probably the religious teachers and leaders of Jerusalem. They had their own system of education. The apostle Paul tells how "under Gamaliel I was thoroughly trained in the law of our fathers" (Acts 22:3). Jesus had no such formal training under the watchful eye of recognized rabbis. This does not mean that Jesus was illiterate or uneducated, only that He was not dependent on the religious education system in Jerusalem for the profound wisdom and insight into the Old Testament and other spiritual matters that He consistently exhibited.

Jesus explained how He came by His insight: the one who sent Him bestowed it on Him (v. 16). "The reason He can teach so well without formal education is that He himself is 'taught of God' (cf. 6:45)."[2] In order to understand His teaching, one must be willing to abide by God's will, since it is God from whom Jesus' teaching derives (v. 17). If Jesus were seeking to further His own ends, His words would be idle. But since He worked for God's "honor" (v. 18; the word is literally "glory"), He was "a man of truth," or literally, "true." In 3:33 and 8:26, the same word "true" is used to describe God Himself. There is "nothing false" or wrong in anything Jesus

2. Michaels, *John*, p. 115.

says, just as it is unthinkable that God Himself should say that which is untrue (Num. 23:19; Heb. 6:18).

Jesus was not content merely to make statements. He sought to provoke His listeners to personal response to what He said. He therefore put His hearers on the spot by pointing out that none of them kept the law of Moses perfectly, a fact made clear in the Old Testament itself (see Isa. 53:6; Ps. 14:1-3). Why should the religious leaders be plotting His ruin for breaking Moses' law (which Jesus was not really guilty of doing anyway [John 8:46])? Even if Jesus were guilty, would that justify plots against His life (v. 19), since they were all similarly guilty?

Many in the crowd were unaware of the schemes of the religious officials against Jesus. They took up the popular rumor that Jesus did His work by demonic power, and they inquired incredulously who Jesus thought was trying to kill Him (v. 20).

Jesus did not directly answer the crowd's question. He rather referred back to His "crime" of healing a man on the Sabbath (5:9, 16). This was apparently the "one miracle" (v. 21) that more than any other had generated such opposition against Him from some among the Jewish leadership.

Jesus pointed out the hypocrisy of their objections to what He had done. They did the same thing themselves when circumstances required. Male children were required to be circumcised on the eighth day after birth (Lev. 12:3). If the eighth day happened to fall on Saturday, they had to deal with the question of which law to "break"—the command to keep the Sabbath holy or the command to circumcise. They chose to break the Sabbath in order to circumcise (v. 22). Why then should they object to Jesus' healing the lame man on the Sabbath (v. 23)?

Although Jesus is sometimes claimed to have taught that no one should ever judge the rightness or wrongness of anything someone else does (see Matt. 7:1, "Do not judge. . ."), in verse 24 Jesus insists that at times discerning moral and spiritual judgments must be made. The key is to make sure they are not shallow and self-serving criticisms. Jesus called on His hearers to "make a right judgment." They needed to move beyond their simplistic traditions and perceive the weightier spiritual matters that were at stake. For, as He would soon state, if they failed to judge Jesus and themselves correctly, they would die in their sin (8:21).

LIVING WATER FROM WITHIN (7:25-44)

In verse 25 yet another segment of the crowd comes into view. These were neither the Jewish leaders (v. 15) nor the crowd that was unaware that Jesus' life was in danger (v. 20). This new group knew of the conspiracy among certain officials to do away with Jesus (v. 25). But they were puzzled because Jesus was being allowed to move about and speak freely (v. 26). Did this mean the leaders suspected that Jesus was the Messiah? But that would be impossible, they reasoned, for they knew that Jesus was from Nazareth, whereas no one will know where the Messiah comes from when He finally makes His appearance (v. 27).[3]

Jesus became aware of their outlook and addressed it. With some irony He repeated their words but implied that they knew less about Him than they thought they did (v. 28). He restated what He had already claimed in various other settings: He had been sent from one who is "true" (see v. 18, where the same word is used to describe Jesus), whom they did not know. Jesus, however, did know Him and had come from Him (v. 29).

It is not clear whether Jesus' words in verse 29 provoke the arrest attempt in verse 30, or whether this just happens to be the moment when authorities try to "seize him." In either case, Jesus eluded their grasp, for it was not yet the time ordained by the Father (see 8:20; 12:23, 27; 13:1; 17:1). Meanwhile, opposition to Jesus was offset by an increasing number who committed themselves to Him. They were convinced that the "signs" Jesus did justified the response He called for—personal commitment to the kingdom of God He announced, through personal devotion to what He said and who He claimed to be (v. 31).

The Pharisees got wind of the increasing support for Jesus (v. 32). Apparently they reported this to "the chief priests and the Pharisees," which probably refers to the Jewish high court, the Sanhedrin.

---

3. A Jewish tradition to this effect is reflected in the writings of Justin Martyr, a mid-second-century writer (*Dialogue with Trypho*, 8.7; cited in Bruce, *Gospel of John*, p. 187, n. 8).

The Sanhedrin included some Pharisees but was dominated by the Sadducees, a wealthy and powerful group of families from whom the high priest was regularly selected. They had trained police at their disposal. These were dispatched to bring Jesus in. "Jesus' opponents are trying to nip any such incipient faith in the bud."[4]

Meanwhile, Jesus continued to teach. He spoke of a time when He would return to the one who sent Him (v. 33). Those who rejected Him would seek Him but in vain, and they would be barred from the realm Jesus would then inhabit (v. 34).

Once again, Jesus' words were not understood. "The Jews," probably the Jerusalem hierarchy, speculated that perhaps He was threatening to take His message to His countrymen living outside Palestine (vv. 35-36). There were large Jewish populations in such areas as Alexandria and Rome, and considerable numbers in most other major cities. These were Jews of the so-called Diaspora.[5] Later followers of Jesus would do just that: they would preach Jesus' message in the synagogues and streets of Jews and Gentiles across the Roman Empire. But this was not what Jesus meant by His statement.

Jesus clarified His point on the last day of the feast (v. 37). During the feast, there were daily ceremonies when water was poured from a golden pitcher at the time of the morning sacrifice in the Temple. This symbolized God's bountiful provision for His people. On the last day of the feast, this ceremony was not repeated. There was rather a prayer for rain and God's blessing in the coming months and years.[6]

Jesus seized the occasion to proclaim loudly an invitation to come to Him for spiritual refreshment (v. 37). His words echoed Isaiah 55:1, where the prophet extends a moving invitation to accept the covenant blessing of Yahweh. Several Old Testament passages imply that the recipient of God's blessing receives a bounty that overflows to others (for example, Ps. 51:12-13; Isa. 58:11). This is the idea that Jesus

---

4. Schnackenburg, *Gospel According to John*, 2:149.

5. The word means "scattering" and referred first to Jews who fled or were deported from Palestine during the Babylonian invasion and conquest of Jerusalem in 587 B.C. After that time, Jews who lived outside of the land promised to Abraham were called the "Diaspora."

6. For details of the elaborate observances connected with this event see Beasley-Murray, *John*, pp. 113-14.

expresses in verse 38. He equates God's richest personal blessing with trust in Himself.

The saving presence Jesus promised comes about through His Spirit (v. 39), who had not yet made the dramatic appearance that He would at Pentecost (Acts 2) and afterward. Of course the Spirit was at work throughout the Old Testament as well as during the life of Jesus. But not until the unfolding of the drama of Jesus' death, resurrection, and ascension (when Jesus was "glorified," v. 39) would the full scope and intensity of the Spirit's work grow to the proportions seen in the ministry of the early church.

The result of Jesus' ministry during the festival week was mixed. Some hailed Him as "the Prophet" (v. 40; see Deut. 18:15). This claim was made earlier (6:14), but that was in Galilee, not Jerusalem.

Others took things a step further—Jesus must be the Christ (v. 41). Others were not so sure, for they were unaware of Jesus' birth in Bethlehem in accordance with Old Testament prophecy (v. 42; see Micah 5:2; Matt. 2:6). They took Him to be from Galilee, which is partially true, and they followed many of the ruling officials (see v. 52) in concluding that this disqualified Him from being the Messiah.

An acute division arose, as Jesus said it would (Luke 12:51). "From now on the division (*schisma*) in the crowd on Jesus' account becomes a recurring note in the narrative (cf. 9:16; 10:19); people range themselves inevitably on this side or that according to their estimate of him."[7] Yet His opponents did not succeed in squelching either His preaching or His popular support (v. 44). Jesus remained at large.

NO PROPHET FROM GALILEE (7:45-52)

John concludes the chapter by returning to the guards who had been sent to arrest Jesus (v. 32). These returned empty-handed and were upbraided by officials of the Sanhedrin (v. 45). In their own defense, they confessed to having been captivated by what Jesus said (v. 46). This was a powerful testimony to the force and eloquence of Jesus' address, for these were trained law enforcement officers under direct orders. But they had encountered a higher authority.

7. Bruce, *Gospel of John*, p. 184.

The Pharisees were utterly without sympathy and reproved them bitterly (v. 47). Their unfavorable assessment of Jesus ought to be binding on everyone else (v. 48). They failed to note that God often reveals the truth to those of lower social or educational status, perhaps because their relative lack of pride and self-sufficiency renders them more open to what God has to say (see Matt. 11:25; Luke 10:21).

They accused the police of succumbing to the stupidity of the accursed "mob that knows nothing of the law" (v. 49). This was a reference to the "people of the land," the large majority of the Jews in Jesus' day who belonged to no organized sect like the Pharisees and who were therefore looked down upon for their lack of piety. It was often precisely these who heard Jesus gladly (see Mark 12:37).

Yet not even all the leaders placed the confidence in their judgment and traditions that these verses reflect. Nicodemus, the nocturnal inquirer of chapter 3, questioned the wisdom of such an attitude.[8] On the grounds of the very law by which they sought to condemn Jesus, they ought to give Him a fair hearing (vv. 50-51).

The reply of Nicodemus's colleagues was not exactly charitable. They had a tendency to overlook the intent of the law they claimed to abide by (Matt. 23:23). Venting the same contempt toward Nicodemus that they had for Jesus, they scoffingly asked whether Nicodemus was also from Galilee, a land looked down on by the proud leaders of Judea (v. 52).

They were not quite right that no prophets came from Galilee. Jonah was one exception (2 Kings 14:25), and Elijah was another (1 Kings 17:1; Gilead extends northward to Galilee). But perhaps they referred to future, not past, prophets, especially "the Prophet" of Deut. 18:15. They were convinced that He must come from Judea. They were unaware that this was precisely where Jesus was born.

8. Calvin, *Gospel According to St. John*, 1:204, takes a surprisingly critical view of Nicodemus's intervention on Jesus' behalf. Yet there is wisdom, though not much charity, in his remarks. Schlatter (*John the Evangelist* [German], p. 205) suggests that Nicodemus "did not forget the command he received from Jesus; he is at pains to 'do the truth' [see 3:21], to act in such a way that truth will emerge as a result of his action."

TROUBLE BREWING

Chapter 7 reports opposition to Jesus from His family, from many of the common people, and from the religious leaders. Yet it also shows that a growing number were becoming convinced by His deeds and claims. The leaders grew more angry at their inability to corral this upstart from up north, and Jesus became more open in His challenge to their authority and His call for full acceptance of Himself and His message.

A showdown was in the making. The intensity of the antagonism Jesus already faced climbs to the danger zone in the next chapter.

8

SON OF GOD
OR SON OF THE DEVIL (8:1-52)

Chapter 7 concludes with Jerusalem authorities fuming at Nicodemus for daring to suggest that Jesus deserved a fair hearing (7:50-52). Chapter 8 traces a fierce confrontation between these same authorities and Jesus Himself. Jesus will make His boldest assertions yet regarding the uniqueness of His relationship to the Father. His opponents, who so far have only sent police to arrest Him, will seek to take the law into their own hands in the hope of at last being rid of their foe.

The drama that John relates in order to move the reader to informed personal commitment to Christ (20:31) reaches one of its most intense and engrossing levels of conflict in chapter 8.

HYPOCRITES FACE AN ADULTERESS—AND JESUS (8:1-11)

HISTORICITY AND AUTHORITY

As marginal notes in most modern translations indicate, John 7:53–8:11 is absent from many important Greek manuscripts. In some ancient copies the account is inserted after 7:36, after 7:44, or after 21:25. In still other copies one will find it after Luke 21:38. Many of the manuscripts that do include it contain special scribal notations indicating the uncertainty of the passage.[1]

---

1. For these and further details see Metzger, *Textual Commentary*, pp. 219-22.

Many modern commentaries treat the passage as historical,[2] though there is strong doubt that it belongs to the original version of John.[3] Since there is considerable probability that John did not write it, there is reason to avoid according canonical authority to the incident. In the remarks below we will treat the verses as if they accurately describe an actual event,[4] without thereby implying either Johannine origin or canonical authority for the passage.

A MEMORABLE LESSON (8:1-11)

The focus moves now from the Sanhedrin and Nicodemus (7:45-52) to an early morning setting in which Jesus addresses a large crowd in the Temple area (v. 2). He sat as He spoke, the normal posture for a Jewish rabbi.

Without warning, Pharisees and "teachers of the law" hauled a hapless woman into their midst (v. 3). "Teachers of the law" are the "scribes" of the other three gospels. The expression appears nowhere else in John's gospel. This woman, her accusers said, had been caught in the act of adultery (v. 4). They reminded Jesus that the Law of Moses (Lev. 20:10) mandated the death penalty for such a crime. They neglected to mention that Moses also commanded that her sex partner receive the same punishment. Either the man had escaped, or they were simply victimizing the woman for the sake of forcing Jesus into making a statement that would get Him in trouble (v. 6).

Their strategy was obvious and ingenious. If Jesus advocated leniency, then He could be accused of undercutting Moses' authority. If

2. A useful, short study outlining the justification for this position is Gary M. Burge, "A Specific Problem in the New Testament Text and Canon: The Woman Caught in Adultery (John 7:53–8:11)," *Journal of the Evangelical Theological Society* 27/2 (1984): 141-48.

3. Defending its originality is Zane Hodges, "The Woman Taken in Adultery (John 7:53–8:11): The Text," *Bibliotheca Sacra* 136 (1979): 318-32. This position has not found wide acceptance among NT scholars.

4. Michaels, *John*, does not comment on the passage. Morris, *Gospel According to John*, does so, but in an appendix (pp. 882-91). Roman Catholic commentators, says Schnackenburg, treat it as part of the canon because it is contained in the Vulgate, though "this does not involve any decision about its literary origin" (*Gospel According to John* 2:162). Ironically, many conservative Protestants join with Catholics in defending its canonicity—not because it is in the Vulgate, of course, but because it is in the King James Version.

He upheld Moses and called for her to be stoned, He would be violating Roman law, which forbade the Jews to execute lawbreakers without their express consent.[5]

Theories abound, but no one knows for sure what Jesus wrote as He knelt and pondered (vv. 6, 8). As they continued to barrage Him with questions, He abruptly rose with a response: Let that accuser who is sinless begin the execution proceedings (v. 7). In this way Jesus upheld the spirit of the law, yet shifted the responsibility for carrying it out to where it belonged: on the people whom God had charged with living out His commandments in covenant with Him.

Beginning with the oldest, and presumably the wisest, leaders, the accusers began to drift away (v. 9). They were not going to trick Jesus into reinstating an ordinance that the Jews of that time were not normally enforcing anyway.

At last only the woman remained. No one dared press the original charge further once Jesus with His usual shrewdness turned the tables on those who sought to ensnare Him (v. 10). Jesus in no way excused her grave error, but neither did He condemn her on the spot. The public airing of her shameless deed may have been punishment enough. It was time for reform and healing to begin.

There was hope for her in Jesus, though she must make a decisive break with the life she had been living (v. 11). Earlier Jesus told the healed lame man, "Stop sinning or something worse many happen to you" (5:14). The message may be similar here. If she hoped to elude the just consequences for violating God's commands, there must be a radical shift in her life, not merely the idle acceptance of God's mercy, as if that mercy were not also a summons to personal commitment to the One from whom the mercy had come.

Whether the woman actually followed Jesus or not remains unknown. But Jesus had cleared the way for her, and for countless others whose sin condemns them before God, to receive forgiveness and begin a new life of service and obedience to Christ.

5. There was one exception to this law: Gentiles found within the Temple areas reserved for Jews alone could apparently be put to death on the spot.

CHALLENGE FROM THE PHARISEES (8:12-30)

VALID TESTIMONY (8:12-20)

Some of the same Pharisees, perhaps, who taunted Nicodemus
(7:52) now challenged Jesus face to face. Jesus addressed the crowds,
teaching that the radiant, cleansing, and life-giving presence of God—
"the light"—is available to any who follow Him (v. 12). The Pharisees responded that such self-advocacy is invalid (v. 13). They knew
that according to Scripture two or more witnesses were required to establish the factuality of public testimony (Deut. 19:15). A "tradition
of the elders" expanded on Moses' commandment at this point: "No
man can give evidence for himself."[6] Jesus should not be believed because He was, so to speak, just tooting His own horn.

Even if they were correct, Jesus responded, they would be wrong
(v. 14). He came from God, and God does not need man's corroborat-
ing testimony to know and say what ails man (see 2:25). His accusers
did not accept the implications of Jesus' heavenly origin—"you have
no idea of where I come from" (v. 14)—but their ignorance did not
minimize Jesus' authority over them. His decisions and decrees are
powerful and flawless because they are backed up by God Himself (v.
16). The Father is Jesus' co-witness, and together they satisfy even the
requirements of the Mosaic law of testimony (vv. 17-18).

The Pharisees pressed for a clearer statement regarding Jesus'
"father" (v. 19). If they could get Jesus to say openly that He referred
to God in heaven, then they would have public witnesses of open blasphemy (see 5:18). But their effort failed, in part because Jesus' "time
had not yet come" (v. 20). It would arrive soon enough.

MUCH TO SAY IN JUDGMENT (8:21-30)

Jesus did not let matters rest, however (v. 21). It was important
that even His enemies be faced with the challenge of His identity so
that they, too, would have opportunity to repent—or else condemn
themselves by their willful refusal to respond.

Jesus warned them that they would die without their sins being
forgiven (v. 21). This is because they were unwilling to recognize

6. Brown, *Gospel According to John*, 1:340, n. 13.

God's forgiveness of their sins in the one who stood before them. They ignored Jesus' statement about their sin, raising idle if not frivolous questions about whether Jesus might be contemplating suicide (v. 22), a manner of death abhorrent to the Jews.[7]

Jesus persisted (v. 23). The suicidal behavior was theirs, not His, for they refused to believe who He was claiming to be, and the outcome of their stubbornness would be judgment before God with no mercy: "You will indeed die in your sins" (v. 24). They must stop trying to reduce Jesus to their own proportions. He was from above, not limited by and restricted to the traditions and perceptions of those around Him. They were from below, blind to the divine wisdom and mercy that confronted them. Jesus' claim was reminiscent of what God said centuries earlier to the ancestors of Jesus' opponents (Isa. 55:8-9).

Since Jesus gave no answer that they could use against Him when asked who His father was, His accusers changed tactics. They asked Jesus who He was (v. 25).

Jesus replied that He had already said enough for them to answer that question for themselves (v. 25). He implied that He could be much more harsh and decisive in condemning them for their refusal to respond: "I have much to say in judgment of you" (v. 26). But He would say no more than what the Father led Him to disclose.

Their lack of understanding (v. 27) should probably be understood as willful refusal rather than as intellectual inability. Jesus concluded this portion of His discourse with a summary statement (vv. 28-29). His being "lifted up" (see 3:14; 12:32, 34) would furnish final proof of what they refused to accept—that Jesus is who He claims to be, that He speaks only what God wills, and that His every action is consistent with God's redemptive intention for Him as well as for His listeners. Everything Jesus did is pleasing to God.

Even in the midst of so much confusion and hostility, the light Jesus claimed to bring (v. 12) broke through. "Many put their faith in him" (v. 30). But out of this hopeful development arose yet another bitter series of exchanges.

---

7. Morris, *Gospel According to John*, p. 446, n. 34.

FAITH AND FREEDOM (8:31-47)

Despite the diatribes of those who opposed Jesus, some were inclined to accept Him and His message (v. 30). Jesus informed them that His true disciples remained firmly committed to His teaching (v. 31). The outcome of their perseverance would be freedom (v. 32). In the context this referred, not to political freedom, but to freedom from bondage to the sinful traditions[8] and hard feelings that gripped most of Jesus' hearers.

The resolve of these new believers was immediately tested by those standing around them who were still unbelieving. They challenged Jesus' insinuation that they were not already free (v. 33). They questioned His charge that Abraham's descendants needed Him in order to gain liberty.

Jesus' reply as John's gospel records it was tightly packed with significance. He first reaffirmed His position, adding that the "freedom" of which He spoke involves freedom from sin (v. 34).[9] He may have had in mind both sin's destructive power in the present life and its eternal penalty in the life to come. Next He suggested that descendants of Abraham had the status of slaves in an ancient household. Slaves were not automatically permanent residents (v. 35). This privilege must be extended to them by their master (see Ex. 21:5-6). The son, by contrast, was a permanent resident.

What Abraham's descendants needed, therefore, was to gain the status of a son. Now the Father of the household had sent His Son. He was offering them permanent residence in His household. They must welcome that Son and respond to His invitation. In the words of Ex. 21:5, they must declare, "I love my master. . . and do not want to go free." Then, but only then, they would "be free indeed" (v. 36).

---

8. The traditions were not necessarily sinful in themselves. But they became sinful because they displaced or distorted God's written commands (see Mark 7:8; Matt. 23:23).

9. Bruce, *Gospel of John*, p. 197: "Jesus reminds them that there is another kind of slavery than social or economic slavery. Sin is a slave-master, and it is possible even for people who think of themselves as free to be enslaved to sin."

Jesus realized that His hearers cherished proud notions of their Abrahamic descent (v. 37). But He also knew that they were out of sympathy with their forefather, who would not seek to kill the Son (v. 40) but rather rejoiced at what the Son had come to do (v. 56). Their murderous resentment and rejection of His preaching told the real story of their ancestry and loyalty. Jesus acted in accordance with His Father, whereas they responded out of devotion to theirs (v. 38).

Jesus' provocative assessment of their parentage drew a predictable outburst (v. 39). But Jesus disagreed with their claim to be Abraham's true children. Here Jesus anticipated an observation that Paul later makes (Rom. 2:28-29). Their hostile behavior toward Jesus implied that they had a father other than Abraham (v. 40). Their actions were in keeping with that father (v. 41).

They well understood the implications of Jesus' pointed charge. They protested vehemently. They resented being called "illegitimate children" (v. 41). Not only were they Abraham's children—they were children of God Himself! Westcott paraphrases their sentiments as follows: "We are the offspring of the union of God with His chosen people. Our spiritual descent is as pure as our historical descent."[10]

A primary source of conflict between them and Jesus was finally in the open. Jesus claimed that God was His own father and that they must therefore listen to what He said if they wished to know and do God's will. They insisted that God was their own father, that they had equal if not superior access to God. In this sense, they did not need Jesus to tell them what God expected from them—they knew directly from the source, quite apart from any mediation on Jesus' part.

This stark conflict between basic viewpoints sets the stage for a breathtakingly strong denunciation of the unbelieving Jews' recalcitrance in the next verses.

UNABLE TO HEAR (8:42-47)

Jesus replied concisely but forthrightly. He repeated that their animosity toward Him actually reflected animosity toward God, for He was from God (v. 42). He takes up the problem posed by their rejection of His teaching. Why did they not understand? They were "un-

---

10. *Gospel According to St. John*, p. 136.

able to hear" what Jesus said (v. 43). This inability was, however, not primarily of the intellect but of the will. They could not hear because they would not turn loose of their own cherished convictions.

If there was any hope of their abandoning their disastrous position, they must be confronted with brutal clarity. Jesus did what was necessary for God's truth and steadfast love to go forth in such a hostile setting. They were following a murderous, truth-repressing policy in their aggressive opposition to Jesus. In doing so they mimicked the archenemy of God through all human history: the devil, the father of lies and murder (v. 44).[11] This was not a pleasant disclosure, but it was true. And precisely for that reason, Jesus' claims met rejection, and had all along (v. 45).

Jesus concluded by claiming a different basis for the truth of His words than He had previously mentioned—His sinlessness (v. 46). A sinless person would tell no lies; therefore His every utterance would be true. Jesus was sinless, so His words could be relied on. But they held the conviction that Jesus was not sinless (9:24). They "do not belong to God" (v. 47) and did not recognize the one whom God had sent. As a result, they rejected the painfully penetrating but life-giving message Jesus brought.

DEITY OR DEMON? (8:48-59)

GREATER THAN ABRAHAM? (8:48-53)

As they do elsewhere in John's gospel (7:20; 8:52; 10:20), Jesus' enemies accuse Him of complicity with Satan or satanic power (v. 48). They also smeared Him by tagging Him with the most demeaning racial epithet they could come up with—Samaritan.

Jesus refused to repay these vicious charges in kind. Instead He dealt with them calmly. It was not demonic power but divine honor that drove Him (v. 49). Their charge against Jesus came back to rest on them, since they dishonored the one God sent. He was the judge in

---

11. Schlatter, *John the Evangelist* [German], p. 215, points out that "just as rabbinic teaching had no doctrine of divine sonship, so it had no doctrine of being a child of the devil, in the sense that Jesus speaks here, where He portrays the devil as the one who produces that will in man which moves Him to destroy life and oppose the truth."

this matter, for He was zealous for the glory that should be shown Him, which Jesus was giving His life to promote (v. 50).

Then, as He did earlier in the debate that raged in chapter 6 (see especially 6:53-56), Jesus met willful opposition by putting an even sharper edge on His teaching than caused opposition in the first place. He asserted that "if anyone keeps my word," another way of saying "holds to my teaching" (v. 31), "he will never see death" (v. 51).

By this expression Jesus may have indicated several things. He may have been asserting that the presence of the abundant life He brought (see 10:10) will dispel some of the deadly effects of sin in this present life. Or He may have been asserting that for the one who trusts Him fully, physical death is a prelude to future bliss rather than non-existence or even punishment. He will "never see death" in the sense that physical death will not have the last word. Or He may have been saying both of these things.

Whatever He meant, His listeners took offense. They concluded that their earlier verdict was now confirmed (v. 52). Jesus was claiming to be someone greater, and bringing something greater, than the patriarchs and prophets of the Old Testament. They all died. Jesus claimed to impart a gift that even they did not enjoy. Did Jesus think He was greater than Abraham? Unthinkable!

Yet this astounding thought was precisely the truth. All that God did earlier was summed up and exceeded by the Son (see Heb. 1:1-2).

"BEFORE ABRAHAM . . . 'I AM'" (8:54-59)

The climax of the intense series of exchanges in this chapter comes, appropriately enough, at the end.

Jesus harked back to their original charge—that He was bearing witness to Himself and should therefore be rejected (v. 54; see v. 13). As He had repeatedly stated, this charge was false. For the very Father they claimed as theirs was actually on His side, so to speak. Although Jesus' stance caused great conflict, He could not soften it without falling prey to the same lying spirit that He met in His opponents (v. 55). Despite their negative verdict on Him and His message, all He did grew out of the Father's will and word. He was so much in tune with the Father, the God of Israel, the God who first covenanted with Abraham, that He could honestly say that Abraham rejoiced at what Jesus was bringing to pass (v. 56). Here it should be recalled that in Jesus' outlook those who like Abraham died trusting God were still alive, so to speak, in God's presence, "for to Him all" who are like Abraham, Isaac, and Jacob, who trust in the Lord, "are alive" (Luke 20:38).

To skeptical listeners this sounded ridiculous. They responded incredulously and mockingly (v. 57).

Jesus answered deliberately and forcefully (v. 58). He used language so suggestive of God's own reference to Himself at the burning bush (Ex. 3:14) that they sought to stone Him on the spot for blasphemy (v. 59; see Lev. 24:16).[12]

It is not clear whether Jesus' escape involved a miraculous deliverance or merely deft and quick action on His part. Perhaps some of both were involved.

In either case Jesus hads now divulged His identity in Jerusalem with greater explicitness than ever before. His hour had still not come, but it had leaped many times closer in a brief span of time. He had gone from relative isolation in remote Galilee (7:1) to notoriety in Jerusalem, seat of religious power, home of those who stone the prophets.

The stage was set for additional priceless lessons from Jesus regarding Himself and the work He had come to do. It was set also for further conflict, along with still mightier acts of power, in the gripping chapters just ahead.

---

12. Schnackenburg's otherwise helpful discussion of Jesus' "I am" statements in John concludes disappointingly that "it would be a misunderstanding of the use of this high claim in the mouth of Jesus if it were interpreted as an identification with God" (*Gospel According to John*, 2:88). Yet this is exactly what the Jews appear to have done. Kysar (*John*, Augsburg Commentary, p. 146) claims that "it is not clear . . . in what sense His words are blasphemous." It seems highly probable that Jesus was, however, making a strong and unambiguous claim to essential oneness with the heavenly Father—in a word, to deity. And that is why the Jews sought to stone Him. See Morris, *Gospel According to John*, pp. 473-74. More cautious, but also more thorough, is Brown, *Gospel According to John*, 1:533-38.

9

SIGHT TO THE BLIND (9:1-41)

The act of "seeing" plays a central role in John's gospel from the very start.[1] Christ comes as a shining light (1:5), the first requirement for visual perception to take place. John testifies, "We have seen His glory" (1:14). He asserts that "no one has ever seen God," though the Son "has made Him known" (1:18). John the Baptist exhorts His followers to see, to regard carefully, "the Lamb of God" (1:29, 36). Jesus promises His first followers, "You shall see greater things . . . You shall see heaven open" (1:50-51).

As "hearing" plays a central role in Paul's letters (see Rom. 10:17: "faith comes from hearing"), so "seeing" is the key to knowing and trusting Christ in John.

Chapter 9 relates an incident in which someone receives physical sight, and ultimately spiritual insight, from Jesus. The account has literal historical value.[2] But it also serves as a sort of parable illustrating the universal, yet personal, need of every member of the human race. That is the need for Jesus Christ to open the spiritual eyes of those who are blind to the sight-restoring message He brings. In Kysar's words, the chapter shows "in an exemplary way how John recites a wonder story and then proceeds to explore its symbolic meaning. While it is a physically blind man who is healed, it is His spiritual sight and the

---

1. Brown, *Gospel According to John*, 1:501-3, surveys five different words used in John some 114 times, all of which carry the connotation of seeing.
2. Surveying the whole chapter, Westcott asserts, "The variety of opinion among the people and the mention of 'the man called Jesus' belong to the experience of an immediate witness" (*Gospel According to St. John*, p. 143).

spiritual blindness of the religious leaders that constitute the central message of this section."[3]

Without receiving the new vision only Jesus can give, there is the sure and frightful prospect of judgment for the sin of willful blindness. Jesus came, He says, "for judgment . . . so that the blind will see and those who see will become blind" (9:39). Chapter 9 serves to illustrate and explain the meaning of this enigmatic but illuminating claim.

MYSTERY MAN (9:1-12)

The exact location where Jesus healed the blind man (v. 1) is not known. It was somewhere in Jerusalem, perhaps near the Temple from which Jesus had just come (8:59).

The disciples' question (v. 2) reflected a view evidently common at the time—physical malady was the direct result of some particular sin.[4] The same assumption helps explain Jesus' words in Luke 13:2. Deut. 7:10 is an Old Testament passage that some may have interpreted to mean that physical sickness is always the result of God's displeasure for one's sin, or one's ancestors' sin.

Jesus' reply (v. 3) seems to address the ultimate purpose of the affliction rather than its cause. The man's condition should not be a springboard for vain speculation about moral causation. It should rather be regarded in its present potential for "displaying" (the same word occurs in 1:31, there translated "revealed") what God can do.

It is important, Jesus went on, to seize every opportunity to "do the work" that will point to the one who sent Him. For "night is coming" (v. 4). This may refer to the brevity of the time left to Jesus on earth or to the fleeting nature of man's opportunity to live life to God's glory (see Eccles. 12:6-7; James 4:14), or to both.

Jesus' statement that He is "the light of the world" (v. 5) harks back to opening verses in the gospel (1:4-5). It may be regarded as a

3. *John*, Ausburger Commentary, p. 148. Kysar's tendency, however, to see John (or some other redactor) as contriving incidents and interpretations rather than reporting substantially factual occurrences is to be resisted.

4. "The idea that sickness or deformity is punishment for sin . . . is an ancient one, and although Jesus rejects it (v. 3), His own interpretation of the man's blindness is scarcely more acceptable to modern humanitarianism" (D. Moody Smith, *John* [Philadelphia: Fortress, 1976], p. 34).

fitting prelude to what He was about to do—give light to the eyes of one who thus far has known only darkness.

In most of Jesus' healings He made no use of such devices as spittle or mud (v. 6). It is not absolutely clear why He did so here. Perhaps this would give the blind man something tangible to remember and reflect on, fostering an unshakable loyalty to the one whose hands daubed mud on his sightless eyes. He would soon be called on to denounce Jesus (v. 24). It was fortuitous that he had such palpable contact with Him now.[5]

Jesus' purpose could also involve the public testimony of ritual washing (v. 7). Many would witness the blind man's action and be forced to take some personal stand regarding Jesus as a result. The man's public act would also serve to confirm his own commitment within himself to be obedient to the one who granted him sight.

The query of amazed neighbors and acquaintances expected a positive answer (v. 8). We might translate, "This is the same man, isn't it!" While some are sure it is, others are skeptical (v. 9).

But the man himself knew very well what he was, and what he had now become. Jesus had touched his eyes, and more, and he would never be the same. Curious questioners barraged him for an explanation (v. 10). He told what he knew for sure (v. 11). They demanded to know the healer's whereabouts (v. 12). But the man could offer no help. He didn't know himself.

Suddenly, what appeared to be such a marvelous blessing turned into a grueling ordeal.

OFFICIAL INVESTIGATION (9:13-34)

ROUND ONE (9:13-23)

The weighty authority of the Pharisees (see comments above on 1:24 and 3:1) caused some to bring them in on the case (v. 13). By this time it was common knowledge that they sought to arrest Jesus (7:32)

---

5. Calvin (*Gospel According to St. John*, 1:241) offers a somewhat different suggestion: "Christ's purpose was to restore sight to the blind man; but He starts the work in what seems a very absurd way; for by anointing his eyes with clay He so to say doubles the blindness. Anyone would have thought He was mocking the poor man or carrying on senseless fooleries like a madman. But by doing this, He meant to try the faith and obedience of the blind man, that he might be an example to all."

if they could do so without causing a public stir. The healing had taken place on the Sabbath (v. 14), the focal point of much of the Pharisees' teaching. Although the blind man did not know who had healed him, the Pharisees knew exactly who was causing all the trouble (vv. 22, 24, 29). It is thus understandable that their involvement was solicited.

The verb tense of "asked" (v. 15) implies repetition. The man was being interrogated, not merely addressed for informational purposes.

For some of the Pharisees, the fact that the healing took place on Saturday was proof enough that Jesus was in violation of God's revealed will. Others were not so sure. Ironically, the Pharisees were rent by the same division that characterized the common people whom they so roundly denounced (v. 16; see 7:43, 49). The "signs" (v. 16) may be pointers to God's saving grace in Christ, but they can also cause people to take offense and reject the one who works them.

Perhaps out of desperation, they turned again to the man who was once blind (v. 17). He suggested that Jesus was a prophet. This is understandable, for Old Testament prophets like Elijah and Elisha were known for healing miracles. Since Jesus did similar acts, perhaps He had a similar calling and power.

The Pharisees' skepticism was not limited to Jesus. Obviously they rejected the man's suggestion that Jesus was a prophet from God. But they were reluctant even to grant that the man was blind in the first place (v. 18). So they called for his parents and cross-examined them (v. 19).

They cautiously stated what the Pharisees already knew (vv. 20-21). They feared to say more, aware of an apparently informal decision on the part of the Jerusalem religious leaders to bar from the synagogue anyone who "acknowledged that Jesus was the Christ," the God-appointed regent of the Jews (vv. 22-23).

Ejection from the synagogue[6] might have been either temporary or permanent; further details are lacking. In either case, such a mea-

---

6. Much contemporary scholarship builds on the theory of J. Louis Martyn (*History and Theology in the Fourth Gospel* [Nashville: Abingdon, 1979], pp. 24-62) that followers of Jesus were first cast out of the synagogue when Jewish leaders incorporated a prayer against "heretics" (Christians) into the synagogue liturgy. There is evidence that this occurred late in the first century. Some conclude that chapter 9 of John is, accordingly, not really about a historical incident in the life of Jesus but rath-

sure would have meant severe humiliation and ostracism. It might even have called in question one's place in the future heavenly kingdom. The Pharisees' threat was not a light one.

Yet although they had thus far kept public acclaim for Jesus' act from surfacing, the stubborn evidence of the man before them could not simply be dismissed. Plainly Jesus had effected an amazing physical change. If they could not explain it away, perhaps they could denounce it as the deceitfulness of a "sinner" (v. 24) and ultimately someone in league with the powers of darkness (see 7:20; 8:48). This seems to be the motivation behind a second round of questioning for the man whose healing was bringing such hostile attention.

ROUND TWO (9:24-34)

Some suggest that the order "Give glory to God!" (v. 24) was a legally binding command to tell the truth (see Josh. 7:19). Others think that they want him to attribute the healing to God, not to Jesus, whom they characterize as "a sinner." In either case, the intensity of their questioning and the pressure they were exerting on the man were unmistakable.

To the man on trial, the Pharisees' theories about Jesus' sinfulness in the light of their Sabbath rules must have sounded somewhat pedantic and hollow. "One thing" was utterly irrefutable—"I was blind, but now I see" (v. 25). He had no need or wish to quibble about the light that had invaded and dispelled the darkness that had once engulfed him.

The Pharisees persisted, seemingly grasping for any straw they could to construct a case against Jesus (v. 26). The man's patience wore thin, perhaps because he was weary of being badgered and perhaps because he resented the slurs against the man who had shown him such powerful mercy (v. 27). He baited his inquisitors with an aggres-

er about conflict between Jews and Christians some half-century after Jesus passed from the scene. It is then further supposed that the whole of John's gospel is primarily a reflection of the life setting of the person or community that put the gospel narratives in their present form, not a historically reliable account of incidents and discourses in the life of Jesus. Explaining, and sometimes questioning, this point of view is Beasley-Murray, *John*, pp. 152-54; also xliv-liii. See also Robinson, *Priority of John*, pp. 72-81.

sive, somewhat arch question of his own—are they intent on gathering data so that they may become the disciples of this Jesus fellow whom they so heartily despised?

"Hurled insults" (v. 28) is a verb denoting extreme verbal abuse (the same word occurs in Acts 23:4; 1 Cor. 4:12; 1 Pet. 2:23). They accused the man of being Jesus' disciple, to them a cutting accusation. They insisted that Moses, not Jesus, was their mentor. This points not only to their adherence to the Old Testament but also to their reliance on oral tradition, some of which they claimed had its origin in Moses himself.

In order to believe that Jesus was really the fulfillment of Moses' teachings (see 5:46), the Pharisees would have to be convinced that God spoke to Jesus as "God spoke to Moses" (v. 29). This helps explain why Jesus expended so much effort in John's gospel telling "the Jews" that He was sent from God and spoke the words that God had given Him. In the end it seems that few among the religious hierarchy were persuaded by His claims. But He could not be accused of dodging or overlooking this issue, so central in the minds of His most studied opponents.

The man replied with sarcasm yet conviction. He ridiculed the Pharisees' unwillingness to admit the obvious (v. 30). He cited the popular view, one with some Old Testament support (e.g., Ps. 66:18), that God does not answer the prayers of those who willfully rebel against Him (v. 31).

Continuing his brief and risky lecture to the learned, he concluded that the miracle whose integrity they questioned was unprecedented (v. 32). The only satisfactory explanation for it was that the one who did it was "from God" (v. 33). Otherwise He would lack such remarkable ability.

Such logic seems hard to resist, but the Pharisees managed. The man's forthrightness gave them a welcome chance to shift the focus of their attack from Jesus to the man himself. How dared he lecture them (v. 34)! "Steeped in sin at birth" may hark back to the belief seen in verse 2: congenital handicap must imply sin on the part of parents. Or it may reflect the sentiment seen in Ps. 51:5. Either way, the insult is intentional and scathing.

The final outcome was not merely insulting. In the Jerusalem setting of the day, to be barred from the synagogue could have devastating consequences for both family and other social ties.[7] Apparently in the course of a few short hours, the man had gone from dependent beggar to popular though controversial celebrity to social reject.

Was feeling Jesus' touch, even if it meant regaining one's sight, worth such a high price? The question could not have been far from the man's musing as the religious leaders announced their stern decree.

Sight and Insight (9:35-41)

Jesus is the one who not only saves the lost but also seeks them (Luke 19:10). When He heard of the expulsion from the synagogue, He found the victim and confronted him with the question, "Do you believe in the Son of Man?" (v. 35; on "Son of Man" see remarks on 1:51).

A person blind for so many years, and thus possessing heightened auditory powers,[8] would immediately have recognized Jesus by the sound of His voice. He knew Jesus was the one who healed him, but he was not sure who or what the "Son of Man" was. So he asked (v. 36).

In words reminiscent of the ones He spoke to the Samaritan woman (4:26), Jesus identified Himself as the bearer of the title (v. 37).

It is possible, even highly likely, that the man had heard for months about Jesus of Nazareth, who called Himself the Son of Man. Now he discovered that this famous, though bitterly opposed, prophetic figure was the one who opened his eyes. His responded immediately with an expression of personal commitment and religious veneration (v. 38).

Jesus replied with a statement summarizing the importance of His ministry (v. 39). His immediate task was not to judge (see 3:17), but His ultimate task was. As 5:27 indicates, final judgment rests in the hands of the Son of Man (see comments on 5:27).

7. Heb. 10:32-34 does not explicitly mention expulsion from the synagogue, but in other respects it may sketch the grim prospects that awaited descendents of Abraham who decided to declare allegiance to Jesus.

8. See John M. Hull, *Touching the Rock: An Experience of Blindness* (London: SPCK, 1990).

Jesus reiterated that truth here. And He expanded on it. Through Him the blind will receive sight. Jesus' meaning is similar to what He says in the Sermon on the Mount (Matt. 5:3-6): those who are poor in spirit, who mourn, who are meek, who hunger and thirst for righteousness—they are the ones whom God is able to speak to, forgive, and satisfy. Those who own up to their blindness, who confess the darkness enshrouding their hearts—they are the ones whom the Son of Man gladly pardons and saves.

Paul expresses the same truth with respect to the self-examination of believers readying themselves for Communion: "If we judged ourselves, we would not come under judgment" (1 Cor. 11:31).

But there are those who refuse to pronounce a negative verdict on themselves. They refuse to bemoan their sorry state, or to be humbled by the stark truth about themselves pronounced by God's Word (see Rom. 3:19-20), or to yearn for the righteousness God alone imparts through His Son alone. "Those," said Jesus, "who see will become blind" (v. 39). There is no hope for those who refuse to recognize their hopelessness without Christ, preferring instead to fix their gaze on the mirage of their supposed uprightness and sufficiency before God.

Some Pharisees, perhaps still hoping to catch Jesus in a statement or action they could use against Him, overheard Jesus' remarks. The literal force of their accusatory question (v. 40) is, "You don't mean to imply that *we* are blind, do you?"

Jesus' reply was simple but devastating.[9] If they were willing to admit their blindness by acknowledging the light Jesus brought, they "would not be guilty of sin" (v. 40). By "sin" Jesus may have meant their most recent assault on Jesus' integrity: their refusal to see the blind man's healing as the good work of God through Jesus. Or He may have been speaking more generally of the sinful condition that was the plight of every Pharisee, as it is of every son or daughter of Adam generally.

But they did not acknowledge their faulty vision. They were therefore blind to the saving light that confronted them, light that they

---

9. William Temple calls it "a crushing, overwhelming retort" (cited in Morris, *Gospel According to John*, p. 497, n. 59).

even dared to call error and darkness. Through their own choice, therefore, their "guilt remains" (v. 41).

This grim verdict on the leading sect of religious leaders, the group that was widely viewed as the definitive interpreters of Moses for the entire Jewish people (see Matt. 23:2), forms the background for the next chapter. There Jesus will contrast the style, content, and result of their leadership with the outcome of the watchcare He exercises over those who come to Him for refuge and guidance.

As far as chapter 9 itself is concerned, the main message remains one of light, life, and hope because of the one who sees and responds to the plight of the blind. Because of Jesus Christ, the light of the world, those who once walked in darkness can rejoice with the man born blind that "a light has dawned" (Isa. 9:2) that will transform their lives, presently and without end.

10

WOLVES VERSUS GOD'S SHEPHERD
(10:1-42)

It is possible to read much of chapter 10 as a sweet and peaceful meditation on Jesus, the gentle Good Shepherd of His beloved sheep. But such a reading isolates the chapter and misses its close ties with chapter 9. At least three important clues suggest that as John wrote, he was explicitly relating Jesus' statements in the tenth chapter with what had taken place in the ninth.

First, 10:21 harks back directly to the healing of the blind man in chapter 9.

Second, although 10:22-39 reflects a different temporal setting from 9:1–10:21, Jesus' mention of sheep in 10:26-27 suggests that there is a close relationship between those remarks and the passage preceding them, even though the remarks were made in different circumstances.

Third, in 10:31 and 10:39, "the Jews" attempted once more to stone Jesus or at least to take Him into custody. But Jesus eluded their grasp. This is reminiscent of 8:59, the verse that sets the dramatic stage for the healing of the blind man in chapter 9. From 8:59 to 10:39, the reader travels full circle from one heated rejection of Jesus to another. In this instance it seems reasonable to read everything within that circle as composing a single literary unit.

We will view most of chapter 10, therefore, as an extended contrast made by Jesus between the authority and leadership He represented, on the one hand, and the very different authority and leadership exercised by His influential opponents, "the Jews," on the other. As already mentioned, in John's gospel the term "Jews" often represents the religious hierarchy in Jerusalem who tended to oppose Jesus and His message because they feared it would lead to social unrest and the destruction of the religious system to which their loyalty was greater than their openness to Jesus (see 11:48).

THE BLIND MAN'S SIGHT AND THE
PHARISEES' BLINDNESS (10:1-21)

THIEVES, ROBBERS, STRANGERS (10:1-6)

Jesus' words in 10:1 follow without interruption from the end of chapter 9. With the sober authority of one who speaks God's words (v. 1, "I tell you the truth"; see remarks at 1:51), Jesus began to describe the leadership style and character of those highly influential Pharisees who denied their need for the light and life Jesus offered (9:40).

Jesus suggested that they had not come in by "the gate" but had entered by some alternate means (v. 1).

This made them thieves and robbers. Jesus drew on the image of a large pen or stone enclosure with one entrance, guarded by a watchman. Legitimate shepherds would use the normal entrance. Someone up to no good would try to find some other way. Jesus implied that the Pharisees who rejected Him and insisted on their own very different way to God were false and dangerous (mis)leaders.

Figuratively, "the gate" of which Jesus spoke refers to Himself (v. 7). He is the Father's sole and sufficient means of access to participation in the life of the flock. This flock is the diverse yet unified people of God existing through the various epochs and cultures of biblical history (see v. 16).

Verses 1-5 are a "figure of speech," or Johannine parable,[1] whose double meaning the listeners did not grasp at the time (v. 6). In retrospect, however, its message is clear.

The true shepherd enters by the gate, not by some devious avenue of his own making (v. 2). Describing a scene familiar to many of His listeners, Jesus recounted how a watchman at the gate of a sheep pen would admit a shepherd. The shepherd would then call his sheep from among the various flocks in the pen (v. 3). They would follow him as he walked ahead and continued to call to them (v. 4). They would fol-

1. Hunter, *According to John*, pp. 81-82.

low because they could identify and respond to his voice.[2] They refused, however, to follow someone whose voice they did not recognize. "In fact, they will run away from him" (v. 5).

The blind man, like an increasing number of those catching reports about Jesus in the course of His Jerusalem visits, heard Jesus' voice and followed. He followed the voice of the true shepherd and not that of strangers who did not come in by the main entrance. There is little doubt that the strangers Jesus had in mind were the Pharisees and other leaders of "the Jews" who so steadfastly opposed His teaching, and who used every means at their disposal to make the blind man acknowledge their authority in spiritual matters rather than that of Jesus.

THE GATE TO ABUNDANT LIFE (10:7-10)

No one grasped what Jesus said (v. 6), so He spelled it out more explicitly. He Himself is like the gate just described in story form (v. 7). Those who came prior to Him were treacherous imposters, not loving shepherds; many had the wisdom not to follow their lead (v. 8).

By "all" (v. 8) Jesus does not refer to figures like John the Baptist or the Old Testament prophets, upon whose message He based His own (see, e.g., 5:46). He refers rather to "all" whose ways were in opposition to the leading of those whom God faithfully sent in past times.

In the same vein, Jesus' words "the sheep did not listen to them" (v. 8) do not mean that none of the Jews had ever been misled by misguided leaders. On the contrary, many were. But not all were. A remnant of faithful worshipers, harking only to the voice of God Himself in the Scriptures and in the prophets, bucked the popular tendencies of each generation to serve some religious structure rather than the true and living God.[3]

2. "The intimacy between shepherd and sheep is a well-known Palestinian phenomenon. Sheep can even bear personal names!" Gary Burge, "John," in Elwell, ed., *Evangelical Commentary*, p. 861.

3. Luke's gospel refers to a number of such individuals who maintained steadfast trust in God in the midst of widespread unbelief and shallow religiosity. See, e.g., Luke 1:6; 2:25, 36-38; 23:50-51. Broader evidence for the existence of persons with similar views is provided in the form of numerous others from Jewish backgrounds in NT times who declared their ultimate loyalty to Jesus despite the opposing sovereign claims of the several Jewish sects who denied His message.

Whoever makes Jesus their gate, He continues, "will be saved" (v. 9). "Saved" carries the idea of deliverance from danger. False shepherds do not bring deliverance, but theft, death, and destruction (v. 10). Jesus, in contrast, provides a life of abundance.

"Life . . . to the full" (v. 10) should not be confused with material prosperity, freedom from difficult circumstances, uninterrupted emotional ecstasy, or perfect physical health. Consider what this "life" brought the blind man: insults, ejection from the synagogue, and, as a result, probably rejection by his peers and family. Later Jesus would promise His followers, "In this world you will have trouble" (16:33). "Life . . . to the full" does not denote problem-free, painless bliss. It refers rather to the quality, ultimate value, and eternal reward of life lived in relationship and obedience to God through Jesus, who is the gateway to such life.[4]

THE GOOD SHEPHERD (10:11-18)

Having contrasted His leadership with that of His opponents, Jesus now described how His character was different from theirs.

He is "the good shepherd" (v. 11). The mark of the Good Shepherd is His total commitment to the flock. He lays His own life on the line when circumstances require it.

Others, however, value their own survival more highly than that of the sheep. When danger threatens, they flee (v. 12). Wild beasts are then free to do their worst. The hapless sheep are without protection. This is a secondary matter to the person who works for wages rather than out of commitment to his responsibilities and his flock (v. 13). His priority is his own life; he "cares nothing for the sheep."

But Jesus is not like that. There is mutual personal understanding and commitment between Him and those He shepherds (v. 14). They "know" each other. Here the word implies interpersonal trust, not just intellectual awareness. The same close ties that unite Father and Son bind Son and flock (v. 15). It is thus not surprising that He puts

4. On "life" in John's gospel generally, see Brown, *Gospel According to John*, 1:505-8.

His life[5] on the line for them, like a mother braves a burning building and certain death because the children she "knows" are trapped inside.

Jesus takes pains to explain that the Good Shepherd is not the ringleader of some tiny, self-glorifying clique (v. 16). His sheep are far-flung. As He speaks, they have yet to be gathered into His flock. He foretells the time when they will hear His voice through the preaching of the gospel. Then sheep from many quarters will swell the original tiny flock into a vast herd. It will still be one flock, and it will still harken to the voice of its one Good Shepherd.

Jesus underscores the importance of His willingness to give His life for the sheep. This selflessness is the ground of the profound union, the love, He shares with the Father (v. 17). He was sent for this very reason—to be the Good Shepherd who "lays down His life for the sheep" (v. 11). Father and Son enjoyed unbroken fellowship because Jesus was possessed by an uninterrupted willingness to do the Father's bidding, even if it meant death.

Yet He would receive back the life He offered up. And the life He offered, He did so willingly: it was not taken from Him by force or against His will (v. 18). Workers sometimes protect their dignity and independence by declaring, "You can't fire me; I quit!" Jesus could not be killed; He laid down His life of His "own accord."[6] His death would not be a tragic martyrdom. It would be another demonstration of the Father's authority entrusted to Him.

CONTINUING CONTROVERSY (10:19-21)

For the fourth time in recent chapters (see 6:52; 7:43; 9:16), Jesus' listeners were of at least two minds (v. 19). Jesus' "words," which denied legitimacy to the Pharisees and made high claims for Himself, were the source of the problem. The familiar charge of demonic influence was heard yet again (see also 7:20; 8:48, 49, 52). To

---

5. Not the same word for "life" as is used elsewhere in John to denote "eternal life." In 10:15 Jesus speaks not of the transforming dynamic imparted by God through the Son and Spirit—"eternal life"—but simply of the human "life" He possessed that He would be called on to give for the sins of mankind.

6. The underlying Greek words referring to Jesus' personal initiative occur also in 5:30; 7:17, 28; 8:28, 42; 14:10. These verses point to Jesus' subordination to, yet full participation in, the Father's will.

this the charge of insanity was added, a belief some had held since early in Jesus' ministry (Mark 3:21). Such insanity may have been seen as the result of satanic activity.

Others demurred (v. 21). They cited two evidences that refuted the charge of demonic possession. First, Jesus' sayings did not fit the thesis that He was demonically inspired. This may refer to their logical consistency, or to their theological content, or to both. Second, Jesus' works were not those of some malevolent, unseen, spiritual force or person. They were redeeming. They brought honor to God. Would a demon have had the power to grant sight to the blind in such a God-glorifying fashion?

CHALLENGE FROM THE JEWS (10:22-42)

THE UNITY OF FATHER AND SON (10:22-30)

In verse 22 the setting is still Jerusalem, but the time is a couple of months after what took place in 7:10–10:21. Yet it appears that John intends this incident from the Feast of Dedication[7] to serve as the literary conclusion to the extended series of confrontations and discourses stretching back to 7:10.

Average December daytime temperatures in Jerusalem would be around sixty degrees Fahrenheit, so conditions would have been bearable for Jesus to teach in the semi-open colonnade area forming the east boundary of the Temple precincts (v. 23). As He taught, He was surrounded, probably not in an overly friendly manner, by "the Jews" (v. 24). Some of them were likely those with whom He had dealings earlier. They demanded an unambiguous answer to the crucial question of whether Jesus was the Messiah, the deliverer of Israel promised in the Old Testament.[8] Many months before, others of their ranks had put the same question to John the Baptist (1:19).

---

7. Or Hanukkah, the commemoration of the cleansing of the Temple in 164 B.C. after its defilement by the Seleucid ruler Antiochus Epiphanes in 167 B.C. The feast takes place on the twenty-fifth of the Jewish month Chislev (December).

8. Their intent was probably not innocent: "The question asked in verse 24 . . . represents not a genuine popular longing for the deliverer, but rather the efforts of the authorities to trap Jesus into embracing the messianic role. To say 'I am the Messiah' in just those words would be to welcome any and all attempts to make Him king (6:15) and so to place Himself in jeopardy from the Romans" (Michaels, *John*, p. 171).

Jesus' response implied that their question had already been answered, though they refused to admit it. He accused them of unbelief (v. 25). The "miracles" (literally "works") He had done, like healing the blind man, should have told them all they needed to know. But because they were not part of Jesus' flock, they did not respond to His voice (v. 26).

Referring back to statements made several weeks earlier (though He could have been saying similar things in the current setting, too), Jesus affirmed that His followers need not have asked such obvious questions— they knew who Jesus was, and they followed His lead (v. 27). Examples may be found in chapter 1, when His disciples hailed Him (though with very limited understanding) as Messiah, and in chapter 4 when the Samaritans credited Him with the same title.

Jesus continued His reply. His followers, unlike the skeptical questioners, were recipients of a spiritual vitality that would never fail (v. 28). No opponent or opposition (such as that represented by the detractors He faced) has the power to pluck believers from Jesus' sustaining and protecting grasp. Or to put the same thing in other words: they cannot be plucked from the Father's grasp (v. 29).

Jesus could liken His "hand" to that of the Father's because, as He put it, "I and the Father are one" (v. 30). This is not a claim that the Son is identical in every respect to the Father (though it is an important verse for the doctrine of the deity of Christ). Jesus referred rather to their essential unity of will and being but did not obliterate important differences in their respective functions.[9]

THE WITNESS OF THE WORKS (10:31-39)

Those surrounding Jesus must have rejoiced inwardly at Jesus' statement. They had wrung from Him an incriminating public confession, for to claim oneness with God was blasphemy (see 5:18). "Again" they picked up stones (v. 31), as they did earlier in 8:59.

9. Calvin shows prudence and independence of thought in stating, "The ancients misused this passage to prove that Christ is *homoousios* [Gk, "of one substance"] with the Father. Christ is not discussing the unity of substance, but the concord He has with the Father; so that whatever Christ does will be confirmed by His Father's power" (*Gospel According to St. John*, 1:273).

Jesus maintained composure and control of the situation by forcing His accusers to examine what they were about to do (v. 32). In reply, they denied taking offense at Jesus' mighty works. What they resented was His implicit claim to represent God (v. 33).

Jesus had an ingenious response to their complaint.[10] Referring to Psalm 82:6, He pointed out that God has always delegated His power and authority to chosen members of His people in such a way that they could be called "gods" in their own right (v. 34). The "gods" of Psalm 82:6 appear to be unjust leaders of Israel who neglected to uphold righteousness; a more noble example of what Jesus referred to might be Moses, about whom God said: "I have made you like God to Pharaoh" (Ex 7:1). But His point remained—why should "the Jews" have taken such offense at Jesus for claiming a status that God Himself—in the Old Testament Scriptures, which make no mistakes (v. 35)—said He granted to others in the history of His people?

True, Jesus was making a claim for Himself that exceeded the claims made by or about saints in Old Testament times (v. 36). But He was authorized to do so, because the Father had set Him "apart as His very own" and "sent [him] into the world" as He had sent no other. Their charge of blasphemy was, therefore, an unfounded and grave error.

With remarkable poise considering that they were on the verge of stoning Him, Jesus confronted His would-be executioners with an ultimatum. If His activities did not mirror the redemptive interests and activities of the God they claimed to serve, then they were free to reject Him (v. 37). But if they did—even though they may have felt personal animosity toward Jesus—then they were bound to let Jesus' "miracles," His deeds of mercy and healing, quell the opposition that seethed in their hearts (v. 38). They were required by the force of God's presence through the miraculous signs worked by Jesus to recognize that God was uniquely and savingly present, not in the religious system that held them captive, but in Jesus, and in Him alone.

They remained unconvinced and tried to detain Him (v. 39). But once more (see 8:59) He frustrated their fierce desire.

10. See Bruce, *Gospel of John*, pp. 234-35.

MANY BELIEVE (10:40-42)

The last three verses of the chapter furnish a concluding commentary on the swirl of activity related in 7:10–10:39. Having completed the last great direct confrontation with the Jewish leaders that John records, Jesus withdrew to the area where John the Baptist had started the movement that Jesus had inherited and vastly furthered (v. 40). In part because of the Baptist's preparatory labor, in which he did no miracles but accurately pointed others to Jesus, and in part because of Jesus' own widespread fame, "many people came to him" (v. 41).

And they not only came; they believed (v. 42). Their stance toward Jesus became that which John's gospel urges on its readers—to know and personally to trust in Jesus Christ as God's deliverer (20:31).

The final verses of chapter 10 suggest that Jesus had already given ample grounds for many to declare their full personal loyalty to Him. But a still greater sign of Jesus' identity and power awaits in the next chapter. Jesus will accomplish an act that will demonstrate His power over man's greatest enemy. It will also set the stage for the deadly opposition of the Jews that will eventually bring Him to a rigged trial—and a rugged cross.

11

THE DEFEAT OF DEATH (11:1-57)

Life (Gk. *zoe*) is one of the distinctive themes of John's gospel, in which the word occurs some thirty-eight times. By comparison, it occurs in Matthew only seven times, in Mark four times, and in Luke five times.

From the earliest verses of John, the reader is informed that "in him was life, and the life was the light of men" (1:4). Jesus' famous words to Nicodemus (3:16) promise "eternal life." Jesus is "the bread of life" (6:35). People do not have life in themselves; they must receive it from an outside source (6:53). Jesus is the one having words that impart life (6:68). He came to infuse with life (10:10). He gives life to those who give Him trust (10:28).

In chapter 11 Jesus is seen to be "the resurrection and the life" (v. 25). His show of power over "the last enemy" (1 Cor. 15:26) is depicted with dramatic force "as the climax of Jesus' ministry."[1] John's goal for the reader, "that by believing you might have life in His name" (20:31), receives one of its most powerful supports in the account of how Jesus raised and restored Lazarus, not only from death, but also from the bodily deterioration of four days in the tomb.

Jesus' act also foreshadows the display of the resurrecting power of God that will raise Jesus Himself after His atoning death by crucifixion.

1. Morris, *Gospel According to John*, p. 536.

BACK TO JUDEA (11:1-16)

During the brief time of Jesus' withdrawal from hostile Jerusalem (10:40), an incident took place that led to His return.

The incident involved Lazarus, Mary, and Martha (v. 1), none of whom John mentions previous to this. They lived in Bethany, a village less than two miles from Jerusalem (v. 18). Mary and Martha are mentioned in Luke 10:38-42. Mary's show of devotion to Jesus, in which she anointed His feet and wiped them with her hair, is recorded in the next chapter (John 12:3).

Lazarus fell ill (v. 1), and the sisters sent a message to Jesus (v. 3). Apparently Jesus and Lazarus enjoyed a close friendship, for the message identified him as someone Jesus loved.[2]

Jesus' response (v. 4) calls to mind His earlier words about the man born blind (9:3). There the man's blindness, while tragically real, was not final. God and His glory would have the last word. Jesus sensed a similar situation now. Death would take place, but it would not have the last word. God and the Son of God would be magnified through the outcome of Lazarus's serious illness.

Jesus held all three of His dear friends in high esteem (v. 5), but He intentionally delayed further action for some two days after He received the sisters' message (v. 6). It is likely that here, as in 6:6, Jesus "already had in mind what He was going to do." Despite the wrenching anguish that He knew His delay would cause the sisters, and the grim experience Lazarus would have to weather, Jesus stayed put, apparently until He sensed the Father's leading in taking action.

When the time was right, Jesus announced His intention to respond to the sisters' message. They must return to Judea, the area around Jerusalem (v. 7).

Jesus' announcement was not received cheerfully.[3] The disciples reminded Him of the hostility He had barely escaped short weeks

2. Stressed by Schlatter, *John the Evangelist* [German], p. 246.
3. Observes Beasley-Murray, *John*, p. 188: "The disciples are aghast."

(10:31) or months (8:59) earlier (v. 8). Their concern for Jesus' safety probably involved fear for their own lives, too, for Jesus' notoriety placed them under suspicion as well. This is confirmed by the observation that when Jesus was finally arrested, He must plead with the authorities to let His followers go free (18:8).

Besides, the disciples might well reason, Jesus had already shown that He was capable of healing from a distance (4:50). Why not do so here?

Jesus was not deterred by their fearfulness. To describe His strategy He used a metaphor involving sunlight (vv. 9-10). As long as there is daylight, one will hardly trip and fall. A person who ventures forth at night, on the other hand, is apt to meet difficulty.

Jesus' point appears to have involved the "light" by which He walked. Earlier He had underscored that all He did was at the Father's bidding and therefore pleasing to Him (8:29). Elsewhere He stated that "the Son can do nothing by himself; He can do only what He sees His Father doing, because whatever the Father does the Son also does" (5:19). There was security in the "light" of the Father's will and direction, regardless of the dangers all around.

It would have been far more dangerous for Jesus to walk in the darkness of human counsel (see 2:24) or a selfish desire for self-preservation. Thus even when danger threatened Him, as it did in the current situation, Jesus proceeded according to the outlook He had already voiced: "As long as it is day, we must do the work of him who sent me. Night is coming, when no one can work. While I am in the world, I am the light of the world" (9:4-5). Jesus remained true to these words despite His followers' well-grounded protests.

Jesus then explained what He intended to do (v. 11). The word for "fallen asleep" denotes literal sleep four times in the New Testament. But fourteen times it is used figuratively to denote death.[4] Jesus' disciples, perhaps seeking reasons that they need not return to Jerusalem, understood Jesus to mean literal sleep (vv. 12-13).

Jesus corrected their false impression: "Lazarus is dead" (v. 14). He expressed gladness that they were about to witness an event that would deepen their trust. Jesus' joy was not some morbid delight in

---

4. The same double meaning existed in rabbinic Hebrew of the time; see Schlatter, *John the Evangelist* [German], p. 249.

human anguish; He Himself would weep at Lazarus's graveside (v. 35). He meant rather that the boost that their faith in Jesus would receive through what He was about to do would make their fear about returning to Jerusalem seem trivial by comparison. They would be glad that they overcame their reluctance to return to unfriendly Judea.

It was Thomas[5] who appears to have turned the tide of opinion in favor of Jesus' proposal. Although His name is synonymous with doubting (see 20:24-25), here He showed courage and admirable, if resigned, loyalty. Other gospels reveal that for months prior to His final journey to Jerusalem, Jesus taught that He would die there (see Mark 8:31; 9:31; 10:33-34). Thomas affirmed brave willingness to face the risks involved in this teaching and urged his comrades to stop waffling, even if they must share in the fate that they feared awaited their leader.

A Lesson in Life (11:17-44)

MARTHA'S FAITH (11:17-27)

As Jesus and His followers approached Bethany, they received word that Lazarus's sickness had long since brought about his death (v. 17). Before they actually entered the village (v. 30), Martha somehow received news that Jesus was approaching (v. 20). She left Mary behind with a large number of countrymen who had come to share the sisters' grief (v. 20; "Jews" in v. 19 likely refers to "Judeans," inhabitants of the Jerusalem area[6]) and went out to meet Jesus.

Martha first expressed her conviction that, had Jesus not been so long in coming, Lazarus would not have died (v. 21). This could have been a mild rebuke (see Luke 10:40) but is more likely a simple expression of regret mingled with continued trust in Jesus.

---

5. "Thomas" is Aramaic for *twin*, and "Didymus" means the same thing in Greek. We know nothing specific about his twin, if he had one. A. F. J. Klijn cites an ancient tradition that understood *twin* (which in an ancient Syriac translation of John was applied to Judas) in terms of Christlikeness: the disciple "was so like Jesus that he could be considered His twin" ("John XIV 22 and the Name Judas Thomas," in *Studies in John*, Festschrift J. N. Sevenster [Leiden: Brill, 1970], pp. 88-96 [96]). Other disciples also went by both Hebraic and Greek names, e.g., "Cephas" and "Peter."

6. Bruce, *Gospel of John*, p. 243, states that "the word is used here with no theological overtones."

Her next remark, that "even now God will give" Jesus whatever He asks (v. 22), is probably not a vote of confidence in Jesus' ability to raise Lazarus now that He had been dead for four days. For in verse 39 she leaves no doubt that she does not foresee what Jesus plans to do. Rather, she intended to assert that her brother's death had not shaken her allegiance to Jesus. She avowed that His unique relationship with the Father endures even though He did not see fit to prevent Lazarus's death.

Jesus' subsequent remark had double meaning (v. 23). It referred both to the final resurrection and to what He was about to do. Martha grasped only the first of these meanings (v. 24).

Jesus pressed His point, preparing Martha's heart in advance for the quantum leap in devotion to Jesus that Lazarus's resurrection would no doubt produce. The "resurrection" was not merely a future event. It was present in the current moment where Jesus Himself was present.[7] He is the resurrection, just as He is also the life (v. 25). Anyone who trusts in Him has already escaped death, seen as a grim finality or an entrée to future punishment (v. 26). As Jesus put it earlier: "Whoever hears my word and believes Him who sent me has eternal life and will not be condemned; He has crossed over from death to life" (5:24).

Jesus inquired: Did Martha really believe this? Her response was admirably insightful: Jesus is the Messiah, God's appointed envoy who would bring about Yahweh's ancient promises to redeem His people (v. 27). With such depth of understanding, no wonder she continued to honor Jesus despite her bereavement.

But there is no sign that her sadness was in any way lessened by any definite sense of what Jesus was about to do. Jesus' earlier statement that "a time is coming and has now come when the dead will hear the voice of the Son of God and those who hear will live" (5:25) remained in the realm of the life to come, or abstract theory, for her.

MARY'S GRIEF (11:28-37)

Martha conveyed word to Mary that Jesus was in the area and wished to see her (v. 28). Mary immediately responded (v. 29) and

---

7. For parallels in world literature dealing with the mysterious interconnection of life and death, see Westcott, *Gospel According to St. John*, p. 169.

went outside the village where Jesus had chosen to tarry (v. 30). She was followed by the mourners who, as was the custom, were on the premises to share the sisters' grief (v. 31). They suspected she intended to visit the tomb.

Instead she went to Jesus, addressing Him with the same words of either mild reproach or regretful confidence that Martha used (v. 32; see v. 21). In either case her words were accompanied by weeping, and Jesus was "deeply moved in spirit" (v. 33). The Greek verb translated "deeply moved" occurs only four times elsewhere in the New Testament (Matt. 9:30; Mark 1:43; 14:5; John 11:38). It is a reminder of Jesus' empathy with those He came to save. As Heb. 4:15 observes, "We do not have a high priest who is unable to sympathize with our weaknesses."

Jesus was also "troubled." The same word, denoting internal agitation and anguish and even visible shuddering or shaking, is also used of Jesus in 12:27 and 13:21. This, too, is a reminder of Jesus' humanity and of the extent to which He identified with mankind in order to live in their midst and lay down His life for them.[8]

When Jesus sought the whereabouts of Lazarus's tomb, it was not Mary but the mourners around her who answered (v. 34). Perhaps Mary was too overcome with a fresh wave of grief to reply. Jesus followed the lead of the group, weeping when He approached the burial site (v. 35).

John does not discuss why Jesus "wept." The word probably denotes discrete shedding of tears, whereas the word used in verse 33 normally means to weep loudly and lament. But if John intends the reader to draw some lesson from the difference, he does not explain what it is.

The mourners standing about were struck by the depth of feeling Jesus showed (v. 36). His affection for Lazarus was obvious. Jesus here gave a practical example of what He teaches His followers in

---

8. The meaning of the word can be pressed in a somewhat different direction; see Kysar, *John*, p. 180: "Jesus is made angry by the destructive force of death among humans. That is, He is angry at the reality of death that produces such suffering and pain as He witnesses in the sisters and their guests." Kysar may overstate, however, when he continues, "The Creator is repulsed and horrified at the way in which death and suffering distort the goodness of creation and mangle the lives of humans." See the full discussion in Westcott, *Gospel According to St. John*, p. 170.

13:35.[9] It seems, however, that some found fault with Jesus for not doing more to prevent the tragedy in the first place (v. 37). They quietly murmured against Jesus because He did not save Lazarus from death. Ironically, and no doubt to their acute shock, that is precisely what Jesus was about to do.

LAZARUS GOES FREE (11:38-44)

As Jesus actually walked up to the tomb, He was once more visibly shaken (v. 38). This may be another natural human response to the actual sight of the tomb of His beloved friend, another expression of the grief Jesus shared with Mary, Martha, and the other mourners. It has been suggested, however, that Jesus' emotion was not so much one of grief as of stern indignation. In this view, Jesus was not weeping primarily out of sadness; His tears rather reflected intense displeasure, even outrage, that death brings such disorder and human suffering to His Father's world.

Jesus moved with a resolve that suggests premeditation: "Take away the stone." Martha understandably objected (v. 39). The tomb would not be dug straight down into the ground like a modern Western grave. It was rather a hollowed-out place in the rock or rocky soil into which a body could be carried and laid out. The entrance was then blocked with a large cut stone or boulder.

The "glory" of which Jesus spoke (v. 40) was explicitly mentioned in verse 4 and implied in Jesus' earlier exchange with Martha (vv. 23-25). "Glory" in this setting refers to the powerful personal presence of God, a presence that can transform rank death into hope and joy.[10] For the God who was present in Jesus "gives life to the dead and calls things that are not as though they were" (Rom. 4:17).

Apparently Jesus had inner assurance of what God was about to do before He commanded the stone to be moved, for He thanked the Father that He had already been heard (v. 41). But since many of His onlookers refused to acknowledge that Jesus acted at God's command and with God's blessing, Jesus made a point of showing that His deeds

9. See also Rom. 12:15.
10. Hunter, *According to John*, p. 67, points out the similarity between "glory" in John's gospel and "the kingdom of God" in the synoptics.

were worked by God (v. 42), not by Jesus acting on His own or invoking some occult force or power.

John stresses that Jesus' command went forth with a loud and forceful shout (v. 43). The eerie sight of the former corpse, still in grave clothes, lumbering forth clumsily into the daylight, can hardly be adequately described. Jesus commanded that the wrappings around the body and shroud about the head be removed (v. 44). Here is a graphic portrayal of the truth of Jesus' earlier words: "A time is coming and has now come when the dead will hear the voice of the Son of God and those who hear will live" (5:25).

ONE MAN FOR THE PEOPLE (11:45-57)

STIFFENING RESISTANCE (11:45-54)

It is not surprising that many who witnessed Lazarus's resuscitation[11] were moved to place personal trust in Jesus (v. 45). But not all responded favorably. Throughout John's gospel we see that Jesus' words and remarkable deeds, or "signs," have opposite effects on people who witness them. The same pattern persists in this instance. Rather than believe, some scurried off to the Pharisees with this new piece of intelligence about the man they have opposed so long (v. 46).

This precipitated an emergency meeting of the Jewish high court in Jerusalem, the Sanhedrin (v. 47).[12] This group, about seventy in number, was composed of Pharisees along with a somewhat larger number of Sadducees, to which "the chief priests" mentioned by John also belonged. These two Jewish sects held somewhat conflicting views, especially regarding the resurrection (see Acts 23:8), but served alongside each other in the Sanhedrin and seem to have been largely united in their opposition to Jesus.

They recognized that Jesus' influence was continuing to spread. The Lazarus incident would only add fuel to the fire. They feared that if Jesus was publicly hailed as king, the Romans would perceive that

---

11. Properly speaking it was not a resurrection, which in Christian terms implies both raising from the dead and the putting on of an imperishable, or immortal, body (1 Cor. 15:42). Lazarus simply resumed his earlier existence in normal bodily form.

12. Schnackenburg, *Gospel According to John*, 2:346, disputes that such a high-level meeting would have taken place and asserts that John "is not interested in an accurate historical report." But no adequate reason is given for doubting John's claim.

as a threat to their rule and the social order, which the Sanhedrin were partially responsible to preserve. The members of the Sanhedrin rightly recognized that the situation was grave. Both their "place" (the Jerusalem Temple; see Acts 6:13; 21:28) and their "nation" (their continuing enjoyment of a large measure of self-determination under Roman rule) were threatened (v. 48).

Caiaphas served as high priest from A.D. 18 to about A.D. 36. His reign included "that year" (v. 49) when the Sanhedrin presided over Jesus' condemnation. Caiaphas recommended that Jesus be liquidated for the sake of the public good (v. 50). Better that one person suffer unjustly, He reasoned, than that the whole Judean populace be victimized by the merciless Romans because of another popular messianic uprising.

John notes the irony of Caiaphas's counsel,[13] observing that his words seen in a different light predicted Jesus' death on the cross for the sins of the Jews (v. 51). And not only for the Jews: as Jesus already intimated (10:16), the children of God for whom Christ died are not limited to any one ethnic group or locale (v. 52).

The Sanhedrin found wisdom in Caiaphas's proposal (v. 53). This drove Jesus underground once more (v. 54). He withdrew to Ephraim, some fifteen miles northeast of Jerusalem. In this sleepy hamlet He could elude the dragnet of the Sanhedrin, yet remain in easy walking range of Jerusalem for His dramatic last days there.

ON THE LOOKOUT (11:55-57)

For as much as a week before the annual Passover observance, pilgrims would begin arriving for ritual preparations. These might include the sort of "ceremonial washing" mentioned earlier in 2:6 and 3:25, so much a part of Jewish religion of that day. John mentions this (v. 55) as a prelude to the third Passover recounted in his gospel (see 2:13; 6:4), the Passover during which Jesus would be handed over and crucified.

The masses filtering into the city were "looking for Jesus" (v. 56), much as they had done earlier when they knew Jesus might appear despite an official warrant for His arrest (7:11). The plan to seize

13. "Irony can hardly be richer" (Duke, *Irony in the Fourth Gospel*, p. 87).

and arrest Jesus was no doubt public knowledge (v. 57). The high-level decision to put Jesus to death (v. 53) may have been less well known. But in John's account it brings the narrative tension to a high point.

The stage is set for Jesus' triumphal entry, prediction of death by crucifixion, and final public appeal—all in the chapter just ahead. In raising Lazarus Jesus had shown God's power over death in the life of another. Soon His confidence that God would deliver Him, the eternal sacrifice for the sins of the world, by that same power will receive the sternest of tests.

12

THE HOUR ARRIVES (12:1-50)

Throughout John's gospel thus far, Jesus has spoken repeatedly of His "time" (Gk. *kairos;* see 7:6, 8) or His "hour" (Gk. *hōra,* translated as "time" in the NIV; see 2:4; 7:30; 8:20). He seems to have in mind a particular moment when the work He has come to complete may be viewed as accomplished. That moment occurs in 12:23: "The hour has come for the Son of Man to be glorified."

Just what Jesus meant by this statement will be explored below. Now we may note that chapter 12 is central in John's presentation, for it records that moment when Jesus exclaimed that the work He had come to do was in some sense complete.

The chapter is central for another reason as well. It recounts Jesus' last interactions with the various fickle groups who could seem to make up their minds whether to place trust in Jesus or to continue to oppose Him. After chapter 12 Jesus will address His closest followers privately (chaps. 13-17), and after that He will be betrayed, tried, and condemned (chaps. 18-20). Chapter 12, then, marks the conclusion of Jesus' public teaching ministry. In that sense it sums up all that has gone before. This confers a special urgency and poignancy on all that Jesus is about to do and say, as well as on the various responses, positive and negative, to His final proclamations and invitation.

On the Eve of the Final Week (12:1-11)

DEVOTION AND TREACHERY (12:1-8)

There was widespread expectation that Jesus would lay low during this Passover (11:56) since the officials had made known that they sought His arrest (11:57). Even while the crowds discussed these matters, however, Jesus was taking the next steps of obedience to the Father's will that would eventually lead Him to the cross.

He arrived in Bethany, from which He had found it wise to withdraw not many weeks earlier (12:1; see 11:54). A banquet was held in Jesus' honor (v. 2). Perhaps this was the first chance for Jesus' dear friends, Martha, Mary, and Lazarus, to celebrate together since the day Jesus bade Lazarus come forth from the tomb. As she does in Luke 10:40, Martha takes the lead in practical preparations.

Mary took the unusual and costly step of applying a lavish amount of an expensive scented ointment to Jesus' feet (v. 3).[1] In a striking gesture of humility and affection, she used her hair rather than a cloth to spread the thick oil. It was a servant's task to tend to the soiled feet of guests; this Mary did, but not merely with water. A towel would normally wipe off the feet, not a woman's long tresses. It is not easy to know all that Mary's gesture conveyed in her day and time. Nor is it much easier to determine all that Jesus felt as she acted out her own parable of honor and allegiance.

It is not difficult, however, to determine what Judas Iscariot thought (v. 4). A year's wages had been squandered. The poor could have been aided greatly with such a sum (v. 5). But it was personal greed, not social need, that prompted his reaction (v. 6). The betrayer had started down the road to destruction by giving in to the seemingly minor sin of seeking to profit personally from commitment to Jesus. His dishonesty in a relatively little thing paved the way for deceit in a great thing later on (see Luke 16:10).

Jesus defended Mary's act (v. 7). Whether she or any of the others realized it or not, she had anointed His body for burial. Her gesture was eminently fitting in light of what lay ahead. The continual needs of the poor, which Jesus Himself did much to address and

---

1. For the relationship between this incident and the ones recorded in Mark 14:3-9; Matt. 26:6-13; and Luke 7:36-50, see Schnackenburg, *Gospel According to John*, 2:36-37, and Morris, *Gospel According to John*, pp. 571-74.

meet, must sometimes be seen in light of unique opportunities[2] to honor Christ in other ways that are no less important and appropriate to obeying His call to discipleship (v. 8).

CURIOSITY AND CONSPIRACY (12:9-11)

As in 11:31, the "Jews" of v. 9 are probably local Judean residents like Lazarus and his sisters, not the Jewish religious hierarchy as such. Word spread quickly that Jesus was back in the area. Moreover, Lazarus was there as well. Had He perhaps been in semi-seclusion much of the time since His resuscitation to avoid the bother of curious onlookers? Elsewhere John mentions the presence of a "crowd" (5:13; 6:22, 24; 7:12, 31), but here it is a "large crowd" (as in 6:2, 5).

Another group, smaller but wielding great force, was also interested in this new development. The "chief priests" (v. 10) represented the leadership of the influential Sanhedrin (see 11:47). They had already developed one murderous plan for the public good (11:53). Their earlier departure from justice now required that they hatch a second plot.[3] Lazarus must be liquidated, too, because of the way He was causing many to declare allegiance to Jesus.

There was another problem, from the chief priests' point of view —Lazarus was living proof of the reality of the resurrection, a doctrine that they as Sadducees denied (Acts 23:8). He was not only a testimony to the power of Jesus but also a rebuke to the chief priests' doctrinal base. This could only cause dilution of their authority over the communities under their jurisdiction.

We are not told how the banquet ended. Apparently the officials took no action at that time to stop either Jesus or Lazarus from exerting further influence.

---

2. Calvin notes, "They are absurd interpreters . . . who infer . . . that costly and splendid worship is pleasing to God. In fact He excuses Mary on the grounds that she had rendered Him an extraordinary office which should not be regarded as a perpetual norm . . . They who want to worship Christ with splendid and costly trappings are apes, not imitators. Christ approved what was done that once, but forbade its repetition" (*Gospel According to John*, 2:26-27).

3. Westcott, *Gospel According to St. John*, p. 178: "The sacrifice of the 'one man' (xi. 50) soon involved the sacrifice of more."

JESUS THE KING (12:12-19)

The following morning, at precisely the point when both public interest and official opposition were surging, Jesus approached Jerusalem from Bethany, less than two miles away (v. 12). As in 12:9, it was not merely a "crowd" but a "great crowd" that turned out to meet Him.

In verses 13 and 15 John cites Ps. 118:25-26 and Zech. 9:9 to interpret the significance of Jesus' entry into the city.[4] When the actual event took place, John notes, Jesus' disciples failed to see how His act fulfilled the Scriptures (v. 16). This realization did not come to them until later.[5]

But regardless of how accurately either the disciples or the masses understood at that time the Old Testament basis for what Jesus was doing, the significance of it remains. Jesus entered Jerusalem as conquering king. Palm branches (v. 13) were symbolic of Jewish nationalism, their spirit of identity as a nation as well as their opposition to Roman rule. The outcries in verse 13 hailed Jesus as national deliverer. Jesus refused to rebuke them for according Him this honor (Luke 19:39-40), though He did not accept the political and military roles that they expected Him to fill.

The next verse (14) points to the peculiar nature of Jesus' reign. His entry had regal overtones. As in 6:15 there is excitement that God's anointed ruler is about to exalt God's ancient people in a highly visible fashion. But Jesus entered on a lowly donkey, not a prancing war horse. He was a king, but His kingdom's rule was for the present spiritual rather than crassly political in nature (see 18:36).

This event, coupled with the excitement already in the air due to Lazarus's resuscitation and Jesus' presence during the great festival week of Passover, electrified the whole city; "the crowd . . . spread the word" (v. 17).

At the same time the frustration of the authorities increased (v. 19). Jesus seemed unstoppable. The official fear of social disorder and

---

4. Note the careful description of the OT background in Bruce, *Gospel of John*, pp. 258-61.

5. Michaels argues plausibly, though from silence, "There is no blame placed on the disciples for their failure to understand. The accent is . . . on their clear understanding later (cf. 2:22; 20:8-9)" (*John*, p. 207).

Roman intervention (see 11:48) spiraled yet higher. It was only a matter of time before some measure, however desperate, would have to be implemented to avert disaster.

THE SON OF MAN GLORIFIED (12:20-36)

GENTILES SEEK JESUS (12:20-26)

Just as the religious leaders were lamenting that "the whole world has gone after Him!" (v. 19), Philip was approached by "some Greeks" (vv. 20-21). Here the word "Greek" denotes "Gentile." In the ancient world a number of non-Jews (Gentiles) worshiped the God of Israel (for an example see Acts 10:1-2). Some even underwent circumcision in order to observe the rites prescribed by Judaism as closely as possible. These were called proselytes.

The "Greeks" mentioned in v. 20 may have been visiting Jerusalem for the Passover.[6] They had evidently heard about Jesus. It is not known for certain why they approached Philip rather than some other disciple or even Jesus Himself. Perhaps Jesus was avoiding the public eye to avoid detection by the authorities. In any case, Philip and Andrew relayed the request to Jesus (v. 22).

Jesus responded with a surprising statement: "The hour has come for the Son of Man to be glorified" (v. 23). As mentioned at the beginning of this chapter, John's gospel speaks of Jesus' "time" or "hour" a number of times before this point. Prior to this, His "time" had not yet come. But now, He exclaimed, it is here. Why should the request of the Greeks seem so important to Jesus?

The answer to that question has two parts. First, the request is important because of who makes it—non-Jews. From early in John's gospel, the reader has been reminded that Jesus came to as many as would receive Him (1:12), not just to the Jews. "God so loved the world" (3:16), not just descendants of Abraham. When Gentiles sought Jesus, He seemed to take it as a signal that a central aspect of His mission was on the verge of accomplishment.

Second, the request is important because of how Jesus would fulfill it—Jesus would be "glorified." In John the word refers to Jesus'

6. For full discussion of their identity see H. B. Kossen, "Who were the Greeks of John XII 20?" in *Studies in John*, pp. 96-110.

being "lifted up" (v. 32), His being crucified for the sins of the world (see 1:29). But it refers also to His resurrection. Jesus' glorification is both His death and resurrection, the two events seen as one completed whole.

In other words, verse 23 underscores that the "hour," the crucial time "for the Son of Man to be glorified," involves Jesus' atoning death and resurrection for all who will believe. The query of the Greeks appears to have been a sign to Jesus that the climax of His earthly ministry was at hand.

Jesus used a figure of speech to illustrate how death can bring glory in the form of subsequent life. Only if it falls and dies can a wheat kernel bring forth young wheat plants and an abundant yield (v. 24). So it is in the life of man—to guard one's life jealously for one's own purposes is to squander and "lose it" (v. 25). But to "hate" one's life, to consider it as expendable for the sake of following Christ, is to find life's true meaning. One's old self-centered life must be rejected in order to gain true or eternal life (see Phil. 3:7-11).[7]

Jesus concluded with a brief word of challenge and assurance (v. 26). The one who serves Him must be where He is; this was probably a call to "walk as Jesus did" (1 John 2:6). To serve Jesus in this way brings honor from the Father. Jesus, whose entire life was lived in the light of such honor, knew that no greater reward could be imagined or sought.

NOW IS THE TIME (12:27-36)

Jesus' glory, He knew, would bring great suffering with it. When He realized, therefore, that the time was at hand, His "heart is troubled" (v. 27). The word denotes serious disturbance and is used of Jesus elsewhere in 11:33 (see comments there) and 13:21. He asked rhetorically whether He should request to be relieved from the horror of what lay ahead. But His answer was a direct and unambiguous negative. Showing the same human agony yet courageous resolve as He

---

7. Hunter, *According to John*, p. 84, suggests a more subtle Pauline link: "Scholars have noted how close is the resemblance between the parable [John 12:24] and Paul's words in 1 Cor. 15:36: 'The seed that you sow does not come to life unless it has first died.' If Paul knew the Lord's parable about the Thief, as 1 Thess. 5:2ff. implies, it is very possible that He knew this one about the Grain of Wheat."

did at Gethsemane (see Mark 14:36), Jesus sought deliverance but requested that in any event God's honor be upheld (v. 28).

His request resulted in an audible divine response: "I have glorified it, and will glorify it again." The statement appears to look back on all the Father had already accomplished in creation and redemption through the Son. It probably also contemplated the cross and resurrection, in which the glory of God's judgment, grace, and love would be incomparably manifested.

The mixed response of others on the scene (v. 29) is reminiscent of Acts 9:7 and 22:9, where those accompanying Paul could not understand the heavenly voice though they heard its sound.

Jesus pointed out that the audible confirmation was for their sakes, not His (v. 30; see 11:42). Then He elaborated on His earlier statement that "the hour has come" (v. 23) by asserting that "this world" was about to be judged (v. 31). Here "world" refers to all that pertains to Satan and his influence on God's creation; "the prince of this world" will meet his doom when the Son of God goes to the cross.[8] There He will be "lifted up" (see 3:14), a reference to His death by crucifixion (v. 33). In this way He will rescue many from destruction by drawing them away from the overlord of evil to the savior who grants deliverance and life (v. 32). The power and eternality of God's righteous kingdom would assert itself forever at the expense of Satan's current fleeting reign.

Among the holiday crowd would be many for whom some, if not all, of Jesus' words would sound strange. They would not have heard Him teach day after day about the Son of Man, for example. Yet they had apparently heard rumors that this Jesus fellow might be the Messiah, the Christ, the coming king who would rout the Romans. So they sought clarification (v. 34): "the Law," here referring to such Old Testament passages as Pss. 89:4; 110:4; Isa. 9:7; and Ezek. 37:25 taught that the Messiah's reign would never cease. How does this relate to the Son of Man's "lifting up," and just "who is this 'Son of

---

8. "The sentence of judgment passed on this world is endured by the One whom this world murders. This turns the awful news of judgment on sin at the cross into the good news of deliverance from condemnation through the cross" (Beasley-Murray, *John*, p. 213).

Man' " in relation to prevailing messianic expectations?[9]

Among the crowd would also be many with relatively full knowledge of what Jesus had been saying and doing in their midst over a period of several years. It was incumbent on them to act on the basis of the light they had already been shown (v. 35), lest even what light they had be taken from them (see Luke 8:18). Jesus called, then, to personal trust in Himself, the light of the world (v. 36; see 8:12).

With the authorities working feverishly to apprehend Jesus, it would not be prudent to risk lengthy public debate. Having made His point, He resumed the low profile He apparently had when the Greeks first came looking for Him (v. 36).

THE MYSTERY AND JUDGMENT OF DISBELIEF (12:37-50)

WILLFUL BLINDNESS (12:37-43)

John comments on the stubborn disbelief of many around Jesus (v. 37; v. 42 points out that some, however, did believe). Such obstinacy was a fulfillment of the situation described in Isa. 53:1 (v. 38) and in Isa. 6:10 (v. 40). The first passage simply laments how sparse the reception of God's message is. "The arm of the Lord" refers to His majestic strength. It was present in Jesus, but many refused to acknowledge it.

The second passage gives a scriptural explanation of why so many rejected Jesus. It came about "for this reason" (v. 39): because the Scripture said it would be so. As elsewhere in John (see 13:18; 15:25; 17:12; 19:24, 36), here the Old Testament furnishes the interpretive backdrop for making sense of the circumstances surrounding Jesus. The blinding and deadening of v. 40 need not be understood as an impersonal fating of some to perdition.[10] It rather describes the inevitable consequences of unbelief—God gives the rebellious heart over to the godlessness it insists on having (see Rom. 1:24, 26, 28).

9. Calvin, *Gospel According to John*, 2:43-44, sees malice, not curiosity, in their question: "Without doubt they just intended to carp maliciously at Christ's words. . . . The query 'Who is this Son of Man?' has mockery in it."

10. See Beasley-Murray's explanation in *John*, pp. 216-17, which includes the comment "The statement sounds like naked predestination, even irresistable reprobation, but it was neither so intended nor would it have been so understood."

In a striking affirmation of Jesus' essential unity with the Father, John comments that Isaiah's spiritual foresight was precipitated by his vision of Jesus' glory (v. 41). The reference is to Isa. 6, when Isaiah beholds the glory of God in the Temple and is overcome with awe and dread (Isa. 6:5). Earlier Jesus affirmed that in some sense Abraham was a delighted witness to the Son's redemptive work (8:56). Now John insists that in the Shekinah,[11] the radiant presence of Almighty God in His Old Testament self-disclosures, Jesus Himself was present.

Not all, however, were blinded to the light Jesus brought. Even some of the leaders responded favorably, though the hostility of their peers made them assume a low profile (v. 42). John later cites an example of such a "secret disciple" (19:38). He also disparages such lack of courage (v. 43). His statement that the leaders craved human more than divine approval echoes what Jesus said earlier (5:41-44; see Luke 16:15). Fixation on peer acceptance can stunt, and even prevent, reception of Jesus.

FINAL APPEAL (12:44-50)

The remaining verses of the chapter sum up Jesus' proclamation. It is not clear whether they describe His actual parting words as He withdrew from the public eye (v. 36) for the last time prior to His crucifixion, or whether they are a general summary of Jesus' message at the end of His Jerusalem ministry.[12] Perhaps both possibilities are equally true.

Jesus reiterates that to accept Him is to accept the God who sent Him (vv. 44-45).[13] The point bears repeating in the Jewish context (as it still does today) because so many insisted that they had other ways of gaining access to God and gaining His approval. Jesus' parting words to His generation were an insistence that God is uniquely present in Him, in both His words and His works (v. 46). The light He imparts is not equally distributed in any number of other religious settings. Yet it alone can dispel the darkness that envelopes the human soul.

---

11. See R. A. Stewart, "Shekinah," in Douglas, ed., *The New Bible Dictionary*, pp. 1174-75.

12. Kysar, *John*, Augsburg Commentary, p. 203, assumes the latter option.

13. On Jesus as God's authoritative representative, see Robinson, *Priority of John*, p. 350.

What about those who do not accept what Jesus says about Himself? Here Jesus was content to leave them in the Father's hands (v. 47). There was no need for Him to condemn them, for they condemned themselves (3:18-19; see also Matt. 12:37). True, in other passages Jesus does appear as judge (5:22, 27, 30; 8:16, 26; 9:39). But that is not the primary function of His present work.

Jesus' primary concern is rather to be a faithful mediator of the word of God that brings life to those who willingly hear. To reject that word is to reject that life (v. 48). This rejection is culpable because it defies God Himself, who instructed Jesus "what to say and how to say it" (v. 49). Jesus knew that the "eternal life" God offers comes only through acceptance of His liberating "command" (see 1 John 5:3). For this reason He had spared no effort, He asserted, in conveying "just what the Father has told me to say" (v. 50).

Thus concluded Jesus' message to His countrymen at large. In coming chapters (13-17), Jesus focuses attention on His closest disciples. The fearless clarity and bluntness of Jesus' message to the masses will be matched by His personal compassion and empathy in the most extended and intimate portrayal of the Son of God's will for His followers recorded anywhere in Scripture.

13

THE MARK OF A CHRISTIAN (13:1-38)

Some years ago the late Christian thinker Francis Schaeffer penned a little volume from which this chapter borrowed its title.[1] Schaeffer examined John 13:35 carefully in its context and concluded that the verse contained one of the New Testament's most important messages to believers. That message: the vitality of the church's witness to the world is measured by the depth of active concern believers have, and show, toward one another.

A whole book was written, quite amazingly, about just one verse. Yet as we reflect on John 13, we will repeatedly encounter powerful works and words of Jesus that could occupy our attention for a whole book or more. As Jesus washes His disciples' feet; as He instructs them in servanthood; as He predicts Judas's betrayal and Peter's denial—in each of these areas Jesus will challenge us, as He challenged His first followers, to a profound reexamination of our fidelity to the faith and action that He has summoned us to embrace and live out.

How did Jesus intend for His followers to treat each other? What did being a "disciple" look like in everyday life, according to Jesus? And are we truly His disciples? Those are some of the questions raised by the various episodes recounted in John 13.

DISCIPLESHIP AND SERVANTHOOD (13:1-20)

SELFLESS SYMBOLIC ACT (13:1-11)

His public ministry having practically ended, Jesus in chapters 13-17 speaks in private to the innermost circle of His disciples. The

---

1. Francis Schaeffer, *The Mark of a Christian* (Downers Grove, Ill.: InterVarsity, 1974).

setting is the Passover Feast,[2] the commemoration of ancient Israel's deliverance from bondage in Egypt. This is the third Passover mentioned in John's gospel (see also 2:13, 6:4).

Jesus was aware that the final stages of God's plan for Him were unfolding rapidly (v. 1). He had shown patience and love for His followers throughout His ministry, but He was about to demonstrate the depth of His commitment to them through an unforgettable gesture, an acted-out parable of both loyalty and humility.

Their evening meal together was underway (v. 2). Jesus knew, though His followers did not, that Judas was scheming to hand Jesus over to His enemies. This bit of foreshadowing heightens the drama of the narrative. Is Jesus' love for others so great that He will wash the feet of a known traitor? Does "the full extent of His love" (v. 1) stretch so far?[3]

It does indeed. Jesus's entire life had been spent in preparation for and execution of the Father's will for Him. It was never easy, but He had walked in the light of the Father's strength, guidance, and assurance up to the setting of chapter 13 (v. 3). Thus He boldly steered the right course then.

He interrupted His eating as He arose, removed His outer garment, and knotted a towel around His waist (v. 4). Water basin in hand, He then worked His way around the table and washed the feet of His amazed and chagrined followers one by one (v. 5). This chagrin was expressed well by Peter, who blurted out incredulously, "Lord, are you going to wash my feet?" (v. 6). Foot-washing was a menial task for servants, not something performed by friends for each other. Far less was it thinkable for a rabbi to do it for His pupils.

Jesus gave Peter the opportunity to hold his impatient tongue until a later time (v. 7). "Later" may refer to Jesus' explanation starting in v. 12, or to the time after the resurrection, when Peter would be able to look back and see Jesus' present act in the light of His lowly death, yet

2. Scholars note certain contrasts between the way John reckons the timing of the Last Supper, on the one hand, and the way the other three gospels reckon it, on the other. It is possible that dates were figured on the basis of two different calendars. For a detailed discussion see Morris, *Gospel According to John*, pp. 774-86.

3. See Kysar, *John*, Augsburg Commentary, p. 207: "The contrast between Jesus' love in v. 1 and Judas's intent to betray Jesus is vivid and pathetic, as John wants it to be."

spectacular deliverance. Then it would be clear that servanthood can be the gateway to exaltation (see 1 Pet. 5:6).

For now, Peter stubbornly resisted (v. 8). But with even greater resolve, Jesus sternly reminded him who was the disciple of whom. It is Jesus who sets the terms of discipleship; to refuse to recognize His authority is to place oneself outside the pale of His benefits.

So Peter relented, but in doing so oscillated to the opposite extreme.[4] From early in Jesus' ministry, Peter had shown an awareness of Jesus' noble character and his own unworthiness. An example is when Jesus was responsible for a large catch of fish, and Peter fell at Jesus' knees with the words, "Go away from me, Lord; I am a sinful man" (Luke 5:8). Peter echoed that sentiment now by confessing that it was not merely His feet, but His whole person, that needed cleansing. If Jesus was trying to remind the disciples of their unworthiness, Peter implied, why not go all the way (v. 9)?

But Jesus' point was not to humiliate them. "You are clean," He told them (v. 10)—except for the one who would betray Him (v. 11). This meant that their sins, though real and lamentable, were covered because of their faith in Him, and because of the cleansing power of what He was about to do for them on the cross.

Just what was Jesus' point, then? Jesus Himself patiently interpreted His surprising act.

THE LESSON APPLIED (13:12-20)

Having rinsed off each disciple's feet, including those of Judas, Jesus resumed His place at the table and asked them if they realized what His action signified (v. 12). They probably did not, for we learn from Luke's gospel that the disciples quarreled around that same table over which of them was greatest (Luke 22:24). Perhaps the foot-washing was a direct response to that petty squabble.

Jesus moved to answer the question He had raised. He affirmed that the way they honored Him was appropriate (v. 13). He was, indeed, "the Teacher" and "the Lord." He was not merely a member

---

4. H. J. Holtzmann captures it well: "Now the behavior veers precipitously from coy reserve to its total opposite." *Gospel of John* [German] (Tübingen: Mohr [Siebeck], 1908), p. 234.

of the group but also its head. By washing their feet Jesus was not implying that He had no authority over them.

Yet they should have noted that he, their head, had performed a symbolic act to dramatize that He stood solidly among them as a servant rather than loftily above them as a bossy commander (v. 14). Spiritual leadership, Jesus is saying, is not a matter of barking out orders to underlings and pressuring them to comply. Rather it involves leading by costly example, putting the interests of others ahead of one's own (see Phil. 2:4). He had just performed an object lesson that should have burned this truth into their hearts forever.

Even more pointedly, however, His act was an example for them to ponder and to imitate (v. 15). It was not merely a lesson for them to remember and talk about. Servants never outgrow their responsibility to submit to their masters. Messengers convey the information they are told to; they do not usurp the authority of the person who sends them out with news (v. 16).

Yes, Jesus was their servant. But He was also their teacher and master. He had acted out servanthood in an unforgettable fashion. Now the ball was in their courts to do the same (v. 17). Fidelity to Jesus in true discipleship involves not merely seeing and knowing but also doing. The Beatitudes of Matthew 5 speak of how "blessed" (Gk. *makarioi*) certain groups of persons are—the poor in spirit, those who mourn, the merciful, the peacemakers. In 13:17 Jesus uses the same word. "Blessed" are those who act out the example of Jesus.

Does this mean that Christians should literally wash each others' feet today? It might be a fitting ceremony to reenact from time to time as a reminder of what Jesus did. But there is no evidence that footwashing became an ordinance in the apostolic church the way the Lord's Supper itself did. To honor Jesus' example, it is probably most fitting that believers be diligent to serve each other in the many ways that Jesus served those around Him. He did not always wash their feet; that was a one-time lesson to a make a very specific point. Christians need not always wash each others' feet in the literal sense. They do, however, need to grow in exercising the consistent, tangible, selflessness of the Lord who came to serve.

As Jesus exhorted the twelve, He prepared them for the shock they would soon receive from His betrayal and arrest. In general terms

He identified Judas Iscariot and how he would fulfill that which Scripture had foretold about Him (v. 18; see Ps. 41:9).[5] "Lifted up His heel" refers to a treacherous kick or other action that causes someone hurt or grief.[6]

Jesus continued giving advanced warning by underscoring His knowledge of certain future events like His betrayal (v. 19). The morale-shattering hours ahead would be followed by days of contemplation; as the disciples reflected on Jesus' final words, they would be borne up by the realization that He was not taken by surprise. They "will believe that I am He"—that in Jesus God has visited His people, and that those who trust in Him will not be put to shame. After Calvary comes Easter.

Jesus reiterated the significance of the disciples' calling and future mission (v. 20). This may have been to bolster their confidence in an hour when the fabric of their lives seemed to be unraveling. Whereas verses 14 and 16 highlight the humble role they were called to fill, verse 20 affirms the noble status they were privileged to share. In coming days as they would go forth preaching, whoever would accept them would accept Jesus, and whoever would accept Jesus would give place to the Father Himself. Jesus' betrayal, death, and departure were not to obscure the disciples' status as strategic envoys of both Father and Son.

DISCIPLESHIP AND FIDELITY (13:21-30)

Though Jesus counseled confidence, He was profoundly agitated by the prospect of what lay ahead. One of His own flock, whose feet He had just washed, was about to turn traitor (v. 21). This came as a shock to at least eleven of the twelve disciples, and perhaps to Judas himself (v. 22). For although "the devil had already prompted [him] to betray Jesus" (v. 2), that prompting may not yet have grown into full consciousness of the deed he was about to do.

---

5. Westcott, *Gospel According to St. John*, pp. 199-200, devotes a special note to the origin of Judas's choice: was it God's choice for him, or his own choice for himself? Westcott describes the matter as a "concrete mystery."

6. "The metaphor represents an animal which is being fed, kicking its owner." R. H. Strachan, *The Fourth Gospel* (London: SCM, 1941), p. 269.

Overcome by curiosity, Peter took action (v. 24). Next to Jesus, reclining at the low table containing the food and drink,[7] was "the disciple whom Jesus loved" (v. 23). Careful investigation of this and other passages where the phrase occurs (19:26; 20:2; 21:20) indicates that this figure was John, the son of Zebedee, the author of the gospel bearing his name. John discreetly made inquiry (v. 25), and Jesus told him how to recognize the person who would betray Him (v. 26). John was close enough to Jesus to receive Jesus' answer without being overheard by the others (see v. 28).

Satan, who had already "prompted" Judas (see v. 2), now escalated his influence (v. 27). This does not mean that Judas was a helpless pawn; it merely identifies the personal nature of the evil that held him in its thrall because he had, apparently, refused to entrust himself fully to Jesus. One is a slave, Paul wrote later, either to sin or to righteousness (Rom. 6:16). As many Pharisees did the bidding of the master they willfully chose to serve (John 8:38), Judas in going his own way also did the will of the one he had elected to follow.

The other disciples did not hear what Jesus told John, nor did they understand the significance of Judas's exit (v. 28). They thought he might be on an official errand as treasurer (v. 29). But "he went out. And it was night" (v. 30). "Night" has obvious literal meaning but may also be a literary touch bespeaking the darkness of soul into which Judas had plunged. Or one may think of the blackness of the moment when one of Jesus' very own (see 1:11) moved to hand Him over to the ravages of hostile authorities.[8]

DISCIPLESHIP AND STEADFASTNESS (13:31-38)

At the darkest of moments, Jesus soberly exults (v. 31). Judas's departure set in motion the chain of events leading to Calvary and the

7. The custom was to lie on carpet or cushions around a low table, leaning on the left elbow and eating with the free right hand. Legs would extend away from the table rather than under it. See also C. K. Barrett, *The Gospel According to St. John* (London: SPCK, 1962), p. 372.

8. See Michaels, *John*, p. 236: "The narrator adds that it was night, probably as a dramatic comment on Judas's fate . . . For Judas, the curtain of night had now fallen; having left the circle of the disciples to do his evil work, he was walking in darkness." Bruce (*Gospel of John*, p. 291) rightly adds that the reference to night also "reproduces the vivid reminiscence of an eyewitness."

redemption of mankind. Jesus saw that the outcome of the next few hours would be, indeed already was, to the glory of God (v. 32). Now as in the foot-washing and through all His ministry, Jesus' concern was not His own welfare but the Father's pleasure.

Moving into an extended series of reassurances and exhortations, Jesus spoke with affection and real concern (see "my children" in v. 33). He was about to leave them, as He had said earlier to the Jews (see 7:34). They would not be able to follow. Later He would have more to say about this. For now, the central truth the disciples needed to heed involved their commitment to each other in His absence. "Christ's revelation of the nature of the crisis as affecting Himself, is followed by a revelation of it as affecting His disciples."[9]

It was imperative that they "love one another" (v. 34). The teaching occurs in Leviticus 19:18 but can be called "a new command" for at least two reasons.[10] First, it takes as its model Jesus' own giving of Himself, both as a servant (as in the foot-washing) and as a sacrifice for sin (1 John 4:10). Second, it is motivated by the spiritual presence of Jesus in His people (see 14:18), not by rote adherence to an external ethical directive. In either case, Jesus' giving of Himself is the standard for the disciples' devotion to each other. And this devotion is a primary indicator that God still uses to impress on the world what it means to be a disciple of Jesus (v. 35). The converse is surely also true: where such love is lacking, it is no wonder if the watching world fails to give credence to what the church claims for itself and its Lord.

Peter seemed more interested in defending his loyalty than pondering Jesus' statement. He went back to the subject of Jesus' departure (v. 33). He did not like Jesus' claim that His disciples would not be able to follow Him where He was going. So he requested clarification (v. 36).

Jesus gave it. What He said to the group applied to Peter personally as well—he could not follow. He added, though, that "you will follow later." This may refer to Peter's own death by crucifixion in the A.D. 60s, or to heaven, or to both (the Gk makes it clear that Jesus is speaking to Peter alone, not to the whole group).

9. Westcott, *Gospel According to John*, p. 197.
10. See Brown, *Gospel According to John*, 2:613-14, for fuller disscussion.

This was not good enough for Peter. Long ago he had placed all his eggs in the basket of loyalty to Jesus (6:68-69; see also Matt. 19:27). He was not going to give up easily now. He would follow, even if it cost him his life (v. 37).[11]

Jesus quickly put such pride in its place. Things would turn out much different from what Peter projected (v. 38). There is a note of rebuke here, but also of reassurance. For if knowing what will happen in advance bolsters confidence after it takes place (see v. 19; 14:29), then Jesus' stern words would later help Peter to recover from the fall he was about to take.

It is fitting that we again state the questions with which this chapter began. For the benefit of John 13 lies not in merely knowing what was said, but in acting appropriately as a result (v. 17). This is in keeping with the goal of the gospel, whose stated aim is not merely informational but also evangelistic (see 20:31).

How did Jesus intend for His followers to treat each other? With the costly, selfless love that He Himself expressed.

What does being a "disciple" appear as in everyday life, according to Jesus? It appears as followers of Jesus mirroring their master's devotion to the Father, and no less to all other disciples around them.

And are we truly His disciples? Perhaps; but probably at most like Peter, eager to assert our loyalty but apt to buckle under real pressure.

Yet there was hope for Peter, as there is for us. In the next chapter Jesus lays a firm foundation for disciples, then and now, to live out the difficult mandate of servanthood and love He has just proclaimed.

---

11. Schnackenburg, *Gospel According to St. John*, 3:56, notes that "Peter's objection . . . is not so fierce as His protest in 13:8 but . . . just as unenlightened."

14

TROUBLED HEARTS (14:1-31)

Chapter 14 opens with Jesus' words, "Do not let your hearts be troubled" (v. 1). Near the end of the chapter He repeats the same counsel, "Do not let your hearts be troubled and do not be afraid" (v. 27).

It is fair to say that the theme of this chapter is assurance. The disciples were profoundly disturbed at the news that a betrayer was among them (13:21-22). Even their intrepid spokesman Peter was suddenly called faithless (13:38). Jesus had long foretold that an hour was coming when He would be arrested, suffer, and die (Mark 9:10, 31; 10:32-34). Now that hour was at hand. The disciples' confusion, perhaps even internal panic, is understandable. It is likewise understandable that Jesus took pains to allay their worst fears.

Throughout chapter 14, Jesus addresses His disciples' uncertainties, seeking to fortify them for the ordeal just ahead when their leader will be arrested and executed. He does this in part by elaborating on themes He finds crucial and in part by answering questions that His disciples raise.

INITIAL CONSOLATION (14:1-4)

They ought not be troubled, first of all, because they could trust Him in the same way that they trusted God (v. 1). From any other person this statement would be blasphemous. Jesus' oneness with the Father (10:30) made the exhortation not only acceptable but justified. Despite the turmoil His words caused, they could take courage: He is as trustworthy as God Himself.[1]

---

1. Augustine writes, "That they might not as men be afraid of death, and so be troubled, He comforts them by affirming Himself also to be God." *Lectures or Tractates on the Gospel According to St. John*, vol.2 (Edinburgh: Clark, 1874), p. 243.

Second, they could take heart because Jesus knew what He was doing and saying, and He had each of their futures under control. Verse 2 makes this plain. It speaks of "many rooms" in "my Father's house." This is a plain reference to heaven and to each disciple's future dwelling place there. Jesus' imminent death and absence was not pointless; it was for the benefit of His followers. Even Jesus' enemies conceded that He was always ruthlessly honest (Luke 20:21); now Jesus exhorted His followers to trust Him because "if it were not so," He would candidly tell them.

Third, they should not be troubled, because Jesus was coming back (v. 3). This was first of all a reference to His resurrection appearances. Those appearances would have the effect of settling their now troubled minds; they just needed to hang on until He returned. God knew, though they did not, that the waiting period would be less than seventy-two hours (20:14, 19). But Jesus' promise had another dimension—His return would make it possible for Him to take His disciples to be with Him "where I am." Once again the reference was to heaven. The resurrection would both bestow present assurance and make possible eternal salvation. Paul speaks in similar terms when He states that Jesus' resurrection was for our justification (Rom. 4:25). Believers need not be banished from God's presence because of their guilt, not even the guilt of betrayal and desertion that the eleven were about to commit. They may rather, through faith in Christ, be acquitted of wrongdoing and granted entrance into God's eternal presence.

Fourth, they should not be troubled because they had at least an inkling of "the place" where Jesus was going (v. 4). The life He had shared with them, His teaching, and eventually His Spirit (v. 16) were sufficient to guide them through their present confusion and to ensure that what they were unable to grasp at the moment would later take on clarity.

For the above four reasons, then, Jesus' disciples should not let their understandable uncertainty strip them of all hope in the wisdom and power of their "Lord and Teacher" (13:14) to sustain them fully in the present murky moment and in the coming black hours.

Jesus intended for His words[2] to settle fears. And perhaps they did; but they also raised questions. Thomas, Philip, and Judas each voiced doubts in response to Jesus' call for steadfastness.

THOMAS ASKS THE WAY (14:5-7)

Previously Thomas expressed a tenacious, even grim, determination to follow Jesus anywhere, even it if meant death (11:16). But as the implications of his courageous stand became more graphically clear, Thomas began to voice the doubt for which he is infamous (see 20:25). He seemed to assume that following Jesus required complete knowledge of where obeying Jesus would lead (v. 5).

Whereas Thomas's question seemed to be calling for specific facts regarding place and time, Jesus' reply directed him to reaffirmation of personal trust in Him (v. 6). Thomas sought more information about where and how Jesus would go to the Father. Jesus Himself was "the way" Thomas sought. Thomas sought facts, the truth about Jesus' destination as well as his own—Jesus Himself was "the truth" Thomas sought. In the hour of Jesus' impending death, and at a time when arrest and even death was also a possibility for Jesus' followers, Thomas was concerned about life, both in this world and in the world to come—Jesus Himself was "the life" Thomas sought.

If Thomas could not grasp this, then there was really no hope at all. For the only access to the Father is Jesus Himself (v. 6). "The 'one Son' becomes the mediator of divine grace for everyone."[3] This is, no doubt, why Jesus was so intently adamant on making the point.

Jesus underscores the preliminary and incomplete nature of His disciples' faith in v. 7. They did not really know Jesus, and for that

2. Schnackenburg, like many modern scholars at most junctures in John, thinks that the words reflect early Christian theologizing and borrowing from ideas that were in the religious air, not Jesus' own words: "The most likely explanation of how the evangelist came to make the statement concerning the dwellings in the Father's house is that he formed it himself against the backdrop of the views that were current at the time," *Gospel According to St. John*, 3:61. But if John the son of Zebedee is the author of the gospel, there is no particular reason why the words could not be Jesus' own.

3. Schlatter, *John the Evangelist* [German], p. 294.

reason they could not really grasp the assurance that the Father offered them through the Son. But "from now on," Jesus predicted, they would both know and see Him. They would receive the insight and assurance they presently lacked. The words "from now on" probably refer to the extended period of Jesus' self-revelation between the cross and the ascension.

PHILIP SEEKS THE FATHER (14:8-21)

JESUS' WORDS ARE THE FATHER'S WORK (14:8-11)

Philip's question is perceptive and follows logically from the exchange between Thomas and Jesus. Thomas sought "the way"; Jesus pointed him to Himself and ultimately to the Father. Philip took Jesus at His word and requested, simply and directly, that Jesus show them the Father. "That will be enough for us" (v. 8).

Jesus expressed at least mild surprise (v. 9).[4] By now, He implied, Philip should understand that anyone who "has seen" Jesus has also seen the Father. "Seen" refers to acceptance, obedience, and trust, not mere physical vision.

Jesus' words in verse 10 were first directed to Philip ("Don't you [singular] believe?") and then to the whole group ("The words I say to you [plural]"). Whereas Philip asked for Jesus to "show . . . the Father" to them, Jesus replied that they were already face to face with the Father through what Jesus said. For His words did not have their ultimate origin in finite humanness—they were the result of the Father's divine work in Him. This characterization of Jesus' speech (and by inference the gospel accounts that record what He said) is reminiscent of how Peter described the words of Scripture more generally (2 Pet. 1:20-21).

Jesus again exhorted them to trust Him, either on the basis of His words or on the basis of the "miracles" He had done (v. 11). Elsewhere He praised faith that does not not depend solely on outward signs for its justification (20:29). Yet He apparently prefers faith on those grounds to no faith at all.

---

4. Kysar, *John*, Augsburg Commentary, p. 224, sees Jesus' response as "clearly a reproach."

PRAYER IN JESUS' NAME (14:12-14)

Their trust in Him would be vindicated when they found later that they would do the same works, and even greater ones, than Jesus had done (v. 12). This would be possible because Jesus was going to the Father. There He would intercede so that what they requested, the Father would bring about (v. 13). Jesus would do anything they ask (v. 14).

Several questions arise from verses 12-14. First, what does Jesus mean by "greater things"? This likely refers to the geographical breadth and numerical results of the preaching of the gospel in the apostolic church and since.[5] It may also refer to the grafting of the Gentiles into the people of God, something many Christians take for granted but that which Paul (and Jesus: see John 10:16) saw as a climactic aspect of God's eternal plan of salvation (Eph. 3:4-6).

Second, what does it mean to ask "in my [Jesus'] name"? W. Bingham Hunter has carefully analyzed the New Testament uses of the expression, almost all of which occur in John 14-16.[6] He concluded that praying in Jesus' name does not mean that one mumbles "in Jesus name" at the end of every prayer, be it grace before eating or a formal prayer in public worship. It rather refers to prayer that has four characteristics: (1) its goal is God's glory (see 14:13); (2) its basis is the promise and merit of Jesus Christ through His crucifixion, resurrection, and intercession at God's right hand; (3) its precondition is obedience to God's commands (see 15:7); and (4) its desire is that which Jesus Himself would ask for in a given situation.[7]

This means that Jesus' promise in verse 14 ("Ask me anything in my name, and I will do it") is not a blank check guaranteeing Jesus' help in acquiring anything from better health to a winning lottery tick-

5. Westcott, *Gospel According to St. John*, p. 204: Jesus' statement refers to "the wider spiritual effects of their preaching which followed after Pentecost."

6. *The God Who Hears*, pp. 191-99.

7. Strachan's conclusions (*Fourth Gospel*, p. 284) are similar: "Thus to pray in Christ's name is to pray that we or others may do or have just what He wills. 'What are the things I may seek in prayer, the limits within which I may pray?' The answer is determined by our knowledge of Christ Himself, and the fact that prayer in accordance with His will is also in accordance with God's will (cf. 9:31; 11:41; 1 John 5:14). Thus prayer in Christ's name is disciplined prayer."

et. It was a sober promise assuring the eleven that He would continue to lead and protect them after He departed just as He led and watched over them in the past (see 17:12).

It should also be noted that Jesus' promise was first of all to the eleven assembled before Him. In chapters 14-16 Jesus promises them special enabling for their ministry as apostles, the "foundation" of the church (Eph. 2:20). Verses like 14:26 are clearly directed to these key co-founders of the church, not to believers at large in future ages—there is, for example, no evidence that the Holy Spirit will remind believers today of all the things Jesus said to His first disciples, as 14:26 promises. This does not mean that Jesus' special instructions to the eleven have no secondary application today, only that we must beware of applying directly to ourselves words that have their original application in the unique context of apostolic responsibility and authority (see Eph. 4:11).[8]

LIFE IN JESUS, LIFE IN THE SPIRIT (14:15-21)

Jesus continued to respond to Philip's request to see the Father. He counseled Philip and the others to remain true to what He was telling them (v. 15). The ultimate expression of devotion to Jesus is obedience to Him. As John writes elsewhere, "The man who says, 'I know Him,' but does not do what He commands is a liar, and the truth is not in Him" (1 John 2:4).

They should obey Jesus despite present uncertainty because Jesus will provide for the demands that face them in the future when He is physically absent. At Jesus' request, the Father will send the "Counselor" (v. 16), another name for the Holy Spirit (see v. 26).[9] "Counselor" could also be translated "Helper," "Encourager," or "Exhorter." In verse 17 Jesus refers to Him as "him," a person, not "it," an impersonal force. He is the invisible but all-powerful third Person of the Trinity, who will continue the work that Christ, the Trinity's second Person, set in motion in the midst of Jesus' followers.

---

8. A helpful discussion of apostolic authority in relation to the canonical books of the NT is H. Ridderbos, *Redemptive History and the New Testament Scriptures* (Phillipsburg, N.J.: Presbyterian and Reformed, 1988). Ridderbos includes extensive discussion of the pertinent passages in John 14-16.

9. See Brown, *Gospel According to John*, 2:1135-44.

He is the "Spirit of truth" in that He conveys truth, an attribute of God, to those who seek it through Christ. Truth is associated with the Father in 4:23-24 and with the Son in 14:6. "The world" means all those who do not know Christ. The world does not accept or recognize the Spirit, but Jesus' followers do, for they recognize Jesus, and the Spirit's presence is the presence of Jesus Himself (v. 18).

Ironically, Jesus' imminent departure would result in His disciples' seeing Him more clearly than when He was physically with them (v. 19). "The world," on the other hand, those who fail to recognize and commit themselves to Jesus, will think that He has departed indeed. They will be strangers to the life Jesus' followers possess, life that derives from the Son's own presence in their midst and at the Father's right hand—"Because I live, you also will live."

Jesus wrapped up His reply to Philip by assuring the eleven that they will understand who the Father is, and how Jesus unites the Father and the disciples, "on that day" (v. 20). This may refer to the time when Jesus appears to His disciples after His resurrection, or to His imparting of the Spirit to them (20:22), or to Pentecost (Acts 2).[10] In the meantime, Jesus advised the eleven to abide steadfastly by what He told them (v. 21). Obedience to Jesus is the sign of love for Jesus. Obedience is also the precondition for enjoying God's covenant favor, His love, and for discovering progressively more of Jesus' will. Jesus will show Himself faithfully to those who show themselves faithful to Him.

JUDAS EXPRESSES CONCERN (14:22-24)

In verse 22, Judas (probably the eleventh disciple Jesus chose; see Luke 6:16; Acts 1:13) raised a question about Jesus' statement in verse 17. Jesus' disciples, like their Jewish countrymen, expected the Messiah to inaugurate a visible, earthly, political reign (see Acts 1:6). It must have been disillusioning, if not frightening, for Jesus to disclose that society at large would not be able to discern Jesus' presence once He left (see v. 17). This would seem to leave the disciples holding the bag, and an empty bag at that.

10. Bruce, *Gospel of John*, p. 303, asserts: " 'That day' is the day when Jesus will have returned to the Father and sent the Spirit to be with and in His disciples."

Jesus did not deny that the times ahead will be difficult ones. But He asserted once more that the disciples need to obey in the known present more than they need to understand about the unknown future. Far from deserting the world, both Father and Son will come to each disciple who loves and obeys Jesus. They will make their "home" (the same word is used in v. 2, where it is translated "room"[11]) with him (v. 23). With the air of an ultimatum, Jesus commented on what rejecting His teaching, difficult though it be to accept, would imply —lack of love for Him (v. 24). This statement too, like everything else Jesus disclosed to the inner circle clustered around Him, is not a merely human utterance but comes from the Father, who sent the Son into the world. It should therefore be heeded with great care and full response.

JESUS REAFFIRMS REASSURANCE (14:25-31)

The rest of the chapter appears to break off from answering specific questions and to concentrate on the theme of assurance, with which the chapter began.

What Jesus had said to them is of obvious importance (v. 25). But the Holy Spirit, who will come later, will enlarge and deepen their understanding of Jesus' remarks (v. 26). This was a reminder that the disciples often did not understand the meaning of Jesus' words or deeds until after the resurrection and the coming of the Spirit (see 2:22; 12:16). The Father would send the Spirit in Jesus' name, that is, at Jesus' request (see v. 16) and for the purposes that will further the work Jesus came to accomplish (15:26).

In keeping with the thrust of the whole chapter, Jesus bids them peace (v. 27). At the moment they were in turmoil and confusion. "Peace" is the Hebrew greeting and farewell, recalling the full enjoyment of God's covenant blessings, shalom. Here and in 16:33 the word denotes the tranquility of heart and inner assurance imparted by Jesus' personal presence, even in the midst of desperate times. Jesus' peace is not like that which the world gives, which depends largely on favorable circumstances. It abounds precisely in the midst of trial and adversity.

11. Holtzmann (*Gospel of John* [German], p. 250) calls attention to 1:14 and the idea of God's dwelling on earth with His people.

Jesus repeated what they had heard Him say (v. 28) so there would be no doubt as to what lay ahead. It was important that they remember later that God had been in control of the proceedings immediately ahead. If they could recall that Jesus had predicted them, their confidence would be greatly strengthened (v. 29; see 13:19). The construction of the words "If you loved me, you would be glad" (v. 28) implies that at the moment they neither loved Jesus as He called for nor rejoiced as they might have. This points to the pressure and confusion under which they labored that night. "The Father is greater than I" (v. 28) is not a denial of Jesus' essential unity with the Father (10:30). It indicates rather that in His incarnate person, His role or function is one of subordination to the Father. Soon He would return to Him again to share the honor and glory He knew in eternity past (17:5).[12]

The time Jesus had for further last-minute instructions ticked away quickly (v. 30). The hour was at hand for Him to face the calling card of "the prince of this world," death. Jesus was not under that prince's power, but His Father had sent Him for the very purpose of submitting to and triumphing through this hour (see 12:27). By His laying down His life, the world would be confronted by the depth of His love for and fidelity to the Father (v. 31). Jesus was a living example, therefore, of His own repeated exhortation to the disciples that they love Him and obey His commandments. For He loved and obeyed the Father willingly and unreservedly.

Jesus called for them to be up and about, perhaps a signal that they were leaving the upper room and departing for Gethsemane (v. 31). The disciples' heads were no doubt swimming with apprehension and alarm. But Jesus had called them to rest in Him as they rested in God, to stand by His commands in trusting love, and to be confident that God's fullest blessing, His peace, rested on them even in this dark hour.

---

12. Calvin notes the similarity of 14:28 to 1 Cor. 15:24 and concludes: "Christ is not here drawing a comparison between the divinity of the Father and of Himself, nor between His own human nature and the divine essence of the Father, but rather between His present state and the heavenly glory to which He was shortly to be received. It is as if He said, 'You desire to keep me in the world, but it is better that I should ascend to heaven.' Let us therefore learn to view Christ humbled in the flesh, that He may lead us to the fount of blessed immortality" (*Gospel According to St. John*, 2:90). See also Bruce, *Gospel of John*, p. 307 n. 15.

Few passages of Scripture are as pregnant with meaning and as packed with insight as this chapter. Yet there is more—Jesus' remarks continue in the same unspeakably full and rich vein in the chapters just ahead. He will continue to lay a foundation to steady their troubled hearts as He prepares to wage the battle that brought salvation to the world.

15

BEARING FRUIT (15:1-27)

In the previous chapter Jesus' concern was to calm the disciples' agitation, to impart steadiness to them at a tumultuous hour. Jesus was about to be betrayed and His disciples scattered (16:32). They stood in dire need of encouragement. In chapter 14 they receive it.

But they needed more than merely comforting words. Jesus was not interested in just imparting a last-ditch survival strategy. They needed to understand that what lay ahead was aggressive and productive obedience to Jesus. They were not called to hallow Jesus' memory secretly in secluded corners, out of reach of public dissent and danger. They must rather draw from the same source of strength that sustained their Master, so that they could move from feeling fright to bearing fruit.

Chapter 15 outlines how they can accomplish this and what the outcome will be.

NOURISHED BY JESUS (15:1-8)

VINE AND BRANCHES (15:1-5)

Jesus likened Himself to a vine, planted and tended by the Father (v. 1). The disciples were branches of the vine (v. 5). In the Old Testament the vine was a symbol for Israel (see, e.g., Ps. 80:8). But that vine often proved faithless. In contrast, Jesus was true to His mission. As He often points out in John, He and the Father labor inseparably together to bring about God's perfect will.

As branches, the disciples must reckon with what the vinedresser will do to ensure that the vine is productive. Branches that are barren

He cuts off (v. 2). Judas Iscariot was perhaps an example of this. Even productive branches, like the eleven to whom Jesus spoke, felt the sharp edge of the divine pruning hook. "Everything is removed from the branch which tends to divert the vital power from the production of fruit."[1] God is not content with minimal effectiveness; He desires those who already bear fruit to "be even more fruitful."

"Clean" in verse 3 is related to the Greek word for "prunes" in verse 2. Those who are "clean" (see 13:10) have been "pruned" by the purifying "word" to which Jesus referred. He probably meant the entirety of His proclamation and teaching, along with its Old Testament basis. That same word is what sanctifies, or sets the disciples apart for service to God, in 17:17. For Christians today, the cleansing word is the whole of canonical Scripture.

But for the word to do its work, the disciples must "remain" in Jesus (v. 4). This means to love and obey Him consistently. As they dwell in vital communion with and responsiveness to Him, He will dwell powerfully in them. As branches they cannot produce fruit; that is the vine's task. The branches only bear, or carry the weight of, the fruit. To do this requires unbroken attachment to the vine. The result will be "much fruit" (v. 5). Detachment from the vine will result in barrenness. Nothing of lasting spiritual value will come from lives lived apart from Jesus.

FRUITLESS AND FRUITFUL BRANCHES (15:6-8)

The person who fails to "remain" in Jesus is courting disaster. "He is like a branch that is thrown away and withers" (v. 6). Such branches are piled up for burning. Paul speaks of apprehension that he, after preaching to others, might not receive the prize for which he labored so long (1 Cor. 9:27). Hebrews speaks of worthless land filled with thorns and thistles that is fit only for devouring flames (6:8). Similarly, Jesus warned His disciples of how total their dependence on Him must be. Although it may be going too far to read verse 6 as evidence that a true believer can lose his salvation—such worthless branches may never have been authentically connected with the vine

---

1. Westcott, *Gospel According to St. John*, p. 217.

(see Matt. 7:21-23)—Jesus' words are a stern warning that should spur true believers to strive daily for a fuller relationship with their Lord.[2]

As the eleven "remain" in Jesus, and allow their lives to be dominated by His "words," they would have the assurance that their petitions to the Father through Jesus would be honored (v. 7). As we saw in the previous chapter (14:12-14), this verse should not be isolated from its historical setting. The eleven were being addressed, not believers at large. Jesus was primarily assuring those who had sat under His teaching and served alongside Him for three years. His claim was that as the Spirit clarified His teachings for them in the days ahead (14:26), they would receive whatever assistance they required for their work of evangelism and church planting. They needed only to ask.

Jesus' words are misused when they are taken to mean that prayer can be used in a casual or self-centered fashion to wrest from God whatever man's greedy whim might desire. On the other hand, believers today can still be assured that God will hear and respond to prayer that is offered with the intent and integrity that Jesus calls for here.[3]

As Jesus' followers heed His instruction, they will "bear much fruit" and thus show themselves to be Jesus' disciples (v. 8). This will bring glory to God. Fruitlessness dishonors God. Although there is danger in supposing that obedience to Jesus will always bring "success"—saints from Jeremiah to Paul, to say nothing of Jesus Himself, lived fruitful lives in God's eyes but met failure by human standards—there is also the danger of aiming too low in the Christian life. Jesus set before the eleven, and believers at large, a high standard of achievement for God's glory. Since Jesus, the vine, furnishes the strength and gives the increase, the standard is eminently reasonable

---

2. For an insightful discussion of the question whether believers can lose their salvation, in the light of this and other verses in John 15, see D. A. Carson, *The Farewell Discourse and Final Prayer of Jesus* (Grand Rapids: Baker, 1980), pp. 96-99.

3. In the event of unanswered prayer, Augustine's wisdom bears repeating: "For if we ask, and the doing follows not, what we ask is not connected with our abiding in Him, nor with His words which abide in us, but with that craving and infirmity of the flesh which are not in Him and have not His words abiding in them" (*Lectures on John*, p. 304). There is also the possibility that the request is in keeping with God's will but that it is not yet time for the request to be granted. In that case perseverance is called for.

and attainable. Acceptance of a less ambitious standard of low or no
fruit-bearing, according to verse 8, may imply that a "disciple" is no
disciple at all.

Fruit That Will Last (15:9-17)

LOVE AND OBEDIENCE (15:9-13)

The reader of chapters 13-17 of John is struck by Jesus' calmness
and imperturbability. It was the hour of His betrayal and crucifixion.
Yet there was a profound serenity and hope behind all He said. In light
of 15:11, it seems fitting to call this inner tranquility "joy" (see comments in the next chapter on 16:20). And 15:11 makes clear that His
words went out in the hope that His disciples would come to share in
that same steadfastness of heart. But how could they, sinful men beset
by uncertainty, attain this inner disposition? Love and obedience by
the strength Jesus gave are the key.

The disciples must love one another (see 13:34-35). Jesus reminded the disciples of His selfless devotion, His love for them (v. 9;
see 13:1). This love was no less than the Father's love for the Son. But
Jesus was about to leave His beloved followers. Therefore the time
had come for them to band together, loving one another with a new intensity and purity.

To do so they must tirelessly abide by, or obey, what Jesus had
taught them (v. 10). Loving Jesus is not an inner mystical experience
alone; it requires also the practical honoring of God in the thoughts
and deeds of everyday life. Obedience to Jesus is crucial to knowing
and communicating His love. Later John wrote to Christians: "I ask
that we love one another. And this is love: that we walk in obedience
to His commands" (2 John 5-6). John's exhortation is much like what
Jesus calls for here: "My command is this: Love each other as I have
loved you" (v. 12). Jesus set the standard for love[4] by laying down
His life for His followers (v. 13; see 1 John 4:10).

---

4. Schlatter, *John the Evangelist* [German], p. 307, notes, "The love in which the disciples are to abide is that love with which Jesus loved them, not the love with which
they love Jesus."

SERVANTS AND FRIENDS (15:14-17)

So intense was Jesus' commitment to the disciples that He deigned to call them "friends." This assumes that they would walk in loving compliance to the terms of the relationship He had established (v. 14). They were servants (v. 20; see Luke 17:10), but they were not merely servants, for Jesus had disclosed to them all that the Father disclosed to Him (v. 15).[5] A key element in Christian fellowship is common knowledge and personal experience of God's revealed will.

They were Jesus' "friends," not by virtue of their superior merit or gifts but because Jesus chose them (v. 16). This did not refer to their predestination unto salvation (Eph. 1:4-5), at least not primarily. It pointed rather to the historical act by which Jesus appointed the twelve (Mark 3:14). Because Jesus chose them, He granted them His blessing and strength. And as they walked in His strength, they would "bear fruit—fruit that will last." This fruitfulness would come about in response to their prayers to God as they sought to further the aims Jesus set before them and to obey the Holy Spirit once Jesus physically departed.

In verses 9-17 Jesus touches on a wide range of topics: joy, commands, obedience, friends, servants, choosing, and fruit. However, lest His hearers forget the major point, He repeats it: "This is my command: love one another" (v. 17). Where His love reigns, fruitfulness is assured.

Coping with Rejection (15:18-25)

HATED BY THE WORLD (15:18-21)

For the disciples, Jesus' talk of death and departure (13:33, 36; 14:2) was frightening because it would seemingly leave them without a leader. They had to weather fierce hostility while their head was still present. How would they be able to stay together once He left? Why would they even want to?

Jesus took up the problem of the rejection they would face. "If" in verse 18 could be translated "since." They should expect the op-

5. Stressed by Holtzmann, *Gospel of John* [German], p. 257, who also points out that Abraham is called God's "friend" in James 2:23.

probrium of those who reject Jesus. Jesus' followers are the object of scorn because they do not share the loves and loyalties of those around them (v. 19). If they were just like worldlings, they would be accepted by worldlings.[6] Conversely, "Woe to you when all men speak well of you," Jesus says elsewhere (Luke 6:26; see also James 4:4). With this advance notice, the disciples would be prepared for suffering when it eventually came (Acts 5:40-41). Was there some connection between Jesus' instruction here and the fact that Paul seems to have routinely instructed new converts that their commitment to Christ would result in disapproval, even persecution, from those around them (1 Thess. 3:4)?

Jesus called on them to bear in mind the words He had already spoken to them (v. 20; see 13:16). They would harass Jesus' followers as they harassed Him. Some will accept the disciples' teaching in the same way that some accepted Jesus' words. Jesus' "name" (v. 21) refers to His true identity and status as God's unique Son; those who are strangers to and enemies of God will likewise reject the Son (see 8:19) and therefore the Son's followers as well.

GUILTY OF SIN (15:22-25)

Those who heard and rejected Jesus were guilty of a grave offense against the loving Father who sent Him (v. 22). "They would not be guilty of sin" is a hypothetical pronouncement, as in Matt. 11:21. The fact is, Jesus "has come and spoken to them." Therefore "they have no excuse for their sin." Rejecting Jesus is an unspeakably weighty offense, because to express contempt, or even indifference, toward the Son is to express those same attitudes toward God Himself (v. 23; see 5:23b). God is a jealous God (Ex. 20:5-6), "a consuming fire" (Heb. 12:29; Deut. 4:24) who deserves and demands nothing less than full devotion.

In verse 24 Jesus restates and expands on verse 22. Jesus had done things before the eyes of God's covenant people that "no one else did" in all their history. This might refer to deeds such as raising Lazarus after four days in the grave (chap. 11), or to speaking the very

6. "This condition, unlike that of the previous verse, is not fulfilled. The disciples have been 'of the world' and they continue to be 'in the world' (17:11), but they have been chosen out of the world" (Barrett, Gospel According to John, p. 400).

words of God (12:49), or to living without sin (8:46), or to dwelling in their midst as God's unique incarnate Son (1:1, 14, 18). Or it might be a proleptic reference to what He was about to do—die on the cross for the sins of the world and after that be resurrected.

In any case, all that Jesus had done and would do would not suffice to produce saving faith in most who heard of and saw His deeds. Truly they stand condemned, just as their own Scriptures declare (v. 25). Regarding Jesus' use of the Old Testament here, F. F. Bruce notes, "The fact that Jesus quotes this 'law' as authoritative indicates that it was not exclusively their law."[7] That is, Jesus accepts the Old Testament as authoritative, too,[8] although His interpretation of it often stands in opposition to that of the Jews.

CONCLUDING CONSOLATION AND CHALLENGE (15:26-27)

Jesus will have more to say on the subject of persecution in the next chapter (16:1-4). For now, He refers once again to the surrogate who will be His representative in the near future, the Holy Spirit (v. 26; see comments above on 14:16, 26). The Spirit "goes out from the Father" but is also sent by the Son; they appear to share responsibility for His presence and activity.

The Spirit will "testify" regarding Jesus. In this context Jesus' words serve to explain how persecution will often come about. In a world that heartily disdains God and His Son, a clear affirmation of the gospel brings on adverse reaction. Acts 5:32 gives a striking illustration of this claim, as Peter and the other apostles declare, "We are witnesses . . . and so is the Holy Spirit, whom God has given to those who obey Him." Shortly thereafter they are all flogged.

But it is not only the Spirit who will "testify." The eleven "must testify" also (v. 27). As those who accompanied Jesus "from the beginning," that is, from the time of His baptism by John the Baptist (Acts 1:21-22), they had received a unique trust. In their discharge of it they were sure to meet opposition. But so did Jesus. They were called to follow Him in all things, whether those things brought gladness or pain. If they would remain in Jesus and walk in the

7. Bruce, *The Gospel of John*, p. 314.
8. Beasley-Murray, *John*, p. 276, cites 5:39, 45-47 in support.

wisdom of the Counselor He was to send, their lives might be difficult, but they would not be barren. They would move from frightened-
ness to fruitfulness. Their highest calling would be achieved as their
testimony to the Son, through the work of the Spirit, redounded to the
glory of the Father.[9]

Their testimony to the Son, the power of the Spirit, the glory of
the Father—these are the notes on which chapter 15 ends. They are
also the themes of the next two chapters of John.

---

9. Carson, *Farewell Discourse*, p. 127, comments, "To view our witness in such light
tends to transform a responsibility into a privilege."

16

GRIEF TO JOY (16:1-33)

As the hour of His arrest, trial, and crucifixion drew near, Jesus quietly but intensely imparted last-minute insights to His closest disciples. They must "testify" to Jesus (15:27) and to God's call to all persons through Him. He therefore instructed them in servanthood (chap. 13), in consolation (chap. 14), and in fruitfulness (chap. 15).

Chapter 16 continues in the same vein. But the focus shifts. Jesus had already pointed out that His followers would bear reproach from "the world" because of their loyalty to Him (15:18). This was most unwelcome news: first they learned that their leader was about to leave them (13:33); then they discovered that they will be the object of scorn and rejection by the culture around them. Now the crestfallen eleven were in desperate need of hope. In chapter 16 they receive it. Jesus outlined the process by which their present disenchantment and despair will be transformed into hope and joy.

In chapter 16 Jesus bridges the gap between the disciples' sorrow and the sense of peace He knows, exudes, and seeks to share with them, even in this dark hour. He accomplishes this in three steps: (1) by confirming that hard times lie ahead; (2) by assuring them that He will always be present with them in the person of the Holy Spirit; and (3) by dialoguing with the disciples to help refine their understanding of what they are about to face.

GRIM PROSPECTS (16:1-4)

As chapter 16 opens, Jesus continues the warning He began in chapter 15. "All this" in verse 1 is literally "these things"; the expression occurs elsewhere in John's gospel only in 14:25; 15:11; and 16:4, 6, 25, and 33. The expression apparently refers more to the content of Jesus' final discourse (chaps. 14-16) rather than to His teaching as a whole.

Jesus told them "these things" so that they "will not go astray" (v. 1). "Go astray" is a word connoting stumbling or taking offense. Gazing on the once-powerful Jesus hanging seemingly helpless on a Roman cross, His disciples might understandably have felt revulsion and shame. They might be tempted to abandon Jesus and the movement He had prepared them to initiate.[1] Jesus evidently believed that, in order for them to rebound from the shock of His crucifixion and the sting of the rejection they will face in the months ahead, they needed to face the hard facts fully and directly.

They would be put out of the synagogue (v. 2), their spiritual home since boyhood. This had already happened to the man born blind (9:22, 34) and would be the experience of many disciples in the years ahead, as the book of Acts attests (see also 1 Thess. 2:14-16; Heb. 10:33-34). They would even be killed, as the example of Stephen demonstrated (Acts 7:54-60). And those who opposed Jesus' followers would do so in the name of service to God (see Acts 6:12-14). Such godless acts are lamentable but understandable when people know neither the true God nor His Son (v. 3).

Rather than suppress the unpleasant details of the near future from His followers, Jesus clearly outlined "these things" (v. 4) so that they would not be taken completely by surprise (see also 13:19; 14:29). From ancient times the God of Israel is the master of circumstances; He tells the future before it comes to pass (Isa. 42:9). Drawing on this same mastery of human affairs and historical events, His Son now steeled the eleven for what they were about to face—or rather flee.

---

1. Kysar's suggestion (*John*, Augsburg Commentary, p. 245) that v. 1 "is spoken out of the experience of apostasy known in John's church" is feasible assuming that this portion of the gospel of John does not recount actual words of Jesus from the night He was betrayed. Carson notes, "It is common in the scholarly community to assert that the historical Jesus was responsible for very little of the teaching recorded in John 14-17" (*Farewell Discourse*, p. 10). But Jesus' words make good sense in the setting John claims for them. There seems to be no need here to resort to the hypothesis Kysar works from.

THE PROMISE OF THE HOLY SPIRIT (16:5-16)

WISDOM FOR THE PRESENT (16:5-11)

In the midst of their grief,[2] there was hope, because Jesus' physical departure was but the preface to a subsequent, more powerful advent of His personal presence and influence. Jesus of Nazareth would soon pass from the scene, only to send from heaven the Holy Spirit. This is the core of Jesus' message in chapter 16.

Jesus began by remarking on their silence: They had ceased to ask Him where He was going (v. 5). Their sorrow had overridden their curiosity, and they could only listen in stunned incredulity (v. 6).

But Jesus solemnly affirmed that it was better that He go, for then He would be able to send His proxy, "the Counselor" (v. 7). The word translated "for your good" in verse 7 is translated "better" in 11:50 and "good" in 18:14; God can use evil schemes to work positively toward His redemptive ends.

In what sense would Jesus' departure be to their advantage? First, it was the fulfillment of God's eternal redemptive plan;[3] God's ways are always best (Deut. 32:4; Ps. 18:30), whether the immediate outcome is recognizably positive to human eyes or not. Second, the disciples would learn to walk by faith without the comforting but potentially limiting bodily presence of Jesus. Their spiritual communion with the Father who empowered them as He empowered Jesus would be deepened. Third, through the Spirit, Jesus' ministry would be greatly magnified (14:12); it would no longer be as spatially, geographically, and ethnically limited as it was in His earthly days.

The Spirit would continue the work Jesus began (v. 8).[4] Like Jesus (see 15:22), He will cry out against guilt and sin. "Convict" car-

2. Notes Morris, *Gospel According to John*, p. 692: "The work of the Holy Spirit in the church is done in the context of persecution. The Spirit is not a guide and a helper for those on a straight way perfectly able to manage on their own. He comes to assist men caught up in the thick of battle, and tried beyond their strength."

3. Beasley-Murray, *John*, p. 280, stresses the salvation-historical dimension of Jesus' statement.

4. The Spirit "duplicates the work of Jesus: Jesus had been His disciples' helper while He was with them, and at the same time His presence and witness in the world had served as an indictment of those who closed their minds to His message" (Bruce, *Gospel of John*, p. 319).

rics the idea of exposing and convincing. The Spirit will confront and unmask the folly of refusing to trust in Jesus (v. 9). He will impart the redemptive reality of righteousness (v. 10), or right relationship with an utterly holy God, because (1) Jesus will have established righteousness by defeating unrighteousness through the cross, and (2) He will have ascended to His invisible but sovereign seat of authority at the righteous God's right hand (Heb. 1:3). The Spirit will also testify to the coming judgment and mankind's ripeness for it (v. 11); He will be free to do this because the ruler of rebellious mankind is about to be judged in Jesus' victory through the cross and resurrection.

Though the disciples were unable at the moment to imagine the significance of Jesus' utterance, it became clear at least by Pentecost (Acts 2). As the gospel goes forth through the proclamation of common and formally unlearned men (Acts 4:13), the Holy Spirit repeatedly furnishes courage, insight, and words (Acts 4:8, 31). Moreover, as Paul later observes, the Spirit takes people who were formerly hostile to God (Col. 1:21) and places, or baptizes, them into Christ's Body, the church (1 Cor. 12:13). The movement Jesus was founding is not based on mere education, human potential, or strategic planning by religious bureaucrats; it is rather the result of God's outstretched hand of salvation at work through His Son's presence in the person of the Spirit. Jesus' brief synopsis in John 16:8-11 is, then, just a precis of the rich and extensive teaching on the Holy Spirit alluded to in many other portions of the New Testament.

GUIDANCE IN THE FUTURE (16:12-16)

For the moment, Jesus could only say so much, because the eleven could only take so much (v. 12).[5] They needed the Spirit to assimilate additional insight and to lead them into "all truth" (v. 13). Jesus referred to the full scope and depth of the information God would deem fit for them to know, not to all aspects of "truth" in the sense of factual scientific knowledge of the phenomenal world around them.

Like Jesus, the Spirit will speak what the Father desires to reveal (v. 13; see 8:28). He will also disclose "what is yet to come" (v. 13;

---

5. Calvin, *Gospel According to St. John*, 2:119, stresses the encouraging force of Jesus' words.

see 13:19, 14:29; 16:4). This may refer to matters about the end times.[6] Or it may refer to the body of teaching that emerged under the leadership and authority of these disciples and their followers after Jesus' ascension.[7] In either case, the Spirit's role is not to call attention to Himself but to point to those things Jesus has taught, accomplished, and commanded (v. 14). When Jesus is not being promoted, it is doubtful that the Spirit of Jesus is at work.

Jesus' final words about the Spirit in the present context emphasize the trinitarian unity between Himself, His Father, and His coming Spirit (v. 15). They are distinct in terms of their roles, but there is no division or disjunction in the truth they corporately embody and reveal. There is unity in purpose just as there is unity in essence.

Perhaps to provoke a question, Jesus concluded with a puzzling remark (v. 16). The disciples "will see [him] no more," for He was about to die and be buried. Yet they will again see Him "after a little while," referring to His postresurrection appearances and perhaps also to His coming in the Spirit.

If Jesus sought to get the disciples talking again, He succeeded. For in the following verses they break the silence they have held since bewildered Judas raised a question much earlier in the discourse (14:22).

THE LIGHT BEGINS TO DAWN (16:17-33)

QUESTIONS AND ANSWER (16:17-24)

The disciples seemed unwilling to inquire of Jesus directly, so they murmured among themselves (v. 17). They simply could not grasp what He was describing in such great length and detail, either in general or with reference to such specifics as the words "a little while" (v. 18). If Jesus intended to found a kingdom, why should there be a delay? It He did not intend to, how could He speak of His return? They were not only fearful and deflated but thoroughly confounded.

Jesus noted their confusion (v. 19), probably through the God-given intuition He seems to have exercised elsewhere (see 2:24-25;

6. Burge, "John," in Elwell, ed., *Evangelical Commentary*, p. 871.

7. See Carson, *Farewell Discourse*, p. 149: "Implicitly, here is an anticipation of what we now call the New Testament canon."

4:16-18).[8] He concurred that their fears were about to be realized, and even worse: not only will they be shattered, but their detractors will be gratified and jubilant (v. 20). Jesus will appear to have been liquidated, removed from the scene in whose midst He created such a disturbance.

But the apparent outcome is illusory. The discomfort and outright pain of a pregnant woman gives way to such joy over her baby that the memory of the agony fades from view (v. 21). The analogy of childbirth is especially apt here, since in the Old Testament it is often used to denote human response to God's judgment (e.g., Isa. 13:8; 21:3; 26:17; Mic. 4:9).[9] As God's Son will bear the Father's judgment on the cross, His followers bear the discomfort and anguish of seeming injustice and defeat. Nevertheless, despair will be short-lived. They will see Jesus again, born anew from the dead, and the impact will be so powerful that from that time on nothing will be able to dislodge it (v. 22).

The fresh joy and confidence that awaits them will change the whole tenor of their relationship to Jesus. At the present they were still blindly berating Him with questions reflecting ignorance and confusion. The time was coming when they would instead approach the Father and ask directly on the basis of Jesus' proved merit, authority, and instructions (v. 23). The Father's response to the eleven's requests will be a source of assurance and joy in the days to come (v. 24).

FIGURATIVE LANGUAGE (16:25-30)

"I have been speaking" (v. 25) is literally "these things I have spoken." Jesus refers to all He has been saying in chapters 14-16.[10] "Figuratively" occurs also at 10:6; Jesus means that He has been making enigmatic statements that both reveal and conceal His intent. The "time" of which Jesus spoke was perhaps the period after His resurrection (see Acts 1:3) when He would teach them things they could presently not grasp or accept (see v. 12).

8. Westcott, *Gospel According to St. John*, p. 232.
9. Noted also by Brown, *Gospel According to John*, 2:731.
10. Holtzmann, *Gospel of John* [German], p. 266.

In the near future, when the disciples' vision cleared, they would have direct access to God through Jesus' name (v. 26). Here as elsewhere in John, Jesus' "name" refers to His true identity and authority as God's unique Son. After Jesus returns it will, in a sense, be unnecessary for Jesus to relay His followers' petitions to the Father (though Jesus does make intercession for believers: Rom. 8:34; Heb. 7:25). This is because they will be fully reconciled to God (v. 27) through Jesus' atoning death. Through it they will enjoy direct access to the Father. "Have loved" and "have believed" in verse 27 are both perfect tense, implying a complete and enduring commitment. In verse 28 Jesus sums up[11] what the disciples have come to affirm about Him; their unrestrained acceptance of these truths about Jesus will make their future experience of His Spirit and joy possible.

Finally the eleven seemed to pluck up courage and respond to their master's sober words. They averred that His message was now clear to them (v. 29). Jesus' response in verse 32 implies that they do not understand as much as they think they do. Still, they seemed to be making progress. They accepted Jesus' complete understanding of the troubling situation, and they realized that their questioning of Him had been unnecessary and perhaps even arrogant (v. 30). The penetrating wisdom with which Jesus had spoken convinced them that Jesus indeed "came from God."

While this affirmation does not sound greatly different from what some of them declared at the outset of Jesus' ministry (see 1:49), it does suggest that they were in a good position to respond to the powerful outworking of the resurrection and Holy Spirit that they were about to experience. Jesus' discourse, while not fully appreciated, had significant effect.

LIMITED UNDERSTANDING— BUT PEACE NONETHELESS (16:31-33)

Jesus' exclamation in verse 31 may also be a question. In either case, verse 32 indicates the limited staying power of the faith they presently possess. The eleven will be "scattered," a word used in

---

11. Barrett, *Gospel According to St. John*, p. 414, calls this "a complete summary, in John's way, of the Christian faith."

10:12 to describe how the wolf disperses the sheep of a hireling shepherd. They will desert Jesus (though He is not a hireling shepherd, for He will reunite His flock after they flee). Only the Father will stand by Him—a reminder that the salvation Jesus won is fully God's doing, with no contribution of sinful man, who lacks both the ability and will to purchase release from His own sin. Matthew 27:46 and Mark 15:34 record that on the cross even the Father distanced Himself from the Son,[12] a stark reminder of the desolation that lay ahead of Jesus as He spoke.

Despite all the uncertainty and fearfulness clouding the disciples' vision as Jesus wrapped up His discourse, He concluded on a high note of "peace" (v. 33). Here the word refers neither to the absence of military conflict nor to the absence of all inner turmoil. It bespeaks rather the experience of God's upholding hand in the midst of difficulty. Paul refers to the reality of this peace when He states, "In all these things we are more than conquerors through Him who loved us" (Rom. 8:37). The "these things" of which Paul speaks include trouble and hardship and danger and even death—the "sword" of Romans 8:35. Yet Paul can speak of perseverance and ultimate triumph through Christ.

In the same way, there was peace for the eleven on that dark night "in me"—in Jesus.[13] It was not in them, in their courage (13:37) or in their understanding (v. 32). Real trouble lay ahead, both in the immediate and in the long-range future (v. 33). But they could take courage. For the one who was about to die for the sins of the world was also the one who "has overcome" the world.

Jesus' use of the perfect tense "has overcome" was a fitting end to His discourse. The favorable outcome of the events just ahead was so secure that He could speak of it as an accomplished fact. If there is no doubt as to the horrors of the cross, there is also no doubt as to Jesus' victory through it. In this victory His disciples, too, found their hope. Their present grief would first intensify, then dissipate, as Jesus' fortunes fell, then dramatically rise in coming hours. His steadfastness will win their salvation; His selfless courage under duress will prove to furnish the peace they presently only glimpsed from afar.

12. Ramsey's remark on 16:32 (*John*, p. 276) seems to overlook this.
13. Schnackenburg, *Gospel According to St. John*, 3:166.

17

PRELUDE TO GLORY: JESUS PRAYS (17:1-25)

Some years ago a number of North American pastors were polled to determine how long they prayed each day. The average figure— about three minutes! The busyness of modern life easily crowds out focused communion with God alone. And if some pastors pray so little, how long does the average casual churchgoer devote to prayer?

Chapter 17 of John implies a different attitude toward prayer.[1] It is not a short or non-existent optional exercise. It is not a perfunctory ritual confined to mealtime or a "devotion." It is rather the core, in fact the climax, of Jesus' final discourse (chaps. 13-17). It is the seal of all He has said. It is the capstone of a presentation designed to steady the shaky disciples and ensure that their imminent scattering (16:32) will be only temporary. Jesus' final instruction to the eleven in chapters 13-17 primes them to expect what lies ahead, but Jesus' prayer empowers them to survive and rise above it.

The importance of Jesus' prayers in the last hours before the cross is glimpsed in Luke 22:31-32, where Jesus notes the havoc Satan is poised to wreak. What prevented Satan from succeeding? Jesus informed Peter: "I have prayed for you, Simon, that your faith may not fail."

In the hour of Jesus' betrayal and death, it was the prayer of chapter 17 that gave point to His instruction and ensured the survival of His

---

1. Westcott (*Gospel According to St. John*, p. 236) points out that chap. 17 "contains what may be most properly called 'the Lord's Prayer,' the Prayer which He Himself used as distinguished from that which He taught to His disciples."

tiny band of faltering followers. Jesus' prayer for Himself (vv. 1-5), for the eleven (vv. 6-19), and for future believers (vv. 20-26) completed the foundation He had laid for accomplishing His purpose in coming to earth: to die for the sins of the world (1:29).

JESUS' PRAYER FOR HIMSELF (17:1-5)

GLORIFY THY SON

The previous chapter ends with Jesus proclaiming His victory over the world (16:33). Through the cross, He would triumph over all persons and forces seeking to thwart the Father's redemptive plan.

Immediately following that declaration, Jesus looked upward and began to pray (v. 1). This was not an uncommon posture for prayer in Scripture (see 11:41; Ps. 123:1; Mark 7:34) and was a reminder that the heart's attitude, not the body's position, is what determines acceptable prayer (see Ps. 66:18).[2] As in the case of Jesus' prayer at Lazarus's tomb (see 11:42), His words were meant not only as communication with God but also as a lesson for onlookers (v. 13).

Jesus prayed first for Himself. He addressed God as Father (v. 1), again revealing a level of intimacy so exclusive that His use of the term was viewed as blasphemous (5:18). The prayer was, however, not selfish. He prayed that He would be glorified to the end that the Father might be glorified through Him. To "glorify" here carries the idea of bringing the honor, acclaim, and worship that belongs exclusively to Almighty God and His unique Son (see Rev. 5:13).

It is altogether fitting that Jesus should pray to be glorified, or exalted, to a level higher than any other person occupies. For the Father had granted Him pride of place, or "authority over all people" (v. 2). And this authority was not one to be clutched at for the prestige it brought to its holder (see Phil. 2:6); it was rather to be poured out in distributing eternal blessedness to all who would receive it. Jesus' statement that "eternal life" comes "to all those [God has] given Him" was a restatement of 1:12-13: spiritual rebirth comes by God's grace, not by human response, merit, or initiative.

2. Yet Jesus' posture was not meaningless; see Calvin, *Gospel According to St. John*, 2:134. But Calvin also warns that "we must take care that ceremonies do not express more than is in our minds."

The "eternal life" Jesus bestows is a matter of relationship, not simply chronological duration. It involves personal knowledge of God and of His Son (v. 3).[3] Knowledge of one is implicit in knowledge of the other, as Jesus has stressed elsewhere (10:30; 14:9). Such knowledge transforms life in the present age, not merely in the age to come.

How had Jesus brought glory to the Father? The question is answered in verse 4—by fulfilling the work God sent Him to carry out. Jesus spoke of His life and death as an accomplished fact, as in 16:33. But in order for this assured reality to become a realized actuality, the Son petitioned the Father to bestow honor on the Son (v. 5). His prayer included reference to His preexistence (see also v. 26), His eternal union with the Father prior to the earth's creation.

THE ROAD TO GLORY

Easily overlooked but highly significant in Jesus' prayer is the means by which the "glory" of which He spoke would be realized. When Jesus in verse 1 speaks of "the time" (literally "the hour") being at hand, He surely has in mind the cross.[4] How could the cross, a tool of execution so brutal that Roman citizens were exempt from it, bring glory? The notion was impossible for many of Jesus' era to accept. Jews boggled at it, and Gentiles simply dismissed it (1 Cor. 1:23). Yet the message of the crucified Christ, "foolishness to those who are perishing," is yet "the power of God" to those who receive it (1 Cor. 1:18).

God's glory in the life of His Son came about through humble, even humiliating means. Implicit in Jesus' teaching (15:20) and explicit in the teaching of the apostles (2 Tim. 3:12; 1 Pet. 4:12-19) is the insight that servants in God's kingdom win the crown of victory through the tempering flames of suffering. The abiding reminder of Jesus' prayer is that those who wish to glorify God must reckon with following Christ's example. This is an example of costly victory

---

3. Schnackenburg (*Gospel According to St. John*, 3:172) agrees that v. 3 is an explanation of "eternal life." But He also insists that it is an editorial addition, not a statement made by Jesus. Holtzmann (*Gospel of John* [German], p. 277) thinks the entire prayer is the creative achievement of a writer in the second-century church.

4. Barrett, *Gospel According to St. John*, p. 418. Tenney (*John*, p. 244) thinks Jesus refers to His achievement of revealing eternal life to mankind.

achieved by the grace of God through the enduring of painful trials, not of cheap triumph bestowed on the indolent who languish indulgently on their beds of religious ease.

THE JOY OF THE ELEVEN (17:6-19)

THEIR NEED (17:6-12)

Next Jesus' meditative gaze turned to the eleven. He prayed so that they, hearing His petition, might share in the joy He knew despite the pressure He labored under (v. 13).

Jesus recounted one of His chief accomplishments: He "revealed" the Father to the ones the Father gave Him (v. 6). Jesus likely had in mind the whole of His ministry, in which He made God known to persons who otherwise might have remained blind to His reality. The disciples had "obeyed [God's] word" insofar as they responded to Jesus' teachings, because the Son did and said nothing of His own initiative (see v. 8; also 5:19; 14:10).

Verse 7 echoes 16:30. The disciples could finally see beyond Jesus as merely a charismatic but human religious leader with good ideas and a daring plan; through Him they had been brought into saving connection with the one true and living God.[5] This had come about through Jesus' words, His teaching, which in turn had its origins in the Father (v. 8). Jesus' words brought about certainty regarding His origin, as well as faith that His coming was not a historical coincidence but rather a willful act of God's personal grace (see 1:17).

Despite their faith and certainty, Jesus prayed for the disciples (v. 9). They had to carry on His work after He ascended. He prayed for them in a way He did not pray for the world at large. Of course Jesus, like the Father, loved the world (3:16), but at this point His primary concern was the disciples, who were about to be sorely tried. The divine love for the world is, however, tempered by the sentence of judgment under which the world stands (3:36). As long as the world spurns the gift of God's Son, it must remain a stranger to the full measure of intercessory acceptance that Jesus showed here.

Though the divine glory was essentially limited to, and totally complete within, the shared dynamic of Father and Son (and by impli-

---

5. Holtzmann, *Gospel of John* [German], p. 271.

cation the Spirit; v. 10), Jesus' followers had now entered that eternal equation at God's own invitation—"glory has come to [Jesus] through them." As Jesus prepared to depart the world and enter into the Father's presence, He pled for God to extend "the power of [his] name" to them (v. 11). "Name" here refers to God's own Person in all His limitless yet compassionate might; Jesus commended the disciples to the surest of hands. Jesus' prayer for the disciples to be one is not a call for ideological uniformity, nor for organizational union, nor for political unanimity.[6] It is rather a request that there be unity among them, that the same internal harmony of being and purpose that characterizes the Godhead might also characterize the people of God. Jesus would have more to say about this below.

There was every reason for the listening disciples to take heart at Jesus' prayer on their behalf. They had all been kept safe by Him, not by their own wiles or talents, in the difficult days already past (v. 12). The one exception, Judas, insisted on a different course.[7] That his demise was predicted by Scripture in no way absolved him of responsibility. It rather underscored that one who failed to seek God's proffered mercy—while others struggled to follow Jesus, Judas's hand was in the till (12:6)—will bear the tragic consequences. And God may use even the evil designs of a Judas to bring about His benevolent and constructive intentions (see Gen. 50:20; Neh. 13:2).

SANCTIFIED IN THE WORLD (17:13-19)

Jesus' imminent departure was the catalyst for the petition He continued to make (v. 13). His followers were already under fire just as Jesus had been (v. 14). Jesus wished to see the same divine protection that preserved Him through numerous dangers overshadow His disciples as well. They were "not of the world"; their allegiance to Jesus marked them as members of a different kingdom than the one served by the vast majority of their contemporaries. They were born "from above," as Jesus put it in His talk with Nicodemus (chap. 3). Their citizenship was elsewhere (see Phil. 3:20; Heb. 11). This attract-

6. Tenney, *John*, pp. 248-49.
7. Bruce, *Gospel of John*, p. 332.

ed both the curiosity and the animosity of peers who did not share their heavenly loyalty.

But although Jesus was keenly aware of the dangers posed by the world, He specifically declined to pray that His followers be removed from the world (v. 15). For then the world would be without a witness to Jesus. He did pray for them to be protected from Satan. "The whole world is under the control of the evil one" (1 John 5:19). Only by divine power can mere humans withstand the snare of Satan's deadly strategies. Even Jesus resisted the Tempter's allurements only by the power of God working through the Scripture He knew so well (see Matt. 4:4, 7, 10). His followers, who now shared Jesus' other-worldly heritage (v. 16; see 1:13), could be preserved only by the same power.

For this reason Jesus requested that they be sanctified by the truth of God's Word (v. 17). "Sanctify" means to separate from evil and dedicate to God and His perfect will. "Truth" here refers to the divinely revealed truth of Scripture that Christ embodies and fulfills.[8] The book of Acts and the New Testament epistles are abundant testimony to the importance of God's Word in the form of the Old Testament Scriptures in the life and teaching of the early church. They "are able to make . . . wise for salvation through faith in Christ Jesus" (2 Tim. 3:15). They impart endurance, encouragement, and hope (Rom. 15:4). They were written, in part, as warning and instruction to Christians (1 Cor. 10:11). The power of the Old Testament writings is mirrored and intensified in the New Testament, written in the decades after Jesus' earthly life. All this should be seen as part of the fulfillment of the prayer Jesus uttered here.

Jesus' request in verse 17 was not merely for His followers' protection; it was also for their equipping in light of their evangelistic mandate.[9] As Jesus was "sent . . . into the world," so were they (v. 18). Their commission was not merely to survive but to thrive, making

8. Burge, "John," in Elwell, ed., *Evangelical Commentary*, p. 873: "Sanctification comes through sustained exposure to the truth found in God's word (v. 17)." Kysar thinks Jesus refers not to Scripture but to "the content of the revelation (i.e., God's character as redemptive love)" (*John*, Augsburg Commentary, p. 261). Bruce (*Gospel of John*, p. 334) suggests that "word" refers to the message that Jesus gave His followers to preach.

9. Carson, *Farewell Discourse*, p. 193.

Jesus, His message, and His ongoing lordship known in a world largely ignorant of it.

In order for the disciples to go "into the world" with hope and life-transforming vigor, divine might must undergird their efforts. To that end, Jesus sanctified Himself (v. 19). That is, He set Himself apart and dedicate Himself to the sacrificial death that was now only a few short hours away. The old revival hymn "Power in the Blood" recognizes that Jesus' death ("blood"), coupled with His resurrection, makes available an infinite spiritual resource for those willing to serve Him (see Matt. 28:18). As Jesus prepared to send His followers out into the harvest with the gospel, it was not their strength, ability, or understanding but rather His own action on the cross that was the basis for their work.

THE DESTINY OF THE CHURCH (17:20-26)

SO THE WORLD MAY BELIEVE (17:20-23)

Jesus concluded His prayer with a sweeping glance across the centuries of church history to come. He prayed for Christians of all ages who have believed in the testimony (literally "the word") of His first disciples (v. 20). Specifically, He prayed for their unity (v. 21).[10] As Father and Son are united in person and purpose, there should be a melding of personalities, livelihoods, and goals among believers for the cause of Christ and His kingdom. This unity is crucial for "the world" to come to faith in Jesus. For the gospel gains or loses credibility in the eyes of unbelievers to the extent that Jesus' followers show forth God's own unity and love (see also John 13:35).

There is potential for God to be personally present among Jesus' followers because God's glory, His transforming personal presence, has appeared in Jesus, and Jesus has transfused that same glory into their lives (v. 22). Again Jesus stressed that unity among His followers is a necessary preliminary to the gospel receiving a serious hearing in a world either apathetic or hostile to it (v. 23).

It is important that the world face the fact that God sent Jesus and has set His special affection on Jesus' followers (v. 23), because with-

10. Brown, *Gospel According to John*, 2:775-77, discusses the relation of this statement to discussions on ecumenical union and church organization.

out recognition of Jesus' unique status and authority as the bearer of the only true message of salvation, there can be no forgiveness of sins or reconciliation to God. It is worth noting that a key element in the widely popular religious outlook called New Age thought is the denial of Jesus' special status.[11] This denial implicitly rejects the Christian claim that the church, the true followers of Jesus, is the primary vehicle of God's saving message. Jesus' prayer in verse 23 lays the groundwork for challenging this rejection and similar ones that have arisen through the centuries since Jesus spoke.

UNITED IN GOD'S LOVE (17:24-26)

Two major notes conclude Jesus' prayer for all believers down through the centuries.[12] First, in verse 24 He asks that His followers be permitted "to be with" their master. This is probably the same as Jesus requesting that they "see my glory, the glory you have given me because you loved me before the creation of the world" in the same verse. Jesus prayed from the standpoint of being "in the world no longer" (v. 11), so His request might be interpreted as simply asking that the disciples would one day behold the Son in His heavenly glory. This was probably not all Jesus sought, however. He also wished for their lives in the present world to be transformed by the graphic realization of their leader's exalted status as sovereign ruler over heaven and earth. When Paul extols Christ's supremacy over the cosmos (Eph. 1:20-23), and when he grounds Christian behavior in the present age in their "life" that "is now hidden with Christ in God" (Col. 3:3), He is reflecting the fulfillment of this aspect of Jesus' prayer.

Second, in verses 25-26 He affirms that He will continue to mediate knowledge of the Father to the disciples in the future as He did during His earthly ministry.[13] He calls God "righteous," a term de-

---

11. A useful introduction to New Age views is Douglas R. Groothuis, *Unmasking the New Age* (Downers Grove: InterVarsity, 1987). See also Peter C. Moore, *Disarming the Secular Gods* (Downers Grove: InterVarsity, 1989), pp. 36-61.

12. Kysar, *John*, Ausburg Commentary, p. 263, sees vv. 24-26 as a virtual summary of the whole chapter. Bruce, *Gospel of John*, p. 337, says the same of vv. 25-26.

13. "The mark of Jesus' divine sonship is not the possession of some secret name but the capacity to make the name of God known" (Schlatter, *John the Evangelist* [German], p. 326).

noting God's perfect justice in all His dealings. Jesus can say, "I know you" (see also 7:29; 8:55), a reminder that Jesus' knowledge of the Father is direct, while that of His followers comes mediated through their knowledge of Christ (Luke 10:22). Specifically, Jesus is concerned that God's love and Jesus' presence be overwhelmingly evident in the midst of His followers.

The confluence of these two elements, divine love and God's Son through the Spirit, transforms the lives it touches. It makes three things possible: perseverance in the current distress, understanding once Jesus appears following His crucifixion, and obedience to Jesus' commission when He eventually sends His followers forth to the nations with the gospel.

Jesus has prayed. The Father has heard. In one sense, victory was already assured. Yet the further outworking of God's would depend on a selfless act of the one person upon whom mankind's hope, if he is to have any, rests. The road to heaven's riches is pocked with betrayal, unjust trial, humiliation, and death, as in the following chapters Jesus puts feet to His prayers.

18

BETRAYAL AND ARREST (18:1-40)

At the conclusion of Jesus' prayer in the previous chapter, He declared that He would continue to reveal the Father through His words and actions as He had done in the past (17:26).

The next step in this revelatory process involved fulfillment of at least three prophetic predictions: that Judas would betray Him (13:26), that Peter would deny Him (13:38), and that His disciples would flee (16:32). It also involved legal hearings before Jewish and Roman officials. Chapter 18 chronicles these developments, recounting events[1] that lead the reader inexorably along the tragic but redemptive road to Jesus' crucifixion—the painful death that through faith brings life (20:31)

JESUS HANDED OVER (18:1-11)

JUDAS THE BETRAYER (18:1-3)

The setting of previous chapters was an upper room in Jerusalem proper. Jesus' prayer ended, He and His disciples left the city heading eastward under cover of darkness (v. 1). They crossed a ravine called Kidron, a creek bed in which water flowed only during the rainy season. They entered a grove of olive trees. This was the so-called Garden of Gethsemane (Mark 14:32; Matt. 26:36). John says nothing of Jesus' agonized prayer there, nor of the disciples' depressed, exhausted sleepiness.[2]

---

1. For a concise summary of issues related to the historicity of John's account, see Burge, "John," in Elwell, ed., *Evangelical Commentary*, p. 873.
2. Tenney, *John*, p. 254.

John is concerned rather to recount the reappearance of Judas. He was last heard of in 13:30 (see also 17:12). Gethsemane was exactly the place where Judas expected to find Jesus (v. 2). Jesus made no attempt to elude His betrayer, who led a sizeable band of soldiers to make the arrest (v. 3). The betrayal fulfilled Jesus' prediction in 13:26. The "detachment of soldiers" (see also v. 12) refers specifically to Roman troops stationed in the Antonia fortress on the northwest edge of the Temple area. "Officials" refers to the Temple guard, some of whom had earlier failed to arrest Jesus when sent without Roman assistance (7:45). They carried various devices for light, since it was by now well into the night. They were also armed. Roman troops probably seldom ventured forth in formation unarmed in volatile Judea where they were so unpopular. In addition, the Jewish authorities had likely warned them of the possibility that armed resistance might be offered, as indeed it was (v. 10).

JESUS IN CONTROL (18:4-9)

In 16:13 Jesus mentioned that the Spirit would inform the disciples regarding "what is yet to come" (Gk. *ta erchomena*, literally "the things coming"). In 18:4, some of those things are mentioned again. Jesus has some form of prior knowledge of them (v. 4; see 13:3; 19:20; also 10:18; 13:19; 14:29; 16:4). He did not seek to escape what He must do but went boldly forth to face His captors.

At the sound of Jesus' voice from the dark garden, the officials responded that they sought "Jesus of Nazareth" (v. 5). Jesus was a common name; specifying that they were seeking the Jesus who hailed from little Nazareth would help avoid arresting the wrong person.

Jesus' reply (v. 5) may be taken two ways. It can mean simply, "I am he" in the sense of "I am the Jesus you are looking for." But it is also the self-designation of the God who revealed Himself to Moses (Ex. 3:14). Jesus has used it elsewhere with this connotation (8:24, 28). He may likewise have done so here.

Why did armed troops draw back and fall to the ground at the sound of Jesus' declaration (v. 6)? Commentators like Calvin explain that John's narrative "relates the great power which [Jesus] breathed with a single word, that we might learn that the ungodly had no power over Him except so far as He permitted. He replies mildly that it is He whom they seek; and yet, as if they had been struck by a violent hurricane, or rather by lightning, He prostrates them to the ground."[3]

Another explanation observes that the troops may have been edgy, sallying forth into the night and fearing a guerrilla attack. Jesus' miraculous powers would have been reported to them by Judas and were probably widely known in the city anyway. When they hear Jesus' fearless voice from the darkness, therefore, their falling back and down may indicate a defensive posture in anticipation of possible physical resistance.

In either case, Jesus' command of the situation is striking. Repeating His identity (v. 7), He capitalized on the apparent uncertainty of the authorities to gain the release of His followers (v. 8). As He previously stated, He is the good shepherd and protector (10:11; 17:12).[4] In verse 9 John quotes Jesus' words from 17:12 in the same fashion that He elsewhere quotes statements from the Old Testament. Jesus' words are no less bound to come to pass than the inspired words of God Himself in Holy Scripture. This is understandable, since Jesus repeatedly insists that the words He shares are given to Him by the heavenly Father (14:24; 17:8).

PETER'S ACTIVISM REBUFFED (18:10-11)

"Sword" in v. 10 refers to a shorter, easily concealed weapon. Peter was not the only armed disciple (Luke 22:38). Earlier He had vowed to lay down his life for Jesus if necessary (13:37). Now with admirable bravery he attempted to make good on his promise. Nothing more is known of Malchus; mention of such an apparently insignificant yet specific detail suggests eyewitness testimony.

Jesus halted Peter immediately, no doubt saving him from being cut to pieces by the combat veterans looking on (v. 11). Man's ways and thoughts are often not those of God (Isa. 55:8-9). Jesus knew He must accept "the cup," a symbol of the outpoured wrath of God (Ps.

---

3. Calvin, *Gospel According to St. John* 2:154. Brown, in *Gospel According to John* 2:818, says that John is depicting the power of God's name "I am" on Jesus' lips (but the incident is, for Brown, a "theological reconstruction" and not "a historical reminiscence" [p. 811]).

4. Barrett, *Gospel According to St. John*, p. 435: "Jesus purchases the safety of the disciples at the cost of His life."

75:8; Isa. 51:17; Jer. 25:15; Ezek. 23:31-34).[5] He must die for others to furnish them a refuge from the sentence of judgment under which sinners stand (3:36). Peter's zeal was laudable but misguided. A disciple's role is to defer to and further his master's aims, not usurp his authority and dictate by impulsive reactions the course the master ought to take.

ON TRIAL (18:12-27)

INTERROGATED BY ANNAS (18:12-14, 19-24)

The arrest was duly carried out (v. 12). The disciples made good their escape (Matt. 26:56; Mark 14:50), fulfilling Jesus' prediction in 16:32. (Peter and another disciple did not, however, flee very far at this point [v. 15].) Annas (v. 13) was high priest in Jerusalem from A.D. 6-15. Thereafter he wielded influence through some five sons and a son-in-law Caiaphas (v. 14; see 11:49-51), who took turns filling the same post, yet were responsive to their predecessor's wishes.

In John's narrative, Peter's triple denial is skillfully interspersed with comments on Jesus' trial. Peter's denials will be dealt with in the next section. Following the arrest, Jesus was remanded to the custody of Annas (v. 19; see v. 24), who served as a sort of emeritus and de facto high priest even though Caiaphas actually held the office. Annas attempted a brief, fact-finding interrogation.

Jesus' response in verse 20 reflected His awareness of Jewish legal procedure. Witnesses could not be required to testify against themselves. Besides, uncorroborated testimony in one's own favor would prove nothing (5:31; 8:13). Most important, as Jesus noted, His dealings have been carried out in the public eye. Annas was legally bound to seek legitimate witnesses if he wished to dispense justice according to established legal standards (v. 21).

But as John has already hinted, Jesus' arrest was not because of demonstrated illegality but political expedience (11:50, 57). Jesus' appeal to legal principle won Him no more than a spiteful blow to the face (v. 22). This violent act failed to silence Jesus, or even rob Him

5. Morris, *Gospel According to John*, p. 746. But see Kysar, *John*, Augsburg Commentary, p. 270.

of His composure. He used the occasion to reprove the offender and call Him to consider his ways (v. 23).

Annas evidently realized that bullying Jesus would not work. He held no binding authority anyway; if the Jews hoped to press capital charges against Jesus, there would have to be a formal ruling from the legally constituted head of the Sanhedrin, the high priest Caiaphas. So Annas, thwarted, had Jesus transferred to his son-in-law's custody (v. 24).

DENIED BY PETER (18:15-18, 25-27)

Apparently Peter and a second disciple did not go far after eluding arrest in the Garden of Gethsemane. They tagged along behind Jesus as He was led to Annas (v. 15). The second disciple, who may well have been John himself, "was known" and perhaps physically related to Caiaphas (v. 16).[6] He gained entrance to the courtyard as Annas interrogated Jesus. He also arranged for Peter to slip in.

The door-attendant's question (v. 17) expected a negative answer and was not so much incriminating as curious. It was easy for Peter to go along with the benign tone of what she asked. "I am not" a disciple of the accused, He agreed. His cowardly words ("I am not"; Gk. *ouk eimi*) are exactly the opposite of Jesus' fearless ones (literally "I am"; Gk. *ego eimi*) at His betrayal (v. 5). The easy way out that Peter took opened the door to subsequent and more serious denials. Grave sins often begin as minor concessions to pressures of the moment.

The details of verse 18 are again suggestive of eyewitness recollection. They also lay the groundwork for the next denials. To stay warm, and to avoid raising suspicion by cowering timidly in the dark, Peter felt compelled to take his place with the others in the dim light cast by a charcoal fire. This very act of casual-looking confidence put him at risk of being recognized[7] by those who moments before saw his dim figure wield the sword in Jesus' defense.

With consummate literary skill John interweaves Jesus' noble defense of principle (vv. 19-24) with Peter's shortsighted and disloyal

6. Schlatter, *John the Evangelist* [German], pp. 331-32; Beasley-Murray, *John*, p. 317.

7. Holtzmann, *Gospel of John* [German], p. 281.

posturing, as He was questioned once more in verse 25. That second query essentially duplicated the tone of the first (v. 17). Again, but this time in a larger company of witnesses, Peter denied association with Jesus. But now a relative of Malchus (v. 10) became suspicious; he restated the question with a more accusatory edge (v. 26). The likelihood of Peter's association with Jesus was apparently inferred mainly from his Galilean accent (Matt. 26:73).

At the moment when Jesus was challenging His detractors to testify to the truth (v. 23), His own disciple disowned the person who is truth (v. 27). The rooster crowed, as Jesus foretold (13:38). Its sound suggested that dawn was not far away. It had been a long and exhausting night. As Jerusalem awakened to the grim day known in modern times as Good Friday, the prophet who had wept over the royal city (Lk 19:41) was in chains, and on His own.

JESUS BEFORE PILATE (18:28-40)

REQUEST FOR DEATH SENTENCE (18:28-32)

John omits details of Jesus' trial before Caiaphas and the Sanhedrin. Verse 28 assumes that a guilty verdict against Jesus had been reached. He had committed blasphemy. The sentence was death (Mark 14:64). But the Jews needed Roman permission to carry out the sentence. So they approached Pilate with Jesus in tow.

They halted just outside Pilate's Jerusalem residence, not wanting to contract ceremonial defilement in a Gentile household. This could disqualify them from eating the Passover, according to their interpretation of various Old Testament passages.[8] There was considerable irony in their meticulous attention to ritual cleanliness when they sought at the same time to convict an innocent man of a capital crime.[9]

Pilate came out to meet them (v. 29) and requested a formal statement of the charges. Their real grievance was stated in 19:7; at this point they appeared to want Pilate to rubber stamp their scheme to put Jesus to death. For they insisted that Jesus was a criminal and implied that Pilate should simply ratify their verdict and be done with the matter (v. 30).

8. Michaels, *John*, p. 299.
9. Duke, *Irony in the Fourth Gospel*, pp. 127-28.

If they could cite no violation of Roman law, then they should judge Him by their own, Pilate replied (v. 31). But the Jews wanted the death penalty that they could not legally carry out in Jesus' case. The two parties were clearly at odds.

John points to the deeper meaning of the Jews' insistence on wringing a guilty verdict from Pilate (v. 32). For it would guarantee that Jesus' death would not be by stoning, as Jewish law required for blasphemy (Acts 7:58), but by crucifixion in accordance with Roman practice, just as Jesus had darkly predicted when He had spoken of being "lifted up" (3:14; 12:32-33). Crucifixion was looked upon as hanging (Acts 5:30; 10:39) and would discredit Jesus as one accursed by God (Deut. 21:23; Gal. 3:13) in the eyes of anyone who accepted the authority of the Old Testament. To crush the popular support Jesus was receiving among so many Jews, it was crucial to the Jerusalem Jewish leadership that this ingenious strategy be carried out.

THE ACCUSED EXONERATED (18:33-38)

Only if Jesus posed some political threat to Roman rule did Pilate have legitimate interest in prosecuting Him. So for Pilate, it was important to determine whether Jesus was actually claiming some sort of political authority or kingship. If so, it would amount to sedition, or fomenting rebellion against Rome's authority in Judea. He brought Jesus inside for a more private hearing to pursue this question further (v. 33).

Jesus replied guardedly with a question of His own (v. 34). If Pilate was inquiring whether Jesus was a political threat to Rome, Jesus' answer will be negative. If Pilate sought to confirm that He had made messianic claims, then Jesus will have to answer in the affirmative.

Pilate's answer was curt (v. 35). He cared nothing for Jewish religious quibbles. Had Jesus violated Roman law or not? Jesus went back to Pilate's original question in verse 33.[10] He stated that there was a kingdom under His jurisdiction but that it was heavenly, not purely earthly, in origin (v. 36). That is why His followers were not battling to liberate Jesus from Roman custody.

---

10. Brown, *Gospel According to John*, 2:852.

By "not of this world" Jesus meant that His mission and authority derive from God, not from earthly powers. He did not mean that His kingdom had no influence on the world (Matt. 5:13), or that His kingdom was on a parallel track with earthly kingdoms, both having equal power and status. In fact, His reign is above all earthly powers (Eph. 1:21). Jesus' point was that in one sense He posed no immediate threat to Pilate and Rome, but that in any case He was not under their control.

Pilate realized that Jesus had confessed to being a king, and Jesus acknowledged that Pilate was essentially correct (v. 37). But He is the Messiah, the king of the Jews, with a salvific role to fulfill, not primarily a political one. He came to "testify to the truth," or to bear solemn witness in both word and deed of God's saving intention for mankind through Him. "On the side of the truth" in verse 37 is literally "of the truth"; the expression is perhaps synonymous with "from above" (3:3, 7, 31; 19:11) and refers to being willing to receive Jesus' testimony, or rather the Father's testimony about the Son. Those who do not accept Jesus' testimony are not "of the truth"; they do not belong to God and will not hear what He says (see 8:47).

Pilate dismissed Jesus with a question that was at least skeptical and perhaps sneering (v. 38). He announced to the Jews outside his residence, the Praetorium, that he found no basis for the criminal charge they tried to press. The ball was back in their court. To help them decide what to do with it, Pilate had a suggestion.

THE INNOCENT FOR THE GUILTY (18:39-40)

In keeping with a local custom of the time,[11] Pilate offered to set Jesus free (v. 39). The custom was apparently designed to curry Jewish favor by releasing a prisoner held by the Romans on the occasion of the Passover, one of the most revered religious observances of the Jewish calendar.

Those waiting outside Pilate's residence, probably a crowd rapidly expanding in the morning light of a new day, clamored for a known

---

11. Morris, *Gospel According to John*, p. 772, notes that this custom "is not attested elsewhere," but adds, "There is nothing inherently unlikely about it."

insurrectionist to be set free instead. They thus gained the release of someone guilty of the very crime of which Jesus is falsely accused before the Romans.

The situation was deteriorating rapidly. But it would grow still worse. It reached its nadir in the next chapter, as Pilate gave in to the manipulation of the Jewish authorities, and as Jesus trudged silently out of the city, His own cross in hand, to lay hold of a glory hidden from all eyes but His own.

19

THE CRUCIFIED KING (19:1-42)

The previous chapter recounted events leading from Jesus' betrayal to His arrest and initial trials before Annas and Pilate. Pilate found Jesus innocent of any crime that would justify a death sentence and so attempted to find a way to release Him. But the Jerusalem religious leaders, who had schemed for many months to remove Jesus from the public scene, were unrelenting in their insistence that He be disposed of. And this must be by crucifixion, in order to discredit Jesus once and for all in the Jewish setting in which He had gained such a formidable following.

Chapter 19 narrates the outcome of these events. Jesus is sentenced, crucified, and buried. We learn of the reluctant decree of Pilate, the brutal ordeal of the cross, and the immediate interment of the body. A major subtheme is the fulfillment of Scripture. All of the main features of Jesus' last hours are prefigured, if not explicitly foretold, in the ancient scrolls of the Old Testament. The writer, an eyewitness of what He describes (19:35), clearly regards such fulfilled prophecy as evidence that Jesus' teachings and claims are true, and that He should therefore be regarded with utmost seriousness.

Here as elsewhere, John could have written a much lengthier account (20:30; 21:25). But His goal is to furnish sufficient, not comprehensive, factual backing upon which to base his summons to personal commitment to Jesus (20:31). Chapter 19, in chronicling the climax of Jesus' earthly ministry leading up to His death on the cross, is central in the evangelistic strategy which underlies the entire presentation of this gospel.

Sentenced by Pilate (19:1-22)

GUILTY OF BLASPHEMY (19:1-7)

Pilate's flogging of Jesus (v. 1), who was formally uncondemned, sounds brutal—and it was. Sometimes victims died from this punishment. Yet Pilate intended to free Jesus afterwards (Luke 23:16). Apparently He thought that by having Him publicly scourged, he might placate the Jews' demands that He be punished still more severely.[1] Then Pilate could release Him after all.

The Roman soldiers, no doubt chronically bored with their duties as occupation forces in hostile and provincial Jerusalem, seized the opportunity for a bit of cruel comic relief (vv. 2-3). Some plaited a makeshift crown from thorns, perhaps from the local *phoenix dactylifera* or date-palm,[2] and pressed it painfully onto Jesus' head. Others dug up a purple robe, symbolic of royalty, and began to mock this pitiful "king." They formed a receiving line and interspersed sarcastic accolades ("Hail, king of the Jews!") with sharp blows to the face.

The Jews had presented Jesus to Pilate as one who unlawfully claimed to be king and was thus a threat to Roman rule. Pilate now made a countermove (v. 4). He exhibited a beaten and humiliated Jesus who could not possibly be taken as a serious threat to anyone, least of all to mighty Rome. The thorny crown and mock royal robe appeared to make a travesty not only of the gravity of Jesus' kingly claims but also of the Jews' exaggerated alarm at His popularity. "Here He is, the guy you are so all-fired worried about," one might paraphrase Pilate's announcement (v. 5). Surely they would have the sense and compassion to relent. Jesus had suffered enough for His sincere but harmless delusions of grandeur.

Pilate misjudged the depth of hostility Jesus had stirred up. No sooner did Jesus appear than His enemies called for His death (v. 6). "Chief priests and their officials" may indicate that they, the leaders, were primarily responsible for instigating the staged riots that called for Barabbas's release and Jesus' condemnation (Mark 15:11-15). Pi-

---

1. Schlatter, *John the Evangelist* [German], p. 343, points out that the flogging would also have the effect of demonstrating Roman power over any messianic claimant.

2. Bruce, *Gospel of John*, p. 359. For other possibilities see *Harper's Bible Dictionary* (San Francisco: Harper & Row, 1985), p. 1067.

late's "You take Him and crucify Him" points to his continued unwillingness to cave in to their pressure; such a course was illegal (18:31).[3] Pilate was opposing them, or at least stalling for time, by setting perversely before them an option that they both knew was unworkable.

The religious leaders, however, were adamant. Pilate may not have taken seriously such incidents as Lazarus being raised, but they had to. For their control over the religious, and ultimately political, loyalty of the masses was being eroded and usurped by Jesus. Jewish leaders had long been suspicious of John the Baptist (1:19, 24) and positively antagonistic toward Jesus because of His treatment of the Sabbath and God (5:18). They had proof, they maintained, from the Old Testament that Jesus deserved death (see Lev. 24:16). They would settle for nothing less than Jesus' execution, for "he claimed to be the Son of God" (v. 7), a claim they obviously rejected. It should be remembered that the stated purpose of John's gospel is to argue for the acceptance of this very claim.

PILATE'S DILEMMA (19:8-16)

The cause of Pilate's fear (v. 8) is not easy to pinpoint. Was it lingering awe at the personal impression Jesus had made on Him in their conversation?[4] Was it the realization that a potentially destructive riot was brewing and that he would be held responsible for it by his superiors? Was it because of his wife's dream and warning (Matt. 27:19)?

In any case Pilate turned away from the shouting crowd to speak once more with Jesus (v. 9). His inquiry regarding Jesus' place of origin may have been an attempt to find a legal loophole—perhaps there was some other official or venue more suited to handle the case. But Jesus was silent (see 1 Pet. 2:22-23). Pilate's emphatic response (v. 10) implied impatience if not anger. He was not known for being a generous or gracious ruler. It would be highly unusual for a prisoner in Jesus' precarious situation to be less than anxious to cooperate with him in any possible way.

3. Michaels, *John*, p. 304, thinks "they had the power to carry out the death penalty if they so decided." But see Beasley-Murray, *John*, p. 337.
4. Barrett, *Gospel According to St. John*, p. 451, concludes, "Pilate's fear is aroused by Jesus' reported claim to supernatural dignity."

With courage and aplomb Jesus corrected His questioner. Pilate exercised authority only because God in heaven allowed it (v. 11).[5] This does not imply that no earthly rulers should ever be disobeyed, since they rule under God's sovereign will (see Dan. 3:18; 6:10; Acts 4:18-20). "The one who handed me over" was Caiaphas rather than Judas. Caiaphas's "greater sin" was his abuse of his spiritual authority as high priest. His involvement in the conspiracy to convict Jesus made His misuse of "power" all the more heinous in view of the sanctity of the office he was sworn to uphold.

Whatever threat Pilate might have implied in verse 10, in verse 12 his only concern seems to be to get Jesus' case off the docket for the day. But the Jews anticipated this and offered a ready response in the form of a threat of their own. If Pilate fails to execute Jesus, they implied, they will raise the matter with the Roman emperor himself. And they will do so in such a way as to call in question Pilate's loyalty to the crown.

Pilate realized he had been trumped. His hand forced, he prepared to pronounce sentence (v. 13). He assumed his place at the *bema*, the official judgment seat of a Roman magistrate. It was Friday of Passover week, John notes (v. 14; see also vv. 31, 42), the hallowed time when a lamb was slain whose blood symbolizes deliverance from death (Ex. 12:21-23). "About the sixth hour" refers to late morning or nearly noon and is compatible with "third hour" in Mark 15:25, which means well into morning.[6] It must be remembered that precision timekeeping instruments did not exist at the time.

To spite the Jews who had manipulated Him, Pilate mockingly presented Jesus, bloody and battered, as their king. As earlier, they called for His death (v. 15). Pilate taunted them with the prospect of their "king" dying so ignobly; "the chief priests" responded that Caesar, not Jesus, was their sovereign. This declaration of loyalty was ironic, for in pledging allegiance to the pagan Roman potentate they

---

5. Westcott, *Gospel According to St. John*, p. 270: Pilate's "right to exercise authority was derived, not inherent."

6. Schnackenburg, *Gospel According to St. John*, 3:265, prefers to find error here, or to suppose that John is intentionally going against the presumably earlier synoptic tradition.

blasphemed the God they were sworn to exalt above any earthly ruler. Yet they accused Jesus of blasphemy.

This portion of the narrative ends tersely with Pilate handing Jesus over to a military detail for execution (v. 16). Gentile ruler and Jewish leaders had become co-conspirators in a drama larger than either of them realized (see Acts 4:25-28).

LIFTED UP (19:17-22)

Jesus trudged laboriously out of Pilate's presence and through the city gate, carrying as best He could the cross-piece of the cross on which He would shortly be fastened (v. 17). John does not record that Jesus' strength soon failed and that He required assistance (Mark 15:21).[7]

The crucifixion itself is related soberly, without melodrama or embellishment. The only added detail relates to the criminals hanging at His left and right (v. 18). They are called *lestai* in Matt. 27:38 and Mark 15:27, the same word used of Barabbas in John 18:40. They were possibly members of his rebel band.[8] Although John does not explicitly mention it, Jesus' death between two brigands fulfills Isa. 53:12: "because He poured out His life unto death, and was numbered with the transgressors."

In any consideration of the facts surrounding the crucifixion, it is appropriate to recall that Jesus saw in His humiliating death the means of bringing the greatest glory to God, as well as redemption to mankind (3:14; 12:32, 34). His declaration to prospective followers that they, too, must shoulder the cross-piece each day (Luke 9:23) is a grim, ironically uplifting reminder of the practical and painful consequences of following in Jesus' steps.

The public notice of Jesus' name and offense (v. 19) may have been a legal requirement. The sentence Pilate chose to inscribe, stressing sedition (promoting a kingship rivaling Caesar's rule) rather than blasphemy, was another jab at the pride of the religious leaders who

7. This is not, as Holtzmann (*Gospel of John* [German], p. 292) suggests, because the author wants to dramatize the fact that "the Johannine Christ requires no human support."

8. Bruce, *Gospel of John*, p. 368.

vehemently denied Jesus' regal status. Inscribed in three languages and viewed by hundreds of passers-by (v. 20), the placard illustrates Paul's statement some three decades later that these things were "not done in a corner" (Acts 26:26). It is likely that some of the "many" who read the sign were among those who heard Peter interpret the cross of Jesus in a different way a few weeks later (Acts 2:22-41).

Official Jewish objections to Pilate were fruitless (vv. 21, 22). Pilate would make them pay for bullying him so ingeniously.[9] Ironically, the public record proclaims the very truth that Jesus' crucifixion was calculated to disprove and which John's gospel is designed to assert: "Jesus is the Christ," the Messiah, the King of the Jews and Savior of the world (20:31).

SCRIPTURE FULFILLED (19:23-37)

DIVIDING THE SPOILS (19:23-27)

A small fringe benefit for the soldiers doing execution duty was the plundering of the victim's few remaining possessions.[10] In Jesus' case this was no more than the clothing He wore. They divided His outer garment evenly among the four of them, but the more valuable undergarment they decided to keep intact (v. 23). They agreed to decide its ownership by the throw of dice (v. 24).

John sees in this event a fulfillment of Psalm 22:18. The soldiers were unaware of this, of course. John's point is to underscore once again God's mastery of apparently perverse circumstances and to trace out His gracious overruling purpose as it prevails in a gruesome and seemingly hopeless setting. As in earlier chapters, telling the future with perfect accuracy before it occurs is a sign of divine superintendence of events and their outcome (13:19; 14:29; 16:4). For John, fulfillment of Old Testament Scripture is weighty evidence that beneath the surface appearance of a tragic miscarriage of justice, the God who loves the world is bringing about His redemptive intentions.

---

9. Morris, *Gospel According to John*, p. 808, points to the possibility that Pilate let his words stand in order to mock Jesus' accusers.

10. Brown, *Gospel According to John*, 2:902: "In Roman practice the soldiers had a right to the prisoner's clothes as their prerogatives."

While the soldiers haggled greedily over scraps of clothing, Jesus' concern, despite His extremity, was for those around Him. Defying the danger of public association with Jesus,[11] a small group of women courageously stood vigil near the cross (v. 25). Noting His mother among them, Jesus commended her to the care of the beloved disciple (v. 26), who was probably John the writer of the gospel. Jesus' brothers would have been more natural candidates, but they apparently remained skeptical of Him (see 7:5). In looking to her needs without compromising His mission, Jesus fulfilled both the letter and spirit of Ex. 20:12. In an important sense Mary's family was not her blood relatives, even her children, but her spiritual compatriots—a lesson that Jesus had imparted, at first to her chagrin, from His own standpoint as an eldest son many months before (Mark 3:35).

LIFE DEPARTS (19:28-30)

Jesus' actual death is related with as little dramatic fanfare as His crucifixion. Just before He died, Jesus expressed the acute thirst He felt due to exhaustion, loss of blood, and the general trauma involved in hanging on the cross in the midday sun (v. 28). John relates this, too, to Scripture, perhaps Psalms 69:21 or 22:15. Bystanders were quick to oblige Him (v. 29). Jesus may not have been so much interested in a drink as He was in having His lips and mouth moistened so that His last words could be uttered and understood. The "wine vinegar" was not a narcotic drink, which He refused earlier (Mark 15:23), but a diluted wine used by laborers and soldiers to quench thirst.

Jesus' last words, "It is finished" (v. 30), had a double meaning. On the surface level they expressed the imminence of His death. But they also made a profound theological statement: He had completed the work the Father sent Him to do. "The Lamb of God, who takes away the sin of the world" (1:29), had been faithful unto death, "even death on a cross" (Phil. 2:8).

---

11. Burge, "John," in Elwell, ed., *Evangelical Commentary*, p. 875, suggests that they were safe "because of ancient oriental chivalry giving them a protected status." See also Beasley-Murray, *John*, p. 349. But while there may have been minimal danger from legal authorities, the possibility of social ostracism should not be overlooked.

The expression "gave up His spirit" is curious and may possibly hark back to Jesus' earlier statement that He would lay down His life at will, not because He was forcibly deprived of it (10:18).[12] John may be indicating that at the moment of death, Jesus was in the powerful hand of the Father rather than the rapacious clutches of Satan. As the Father gave Him leave, He returned to the heavenly realm He had temporarily given up. By God's grace death is triumphal release, not unmitigated loss and terror.

NO BONE BROKEN (19:31-37)

Roman practice was to leave bodies on crosses for extended periods.[13] This would serve as a deterrent to other members of the populace contemplating defiance of Roman authority. Yet the Jews did not wish their holy festival to be marred by the spectacle of fellow sons of Abraham, criminal or no, exposed to the elements and carrion birds at the hands of their Gentile overlords. If nothing else, this was a violation of Deut. 21:22-23. They therefore requested that the condemned by dispatched (breaking their legs would hasten death) so they could be buried before sunset, the beginning of the Passover (v. 31).

Pilate granted permission, and the soldiers smashed the legs of Jesus' two hapless companions (v. 32). This was not necessary, however, in Jesus' case (v. 33). Just to be sure of His condition, a soldier lanced Jesus' motionless form (v. 34). Attempts to determine the exact cause of death based on the "blood and water" emitted from the wound are inclusive; John's point is that Jesus really died. His participation in humanity was comprehensive. Paul may be making a similar point in a slightly different fashion when He makes one of the three basic tenets of the gospel the fact that Jesus "was buried" (1 Cor. 15:4). Jesus' death, denied by some since the first century and thereafter in the Qur'an,[14] the holy scripture of Islam, was real. His identification with, and His love for, those He came to save could not have

---

12. Michaels, *John*, pp. 314-15.
13. Brown, *Gospel According to John*, 2:933-34.
14. Sura, 4.156.

been more total.[15] And the dramatic reversal of the resurrection could not have been more unexpected.

John normally does not intrude into his narrative. But possibly due to the obvious logical difficulty of insisting that Jesus, who will soon be seen and described as quite alive, was for a time quite dead, John solemnly lays down his own "testimony" to the facts he relates (v. 35). As in earlier chapters of John's gospel, "testimony" does not have the modern connotation of personal subjective experience. It signifies rather the sober avowal of publicly attested objective facts surrounding the life, death, resurrection, and teachings of Jesus, a complex of words and events that form the ground for saving faith.

To clinch his assertion, John cites a pair of Old Testament verses (vv. 36-37), one from Ex 12:46 (see also Num. 9:12), the other from Zech. 12:10. His master Jesus tended to support many of his assertions by relating them to revealed Scripture. The disciple who testifies here has learned his lesson well. John looks to the same biblical resource for corroboration of the truth he writes.

JESUS ENTOMBED (19:38-42)

Joseph of Arimathea, heretofore not publicly associated with Jesus, bravely risks the displeasure of Jewish authorities by seeking permission to dispose of Jesus' body (v. 38). He donates his own tomb to Jesus' last earthly need (Matt. 27:60). He is joined by Nicodemus (v. 39), like Joseph a member of the Jewish Sanhedrin, which voted as a group to push for Jesus' crucifixion. Neither of them, however, appears to have gone along with this decision. Certainly Joseph did not (Luke 23:50-51).

Nicodemus, perhaps with the physical aid of servants, furnishes the aromatic material[16] that would surround Jesus' body on the inside of the linen grave cloths in which He was buried (v. 40). Jewish embalming in Palestine did not include removal of organs and substitution of preservative substances as was practiced in Egypt.

---

15. Barrett, *Gospel According to St. John*, p. 463, thinks that John's point is that "the real death of Jesus was the real life of men."

16. On the reason for such a large amount, see Morris, *Gospel According to John*, pp. 825-26.

The story of Jesus' life appears to be at an end. His resting place is Joseph's new tomb (v. 41), selected in part because of its proximity to the crucifixion site (v. 42). Jesus could therefore be buried quickly, before sundown heralded the next day,[17] Passover, during which no such work could be legally performed.

The clear expectation of friend and foe alike is that Jesus' vision of a new, coming kingdom had been shattered. The messianic hopes of Abraham's seed lie dashed again. Those like Joseph who long for the kingdom of God (Luke 23:51) prepare yet once more to huddle in patient longing for the deliverance of God's people of which the Old Testament powerfully speaks, and about which John the Baptist and Jesus stirringly preached.

But as is often the case where God's saving work is concerned, human expectations and perceptions in themselves are not to be trusted. In a profound sense, as chapter nineteen ends with Jesus' burial, the real story of Jesus' life is only on the verge of beginning.

---

17. Jewish custom recognized sunset, not midnight or dawn, as the beginning of the next day. See Lev. 23:32. This appears to have been a common practice in antiquity: see *The New Unger's Bible Dictionary* (Chicago: Moody, 1988), pp. 1285-86.

20

RISEN! (20:1-31)

"If Christ has not been raised, your faith is futile; you are still in your sins" (1 Cor. 15:17). The necessity and reality of Jesus' resurrection following His brutal and public death is undeniably a component of the apostle Paul's preaching. It has remained the cornerstone of Christian understanding of Christ through the centuries of the history of the church.

Jesus' resurrection receives its primary attestation in passages such as John 20. True, the New Testament evidence is considerably broader than this. In addition to various incidents related in John 20, it mentions the following appearances of Jesus following His death: to the eleven on at least two occasions (Matt. 28:16-20; Acts 1:3-8), to women at the tomb (Matt. 28:9f), to Peter (Luke 24:34; 1 Cor. 15:5), to disciples on the Emmaus road (Luke 24:13-32), to James (1 Cor. 15:7), and finally to a crowd of some five hundred (1 Cor. 15:6).[1]

John 20 adds three more: to Mary Magdelene (vv. 11-18), and to the eleven on two separate occasions (vv. 19-23 and 24-29 [= Luke 24:36-49?]). In addition, John 21 speaks of yet another appearance on the shore of Lake Galilee.[2]

---

1. The three incidents related in Mark 16:9-14 seem dependent on the other gospel accounts and probably do not belong to the earliest version of Mark's gospel. See Metzger, *Textual Commentary*, pp. 121-26.

2. For a painstaking attempt to integrate the various accounts in a coherent fashion, see John Wenham, *Easter Enigma: Are the Resurrection Accounts in Conflict?* (Grand Rapids: Zondervan, 1989).

Whereas some scholars scoff at the possibility of Jesus' resurrection,[3] John joins other witnesses and writers in insisting on it. If John 19 presents the climax of Jesus' earthly mission in terms of His death for mankind's sin, John 20 is also climactic in proclaiming that Jesus' death was not the end, either of His life or of the hope, identity, and mission of His followers.

BODY MISSING (20:1-9)

MARY MAGDALENE'S DISCOVERY (20:1-2)

By early Sunday, the first day of the new week, Jesus had been entombed three days by Jewish reckoning. Friday counted as the first day (His burial was late in the afternoon, before Passover or "Saturday" commenced at dusk), Saturday (from sundown Friday to sundown Saturday) as the second, and Sunday (from dusk Saturday evening to anytime before the following dawn) as the third.

From the standpoint of Sabbath laws, friends of Jesus could have arrived to anoint His body with spices (Mark 16:1) on Saturday anytime after dusk, for at that point the Sabbath had ended. But there would have been no light for their work. In addition, such a small group of local women may have wished to avoid a night-time encounter with the military guard posted at the site (Matt. 27:66). So they awaited the first daylight of the new week instead.

Mary Magdelene (v. 1) was part of a larger group, which John does not explicitly mention (Mark 16:1), though the "we" in verse 2 implies that John knew she was not alone. She had long been an active follower of Jesus, contributing financially to His support, no doubt out of profound gratitude for her freedom from the "seven demons" that once plagued her (Luke 8:2-3).

As soon as she glimpsed the tomb, she knews something was amiss. There were no soldiers, and the heavy stone that should have blocked the entrance to the tomb was ajar or missing (v. 1).

3. The twentiethh century's most influential NT scholar denies that the tomb was empty on the first Easter morn; "a corpse cannot become alive again" (Rudolf Bultmann, *"Der Spiegel" on the New Testament* [1970], p. 236). Similarly, British churchman G. W. H. Lampe regards "the story of the empty tomb as myth rather than literal history." (Lampe and D. M. MacKinnon, *The Resurrection* [Philadelphia: Westminster, 1966], p. 17).

Her response was to notify Peter and "the other disciple," in all likelihood John (v. 2). They had remained in Jerusalem, if for no other reason than because Sabbath laws governing travel would have discouraged their departing for Galilee on Friday evening or Saturday. Mary assumed the body had been tampered with, and perhaps stolen. Morris points out the significant fact that "apparently the thought of a resurrection did not enter her head" at this point.[4] In either case, its whereabouts were uncertain. John's narrative reflects her agitation by its use of the present tense in both of the first two verses. Verse 3 will revert to the past tense, more normal in a narrative account.

PETER AND JOHN'S DISMAY (20:3-9)

Mary's troubling report brought Peter and John on the double (vv. 3-4). Attempts to prove the relative age of the two based on John's superior speed are speculative. Upon reaching the burial site, John did not immediately enter but rather peered in (Gr. *parakypsas*) from the outside (v. 5). He could see the grave clothes, which must have struck Him as strange. Why would someone stealing the body take the time and trouble to divest the corpse of its covering first?

Peter took the lead in actually entering the tomb (v. 6). He beheld an orderly scene. The "strips of linen" that had covered the body up to the neck were lying next to, but separate from, the cloth that had been around Jesus' head (v. 7). There was no evidence of the feverish activity of vandals. The body could therefore hardly have been stolen.

Eventually John worked up enough nerve to enter and take a closer look (v. 8). "He saw and believed." Just what did He believe? Apparently John at this moment accepted the fact of the resurrection. He inferred from the scene before Him, no doubt with assistance from what His master taught, that despite His death before John's eyes less than forty-eight hours earlier, Jesus was not dead but living. This implies that Peter was as yet merely baffled by the meaning of the sight before him; it was thus far only John whose eyes were opened to the incredible but inescapable conclusion.

John's conclusion was not yet as far-reaching as it would and needed to be. It was not yet grounded in the Old Testament writings

4. Morris, *Gospel According to John*, p. 831.

(v. 9). He still did not realize the magnitude of what he and Peter were witness to: the unique vindication of all God's promises in the Scripture. Luke's gospel brings out most clearly the centrality of the Scripture to the disciples' fuller understanding of Jesus' resurrection (Luke 24:27, 32, 44). Still, John had taken the first giant step of trust in a seeming impossibility. The great reversal in the hearts and minds of Jesus' followers—from shocked despair to joyful confidence—was finally under way.

SURPRISING APPEARANCES (20:10-23)

TO MARY MAGDALENE (20:10-18)

As Peter and John returned to their quarters in Jerusalem (v. 10), Mary, who must have followed them back to the tomb, tarried by the graveside weeping (v. 11). Like John earlier, she peered into the tomb, but unlike John she saw a pair of white-clad figures sitting where Jesus had earlier lain (v. 12). They asked why she was distraught; her answer makes clear that she had not yet gained the insight that came to John (v. 13).

Something prompted her to turn at least partially around, and suddenly she was confronted with a third figure. It was Jesus, but she did not recognize Him (v. 14). Perhaps her vision was blurred with tears, or perhaps Jesus' physical appearance was somewhat altered, or perhaps recognition of Him following His resurrection required spiritual illumination (Luke 24:16, 31). He asked a reasonable question; her reply made clear that she still assumed that her beloved healer and master was dead (v. 15). She wished only to recover His body so that she could bestow proper respect on it and put an end to the macabre twist that events had suddenly taken.

At the sound of her own name she suddenly recognized Him (v. 16). "Rabboni," a term of respect, was probably the word she had normally used to address Him. John translates it for readers who do not know Aramaic, indicating that He envisioned a readership not entirely made up of Aramaic-speaking Jews.

Jesus' response (v. 17) was enigmatic. What does "Do not hold on to me" mean? The Greek implies that she should stop something that she is already doing. Apparently she embraced Him at the moment she realized who He was. Perhaps He was protecting her from the assumption that He had "returned" permanently.[5] She needed to know that He was, even at that moment, underway to assume His ongoing future role as advocate before the Father (1 John 2:1). He must also return to the Father in order for the Holy Spirit to come in power (16:7). Rather than leap to a false conclusion, Mary was instructed to inform the other disciples that Jesus was returning to the Father as He promised. Jesus' use of "my" and "your" with respect to "God" and "Father" was a reminder that His relationship to God, while analogous, was not identical to that of His followers. They were sons by adoption (hence Jesus' "brothers," as v. 17 indicates), He by very nature.

Mary dutifully complied with Jesus' request (v. 18). The first to relay word of the empty tomb, she was likewise first to ring the tidings of the Lord's physical (she had touched Him!) return.[6]

TO THE DISCIPLES (20:19-23)

For some hours the disciples simply had to take Mary's word for what she said she saw. But that same evening they (except for Thomas; see v. 24) were able to share fully in her experience. Jesus appeared, apparently out of what might be called thin air, as they gathered behind closed doors (v. 19). Rather than rebuke their desertion of Him two days earlier, or perhaps remind them of how He foretold what would take place, He extended acceptance to them with the gracious traditional greeting "Peace be with you."

5. Schlatter, *John the Evangelist* [German], p. 358: "She reaches for Jesus as if His former relationship with the disciples could be reestablished."

6. In modern thought where Jesus' resurrection is taken seriously at all, there is a tendency to discount the corporeality of Jesus' resurrected form. See Hans Küng, *Eternal Life?* (Garden City, N.J.: Doubleday, 1984), p. 111; Leonhard Goppelt, *Theology of the New Testament*, vol. 1 (Grand Rapids: Eerdmans, 1981), p. 243; Wolfhart Pannenberg, *Jesus—God and Man*, 2d ed. (Philadelphia: Westminster, 1977), p. 84. Yet Grant Osborne maintains that "the evidence in fact strongly suggests from the beginning a physical resurrection" (*The Resurrection Narratives* [Grand Rapids: Baker, 1984], p. 292), and the Jewish scholar Pinchas Lapide, who notes that "some modern Christian theologians are ashamed of the material facticity of the resurrection," avers that the four gospels "compete with each other in illustrating the tangible, substantial dimension" of Jesus' resurrection (*The Resurrection of Jesus* [Minneapolis: Augsburg, 1983], p. 130).

Immediately He showed them His wounds (v. 20). This would verify His identity (Luke 24:37 speaks of their shock and fear that He was a ghost). It would heighten their sense of awe at the wondrous fact that He could stand before them alive, for there is no particular reason to suppose that the punctures, contusions, and jagged wounds had already smoothed to inoffensive proportions. It would also etch in their minds the fact that He was no longer simply "teacher," great though that was, but crucified deliverer. The apostolic preaching of Jesus should, and did, make the cross that Jesus' wounds signified its focal point.

Their joy (v. 20) was fulfillment of Jesus' earlier promise (16:20-22).

The sight of His fatal injuries was nonetheless chilling. Jesus repeated His greeting to dispel undue lingering fear (v. 21). He also reported that now was the time for what He prayed for earlier (17:18) to take place. They were being sent forth with a task and message just as He was sent by the Father.

Jesus "breathed on them" (v. 22). The same word occurs in the Greek Old Testament in Genesis 2:7 (when God breathes life into Adam) and in Ezekiel 37:9 (when dry bones are infused with divine life). The full coming of the Spirit with power is later (see Acts 1:8). But this appears to be a real, not merely predictive, bestowal of His presence now. Perhaps Jesus was urging them to open themselves to the fuller dimension of personal relationship with Him that is available now that they know Him in His crucified and resurrected wholeness. Or it may be that to endure the nearly two months between that evening and Pentecost (Acts 2), they needed the Spirit's enabling already.[7]

The terse declaration of verse 23 refers to their unique authority as the apostolic bearers of the gospel. As they proclaim forgiveness of sins through the cross, the Spirit (see previous verse) will make that forgiveness reality for all who receive the message. Conversely, those who reject the message are not forgiven. Jesus' words do not imply that believers now, either as individuals or as some ecclesiastical entity, have it in themselves to extend or deny the privilege of salvation to any truly seeking it.

---

7. Bruce, *Gospel of John*, p. 392, speaks of "empowerment for ministry." See also pp. 396-97, n. 18. Beasley-Murray, *John*, p. 382, appears to suggest that John's narrative is a theological adaptation of the historical event recorded in Acts 2.

From Skepticism to Trust (20:24-31)

THOMAS'S HONESTY (20:24-25)

We do not know just when the encounter described next took place. Thomas had been absent when Jesus appeared in their midst the first time (v. 24; see v. 19). Sometime later, the other disciples attempted to convince Him of what they saw (v. 25). "Didymus" is Greek for twin, while "Thomas" is Aramaic for the same word. Like many others of his time and locale, he had names in both languages, as did Peter (Cephas).

Thomas was capable of tough-minded commitment when the situation called for it (11:16). There is no good reason to see him as particularly skeptical;[8] others were even more so (Matt. 28:17). But in a social setting where continued loyalty to Jesus was apt to bring woe with it—the "fear of the Jews" was justified (v. 19; see 12:10 for the lengths to which "the Jews" were willing to go)—Thomas was justly hesitant to chase what might be an illusion. His refusal to "believe it" is emphatic in the Greek. Only if the impossible were to occur in his personal presence, too, would he change his mind.

It is not clear whether Thomas's ultimatum was uttered prayerfully or not. But his request was honored, probably more speedily and pointedly than He could have imagined.

JESUS' CHALLENGE (20:26-29)

Exactly one week (literally "eight days") later, on the first Sunday night after the day Jesus initially appeared, He suddenly stood in their midst again behind closed doors and uttered the same reassuring greeting (v. 26). This time Thomas is present.

Jesus goes right to the issue that must have been on everyone's mind, Thomas's unbelief. It had surely driven a wedge between him and his fellows during the preceding week. For his position implied that he thought them deceived, if not deluded. From their standpoint, Thomas's questioning of their judgment could not have been pleasant to bear.

---

8. Calvin (*Gospel According to St. John*, 2:209-10) is particularly scathing. He has been followed by many since.

Jesus invited Thomas to satisfy his curiosity as fully as he might wish (v. 27). There is no reason to suppose that Thomas felt compelled to do so; the plain sight of Jesus' presence and wounds was sufficient. Thomas's exclamation, "My Lord and my God!" was neither an oath nor a redundancy. Thomas hailed Him as the honored "lord," or leader and teacher, that Jesus had been for His followers for many months (see 13:13). In addition, he ascribed to Him the divine status that Jesus' actions and outright claims, sealed now by His resurrection, implied.

Thomas's recognition was no doubt but the first step in an awareness that would take months and years to ripen. But it was a first step, and a more definite one than any of his peers seems to have taken at this point. If John's insight marked one miletone (v. 8), Thomas's marked another, and in some ways a climactic one. His elementary yet sophisticated confession marks the high point of that personal response that John's gospel was written to engender—full and ongoing personal commitment to the one true God through recognition of His presence in the person of Jesus Christ.

There is, however, an even higher road to contemplate. Noble as Thomas's affirmation may have been, still more praiseworthy will be the same confession made under conditions that would prevail after Jesus ascends: "Blessed are those who have not seen" Jesus in His actual bodily presence "and yet have believed" (v. 29).

Jesus had already prayed for those who would believe through His first followers' message (17:20). Now He praised the quality of trust they must exercise. He did not belittle the assistance that literal signs and proof may provide when God sees fit to grant them. He rather commended that faith which does not demand actual touch and sight for its exercise but is willing to act on the powerful testimony vouchsafed to the apostles and passed on ultimately by the Scriptures.[9] A

9. Schlatter, *John the Evangelist* [German], p. 362, writes: "When faith arises apart from observation, it does so through the word; and that it can do so is the greatest demonstration of divine grace. Thus is revealed the activity of God within the life of man, that divine instruction and human learning of which John 6:45 speaks. Jesus' closing words [of chap. 20] elevate the communion of those who believe above the apostles. God's work is not lessened but enhanced. The conclusion of the gospel confirms its beginning: 'In the beginning was the word.' The word is the goal and the consummation of the story of Jesus."

hint of the superior merit of trust in Jesus through the testimony of the written Word was already given in verse 9. Centuries later, a well-known hymn expressed the same truth in the form of a moving declaration and rhetorical question:

> How firm a foundation ye saints of the Lord,
> Is laid for your faith in His excellent Word!
> What more can He say than to you He hath said,
> To you who for refuge to Jesus have fled?

JOHN'S PLEA (20:30-31)

As John's testimony to Jesus' initial appearances draws to a close, He takes the unusual step of appealing directly to the reader. He wishes to make two basic points.

First, he asserts that there are many other "signs" that he and other witnesses could relate (v. 30; see also 21:25). But John knew, perhaps through Jesus Himself, that there is a point beyond which further facts and evidence are useless (see Luke 16:31). With the spiritual insight that Jesus had promised John and his companions (14:26; 15:26-27; 16:13-15), John rested his case, as it were. He was confident that the testimony he had already made available was sufficient to accomplish the purpose for which John, or his scribe, first laboriously inscribed it on a papyrus scroll.

His second point relates to that purpose, a purpose referred to repeatedly already in this commentary. John has related "these [signs]" (v. 31), and much more besides, so that readers might transfer the deepest devotion of their lives to Jesus Christ as John's gospel portrays Him. He is not merely "a smart, wise, and certainly a good man,"[10] John insists. He is the covenant King of God's chosen people promised by the Old Testament prophets. He is "the Christ," or Messiah, who would save His people from their sins (Matt. 1:21).

He is also God's Son.[11] To know Him is to know the only true God. Conversely, there is no access to the only true God apart from

---

10. MacLaine, *Out on a Limb*, p. 50.
11. Brown, *Gospel According to John*, 2:1060, brings out the important differences between "Messiah" and "Son of God" in this context.

Him. "Life" (see 1:4 with comments), vitality that is not merely physical and temporal but also spiritual and everlasting in the future, comes through "believing . . . in His name."

This means allowing ownership of one's entire self to be claimed by the living Jesus who early one spring day claimed John's own life (v. 8). It means learning to love and obey the Christ who modeled those virtues (love, obedience) for His disciples, and who promised to empower them to live likewise. To believe in Christ, and nothing less or else, is to experience life. To withhold trust and allegiance from Him is to deny Christ, an option whose consequences John's gospel has already sternly described.

21

THE TRUE TESTIMONY (21:1-25)

A noteworthy emphasis of John's gospel is that he claims to write the truth. Sometimes this emphasis is explicit: "The man who saw it has given testimony, and his testimony is true" (19:35; see also 21:24). More often it is implicit. In either case, there is a strong ring of claimed authenticity throughout the narratives and discourses comprising John's reminiscences.[1]

Chapter 21 concludes John's gospel with an appearance of Christ that authenticates His risen, and therefore divine, status.[2] As Paul (1 Cor. 15:5-8) cites key appearances of Christ that turned cynics into disciples, John records a memorable incident that confirms Christ's identity and continuing personal presence to His disciples.

This appearance would have been a vivid reminder to them of His authority over their lives (see Matt. 28:18). Christ's emphatic "Follow me!" (John 21:22), while originally directed to Peter, had obvious lasting implications for them all. The net effect of the chapter as a whole is to confirm the veracity of the astounding claims Jesus has made for Himself in previous chapters. These claims, John hopes, will have already challenged the reader to acknowledge who Jesus is and to

---

1. Novelist Dorothy Sayers comments that John's is the only gospel "that claims to be the direct report of an eye-witness," then adds, "and to anyone accustomed to the imaginative handling of documents, the internal evidence bears out this claim" (*The Man Born to Be King*, p. 33, cited in Bruce, *Gospel of John*, p. 409. Bruce also notes [ibid., p. 412, n. 27] C. S. Lewis's verdict that John is "reportage" rather than some fundamentally imaginative literary creation).

2. According to Rom. 1:4, Jesus' resurrection, which only His appearances could have validated, formed one basis for the belief in His divine status among early Christians.

find eternal life through commitment to Him. But just to drive that challenge home, He adds the potent postscript of chapter 21.

Some scholars suggest that the gospel may have originally ended at 20:31. Chapter 21 would then be a later addition.[3] There do not, however, seem to be any ancient copies of John that lack chapter 21; there is therefore no documentary evidence that the gospel originally lacked its present ending. Even if the ending was added later, there is no reason why John himself could not have been the party responsible for its inclusion.[4] The remarks below assume both the literary unity and common authorship of chapter 21 and the chapters preceding it. If it is impossible to demonstrate conclusively the logical necessity of this assumption, it is likewise impossible to prove that it is not a reasonable inference from the available data.

THIRD APPEARANCE (21:1-14)

AN AMAZING CATCH (21:1-6)

Verse 1 serves as a preface to the whole chapter. "Afterward" is indefinite; it is impossible to locate with precision the time of this appearance except to say that it was prior to Jesus' ascension (Acts 1:9). John uses "Tiberias" instead of Galilee (see 6:1), a usage documented in both Josephus and ancient rabbinic writings.[5] "It happened this way" can also read "He revealed Himself as follows." John may be stressing the revelatory nature,[6] not just narrative factuality, of what he is about to relate.

John lists a total of some seven disciples (v. 2). John himself was among the group, for he was one of Zebedee's two sons. He does not narrate how the group came to convene on their old stomping grounds in Galilee.[7] He merely relates Peter's declaration to do something familiar and constructive rather than to sit idly in the absence of an ex-

---

3. Kysar, *John*, Augsburg Commentary, pp. 310-11. He thinks that chap. 21 is "anticlimactic at best and to some degree spoils the finale offered in the previous unit."

4. Burge, "John," in Elwell, ed., *Evangelical Commentary*, p. 878.

5. Schlatter, *John the Evangelist* [German], p. 164.

6. The Greek *phaneroo*, used twice in this verse, often has the connotation of divine revelation in both John and Paul.

7. But see Mark 16:7; they may have traveled there in response to this directive.

plicit directive from their risen leader (v. 3). While there is no good evidence that they somehow sinned in returning to their former occupation of fishing, their foray was singularly unsuccessful. It has been noted that the disciples never catch a fish in the gospels without Jesus' assistance (see for example Luke 5:4, a similar but much different account).

Night was the time for fishing. The fish would be active, the hot sun absent, and the morning markets ready when day dawned. But at daybreak there were still no fish—just a lone stranger watching from the shore some 100 yards distant (see v. 8). It was Jesus, but they did not know it (v. 4). John offers no hint how He got there; this appearance was as mysterious as the earlier ones behind closed doors.[8]

The stranger called out to the toiling band, rightly diagnosing their situation (v. 5). His suggestion was met with startlingly immediate success (v. 6). In dawn's gloom at a distance of 100 yards it is unlikely that Jesus could have seen fish on the right side of the boat any better than the seasoned fishermen to whom He called. The incident rather points to Jesus' supernatural insight. In retrospect, it also implies the productiveness of heeding the directives of Him who makes His disciples "fishers of men" (Matt. 4:19).

"IT IS THE LORD!" (21:7-14)

As at the tomb (20:8), so now at the seaside, the fullness of John's recognition of Jesus seemed to run ahead of Peter's. He blurted out to Peter that the voice was that of Christ (v. 7). Peter hurriedly threw his outer garment (obviously not a heavy one) about himself. He had been stripped, probably to his inner garment, for work, and Jewish protocol called for something more than underwear for the sacred greeting of *shalom* (peace) that Peter would exchange with Jesus.[9] The distance to the shore was not far, and Peter outdistanced the boat as it towed the heavily ladened nets (v. 8).

Upon landing, a cheery scene awaited the hungry crew (v. 9). As He had earlier fed multitudes, Jesus now cared for His own. More food was called for, however; or perhaps Jesus simply wished to call

8. Morris, *Gospel According to John*, p. 862.
9. Schlatter, *John the Evangelist* [German], p. 367.

attention to the staggering proportion of their catch. Either way, He asked for the fish to be landed (v. 10). The command was addressed to the group, but it was Peter who responded (v. 11).[10] The number of fish (153) is surely literal rather than symbolic; if symbolic, there is no clear favorite among the numerous interpretations that have been advanced through the centuries.[11]

Jesus invited them to share the meal He had prepared (v. 12). They apparently felt a strong urge to ask Him who He was—that is, since they had seen the real Jesus die with their own eyes scant days ago, who was this new Jesus? Their minds boggled at His presence, first in the closed room in Jerusalem without Thomas, then again with Thomas, and now on the Galilean seashore, the third time He had appeared to His disciples (v. 14).[12] But they all, even Peter,[13] managed to hold their tongues and accept the manifest though mysterious reality before them. As Jesus broke bread and fish with them, and perhaps partook Himself, His physical presence was affirmed beyond any doubt (see Luke 24:40-43). This was truly the Lord, not a deceiving spirit or the cruel misjudgment of overactive imaginations.

INTERROGATION AND RECONCILIATION (21:15-19)

Peter had been especially eager to greet Jesus (v. 7). He may well have been wrestling with the continuing condemnation of a guilty conscience in the wake of his threefold denial of the master. Now Jesus moves to make their mutual reconciliation public and complete. As breakfast ended, He asked Peter three times (as Peter had denied Him three times) to clarify the depth and quality of his commitment to Christ.

"Do you love me more than these?" (v. 15) may mean, "Do you love me more than these [things lying roundabout us here—the sea,

---

10. Bruce suggests that Peter must have been a man of considerable size and strength to perform this feat (*Gospel of John*, p. 401). But he may have just had the journeyman's knack for handling a difficult task with ease.

11. Brown, *Gospel According to John*, 2:1074, gives a full survey.

12. John does not include the appearance to Mary (20:18) in his reckoning. She was a disciple in the informal sense but not a member of the hand-picked twelve.

13. On other occasions, for example Mark 9:5-6, Peter did not do so well at restraining his impulse to blurt out something, anything, when confronted with an obvious outworking of God's power.

the nets, the boat, your former way of life]?" It is perhaps more like-ly, however, that Jesus reverted to Peter's prideful comments (Matt. 26:33; John 13:37) that set him up for the fall he took on the night Je-sus was betrayed. "More than these" would then mean "more than these [other disciples love me]?"[14] As subsequent verses show, Pe-ter's former pride has been tempered and transformed.

Much ink has been spilled over the shades of meaning attached to the Greek words for "love" and "lambs" or "sheep" in vv. 15-17. Most scholars today agree that the differences are for the sake of sty-listic variation and do not carry the heavy theological freight that some commentators, notably Trench and Westcott last century, once loaded on them.[15]

The point of the exchange seems to be for Peter to have opportu-nity to feel the sting of Jesus' thrice repeated query as Jesus had felt the sting of Peter's triple denial. This was not a vengeful move on Je-sus' part but a cathartic opportunity for Peter. Chastened and humbly vindicated, he could once for all be restored to his former position of leadership within Jesus' inner circle. Having been questioned closely by the risen Christ Himself, then absolved of guilt with a repeated pas-toral mandate (vv. 15-17), any feeling among the disciples that Peter was unfit to lead, and perhaps even to serve, would be impossible to entertain. For the outcome of the painful interview was an unqualified invitation to renew full commitment to the service of Christ—"Follow me!" (v. 19).

Jesus added a parenthetic prophecy to His call for Peter's redou-bled devotion (vv. 18-19). The time was coming when Peter's former spirited independence would give way to dependence and a martyr's death. "Stretch out your hands" may possibly refer to crucifixion, but this is not certain.[16] What is certain is that Peter, like his master, will "glorify God" (v. 19) by dying for the cause he has been commis-sioned to champion. Jesus' "Follow me!" thus takes on a new dimen-

14. This interpretation, and three others, are explained in Brown, *Gospel According to John*, 2:1103-1104. Brown decides to adopt Bultmann's view that "the implica-tions of the clause should not be considered too seriously, for it is only an editorial attempt to bring the other disciples into the picture and thus to bind 15-17 to 1-13."

15. Carson, *Exegetical Fallacies*, pp. 52-53; Bruce, *Gospel of John*, pp. 404-405.

16. Morris, *Gospel According to John*, p. 876.

sion, for it amounts to an initial charge for Peter to embark on a road of obedience sure to end in a painful death.

POSTSCRIPT ON THE BELOVED DISCIPLE (21:20-23)

The exchange between Jesus and Peter apparently ended with the two of them ambling away from the larger group (v. 20). But the beloved disciple, probably the gospel writer himself, had followed closely enough to take in their words. Peter, perhaps thinking that Christ might have a prophecy for John like he did for Peter, asked what would happen to his companion in the future (v. 21).

Jesus' answer to Peter's question raised two issues. First, John's fortunes were not really Peter's business. It was more than enough that Peter be concerned with the integrity of his own walk before the Lord rather than with how God chose to deal with His other servants (v. 22).

Second, Jesus' statement gave rise to a rumor concerning John (v. 23). In the midst of the early church's apocalyptic expectation that Christ would return a second time in judgment, and perhaps very soon, it was asserted that John would still be alive when this event took place. John points out that this interpretation reads too much into what Jesus actually said. Taken in connection with v. 24, John's statement implies that he was still alive at the time he penned these words.[17]

CONCLUDING AFFIDAVIT (21:24-25)

The gospel's final two verses contain a solemn declaration and a graphic disclaimer.

The declaration is yet another categorical assertion that the writer knows whereof he speaks (v. 24; see 15:27; 19:35). He "testifies to these things"; with the sobriety of a man giving legal testimony under oath, John avows that his knowledge is first-hand, his words his own, and his statements true. "We" may be another way of saying "I." Or John may be indicating that "he does not see himself as a solitary

---

17. See Morris, *Gospel According to John*, p. 879.

spokesman but as a member of a larger group that shares in the knowledge he divulges."[18]

The disclaimer is in the form of a delightful overstatement. John has been sparing and selective in what he relates (v. 25; see also 20:30). Already in the first century, the magnitude of what Christ accomplished is clear. Could the whole land mass of planet earth become a repository for books (or, in John's day, scrolls) on Jesus' work and worth, yet more space would be needed to contain the tomes required to do the subject justice. Subsequent developments, including the advent of the printing press and the arrival of today's information explosion, only bear out the aptness of John's assessment. Books on Jesus appear apace, but his importance and relevance seem to expand rather than lessen as new thoughts and findings are published.

Though abbreviated, John's testimony is ample for the purpose he states—"that you may believe that Jesus is the Christ, the Son of God, and that by believing you may have life in His name" (20:31). John has fondly related the way that Jesus made His sovereign claims known in the lives of various unforgettable figures: the disciples, Nicodemus, the Samaritan woman, the man born blind, and many more. Through John's gospel, Christ continues to "give light to every man" (1:9) as the cross that brought Him death yet glory wins eternal redemption for "whoever believes" (3:16).

18. Schlatter, *John the Evangelist* [German], p. 376. Schlatter continues: "It is not ludicrous to propose that John dictated the proceeding, not by himself but in the presence of his co-workers. That is why he says that he speaks in solidarity with those who are in a position rightly to assess his statements ['We know that his testimony is true.']."

SELECTED BIBLIOGRAPHY

Most of the main works cited in this commentary are listed below. For the other main works, journal articles, and specific studies on particular topics see the footnotes of each chapter. Full bibliographical data is given when a book first appears in a footnote; in subsequent footnotes throughout the commentary, a shortened reference note is given.

This lay-level commentary could not interact extensively with a number of important works (e.g., those by Abbott, Barrett, Bernard, Bultmann, Culpepper, Dodd, Haenchen, Lindars, Marsh, Sanders, and many others). A more complete listing of technical commentaries, monographs, and other studies on John is available in D. J. Harrington, *The New Testament: A Bibliography* (Wilmington, Delaware: Michael Glazier, 1985), pp. 99-103; and D. A. Carson, *The Gospel According to John* (Grand Rapids: Eerdmans, 1991), pp. 9-20.

Ashton, John, ed. *The Interpretation of John*. Philadelphia/London: Fortress/SPCK, 1986. Collection of technical essays, many translated from German or French, representative of contemporary critical approaches to the fourth gospel.

Augustine, St. *Homilies on the Gospel of John*. NPNF 7. Grand Rapids: Eerdmans, 1986. Wordy and often allegorical, but rich in theological reflection and pastoral exhortation.

Beasley-Murray, George. *John*. Word Biblical Commentary 36. Waco: Word, 1987. Important commentary by a leading evangelical scholar. Often contains more interaction with critical theories than meditative assessment of John's message.

Boice, J. M. *Witness and Revelation in the Gospel of John.* Grand Rapids: Eerdmans, 1970. Explores the meaning and importance of "witness" in John's gospel.

Brown, Raymond. *The Gospel According to John*, 2 vols. New York: Doubleday, 1966, 1970. A massive scholarly classic, probably the most thorough commentary on John written in English. Roman Catholic perspective.

Bruce, F. F. *The Gospel of John.* Grand Rapids: Eerdmans, 1983. A fine study for the student and layperson. Scholarly yet readable, it is a gold mine of historical and background information.

Burge, Gary. "John." In Walter A. Elwell, ed., *Evangelical Commentary on the Bible.* Grand Rapids: Baker, 1989. Compressed but illuminating treatment. Perhaps the best succinct handling of the entire gospel available.

Calvin, John. *The Gospel According to John*, 2 vols. Translated by T. H. L. Parker. Grand Rapids: Eerdmans, 1961. Lively modern translation of Calvin's lengthy exposition. Calvin remains one of the few truly outstanding Bible expositers in the history of the church. Both beginner and scholar can profit from his seminal remarks.

Carson, D. A. *The Gospel According to John.* Grand Rapids: Eerdmans, 1991. Supersedes all previous candidates (e.g., Morris, Beasley-Murray) as the most thorough modern evangelical commentary on John. Linguistically astute and theologically sensitive. Astounding command of the critical literature; but the message of John, not merely scholarly wrangling about it, comes through loud and clear.

Kysar, Robert. *John.* Augsburg Commentary on the New Testament. Minneapolis: Augsburg, 1986. A popular-level exposition by a leading non-evangelical scholar.

Michaels, J. Ramsey. *John.* San Francisco: Harper and Row, 1984. Popular-level evangelical commentary based on the *Good News for Modern Man* translation.

Morris, Leon. *The Gospel According to John.* Grand Rapids: Eerdmans, 1977. Exhaustive and sensible exposition. Interacts with the previous generation of critical theories.

Schlatter, Adolf. *Der Evangelist Johannes*. Stuttgart: Calwer, 1975. Unique, primarily linguistic commentary by a premier scholar of an earlier generation. Invaluable for pointing up the Palestinian and Jewish roots of John's thought and language. Many a helpful interpretive observation.

Strachan, R. H. *The Fourth Gospel*. London: SCM, 1941. An older but original and insightful study. Excellent on John's theology and the literary flow of the gospel.

Tenney, Merrill C. *John: The Gospel of Belief*. Grand Rapids: Eerdmans, 1948. Dated but useful for both the beginning and advanced student. Tenney, the dean of evangelical New Testament scholars in an earlier generation, shows a command of John's thought and a love for God's Word.

Wenham, John. *Easter Enigma: Are the Resurrection Accounts in Conflict?* Grand Rapids: Zondervan, 1984. An important recent attempt to show how the various gospel records fit together.

Westcott, B. F. *The Gospel According to St. John*. Reprint. Grand Rapids: Eerdmans, 1978. A classic by the famous Cambridge scholar of a century ago.